# THE COMPLETE FISHKEEPER

## EVERYTHING AQUARIUM FISHES NEED TO STAY HAPPY, HEALTHY, AND ALIVE

### JOSEPH S. LEVINE

PRINCIPAL PHOTOGRAPHS BY AARON NORMAN

William Morrow and Company, Inc./New York

## PHOTO CREDITS

All photographs in *The Complete Fishkeeper* were taken by Aaron Norman,
except for the following:
page 69, Lou Ekus; pages 67, 68 and 79, Dennis Osborne for Living Waters Aquarium and Pond, Inc.;
pages 91, 92, 216–219, Fred Rosenzweig; pages 93 and 111, Peter A. Davis;
Hermit Crab and Red Hermit Crab on page 164, Pencil Urchin on page 166, and Anemone on page 168, Alex Kerstitch;
pages 197–200, Paula Chandoha.

It is the policy of William Morrow and Company, Inc., and its imprints and affiliates,
recognizing the importance of preserving what has been written,
to print the books we publish on acid-free paper, and we exert our best efforts to that end.

Library of Congress Cataloging-in-Publication Data

Levine, Joseph S., 1951-
The complete fishkeeper / Joseph S. Levine.
p.    cm.
Includes bibliographical references and index.
ISBN 0-688-10146-1
1. Aquarium fishes.   2. Aquariums.   I. Title.
SF457.L48   1991
639.3′4—dc20                                        91-7415
                                                    CIP

Printed in Italy

First Edition

1  2  3  4  5  6  7  8  9  10

Book Design by Peter A. Davis
Original Illustrations by Jennifer Harper

# ACKNOWLEDGMENTS

To my mentors and guides through the world of underwater life:

Norton Nickerson and Chester Roys, who first took me underwater in the tropics;

John Ryther, who taught me the value of science in aquaculture;

Bill McClarney and John and Nancy Todd, from whom I learned to leaven science with intuition;

Ruth Turner, whose determination inspired me and whose advice steered me to a certain school in Cambridge;

Karel Liem, whose intellectual umbrella sheltered me as he introduced me to the world of ichthyology;

and Ted MacNichol, who, while teaching me to study eyes,

taught me to see a great deal more.

Most of what is good in this book (and in the rest of my life)

I owe to these extraordinary teachers and researchers.

The mistakes it contains are mine alone.

Last, but certainly not least,

this book owes its physical existence, much of its style, a great deal of its accuracy,

and all of its good looks to the talent, enthusiasm, and dedication of

Harriet Bell, Valerie Cimino, and Peter Davis.

The results of their labors have been constant reminders

that publishing, at its best, is a joint effort

whose success reflects the skills of the entire team

rather than any single member.

# CONTENTS

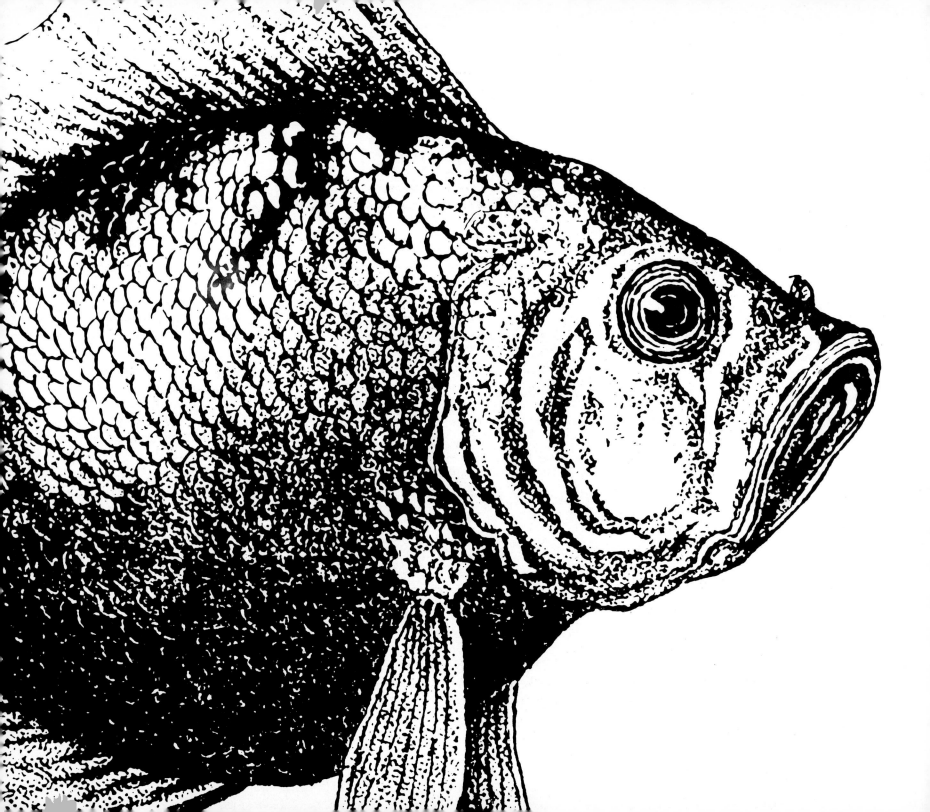

# INTRODUCTION

This book is mostly about fishes, I say "mostly" because it is also about water (as a place for fishes to live), about people (as fishkeepers), about the delights and disappointments of the aquarium hobby, and about my personal views on home fish tanks.

Who am I to be telling you about fishes? A marine biologist by training and an educator by profession, I'm also a fish fanatic who's been keeping aquatic animals since I was nine years old. My love affair with fishes began the moment I won by a goldfish by tossing a coin into his bowl at the Dutchess County Fair. When I trundled home carrying "Oscar" in a plastic bag, my parents were kind—or perhaps foolish—enough to allow us both to stay. Oscar's bowl was traded for a ten-gallon tank, and things soon got out of control.

Thirty years, countless fish tanks, a few undersea expeditions, and two degrees in biology later, I am still keeping (and still learning about) fishes. Among other projects in science education, I design exhibits for public aquaria, zoos, and science museums. But rest assured, although I design seventy-thousand-gallon displays that house two-hundred-pound fishes, I also keep twenty- and fifty-gallon tanks at home. And although my work in professionally equipped aquaculture laboratories serves me well, I still struggle with the vicissitudes of home-aquarium equipment, the problems of locating healthy fishes and plants, and the frustrations of disease outbreaks.

You'll soon find that my approach differs from those found in other aquarium books. I don't claim to present an unbiased view of fish-keeping. I don't try to provide an encyclopedic list of all the fishes in the world. (Lots of authors have attempted that.) Instead, I've assembled a combination of intriguing and useful facts about fishes, and added advice shaped by two decades of training in aquaculture, physiology, ecology, and behavior.

Because I'm a biologist, I view fish tanks as miniature aquatic environments, rather than as water-filled cages. Because I love and respect animals, I feel it is our duty to provide our pets with the best treatment we can give them. Because I've been a "fish farmer," I know that most master aquaculturists—like master farmers and chefs—rely as much on intuition and informed creativity as they do on recipes. And because I know that "real" environments are more hospitable than sterile glass boxes, I'm convinced that home aquaria are more enjoyable, easier to maintain, and less expensive in the long run when they re-create natural—or at least naturalistic—environments.

Why do I feel so strongly about this? Because of my own history as an aquarist. Twenty years ago, my tanks (like those of many other novice fishkeepers) were "decorated" with fluorescent plastic plants, Day-Glo gravel, bubbling scuba divers, animated mermaids, and haunted shipwrecks. I stuffed my tanks as full of fishes as a sardine can and forced my pets to accommodate, not only to each others' habits, but to water conditions that pleased none of them. None of this seemed at all unusual; nearly everyone around me had the same approach.

Not surprisingly, many of those tanks were disasters. Water fouled, and animals died. Big fish bullied and ate little fish, medium-sized fish nibbled each other's tails, and nobody stayed happy for long. Regular doses of aquarium drugs did little to prevent disease and parasites. Scores of dead fish and many dollars later, hosts of well-intentioned fish fanciers either banished their tanks to attics or dumped them at yard sales.

But some of us—though brokenhearted by the death of our pets—were too hooked to let go. With luck, insight, and advice from fellow aquarists, we learned the lessons I'll pass on to you. We learned to treat fish species as individuals whose needs for food, space, and water conditions have been shaped by evolutionary adaptation to their native habitats. We learned to treat aquaria as ecosystems in miniature—networks of life whose energy, food, and wastes must be kept in balance. We learned to navigate our way through the confusing (and often conflicting) claims of aquarium-product advertisements. And we learned, as you will, too, that fish are endlessly fascinating and fun to have around.

## WHY FISHES?

You may be surprised to learn that millions of "fish people" share your hobby. Local aquarium clubs hold meetings across the country. National and international societies publish newsletters and sponsor shows. There even is a forum called FISHNET on the CompuServe computer network that links novices, advanced hobbyists, and professional aquarists into a nationwide support group. And—for better and for worse—there is a sophisticated worldwide aquarium industry.

"Why," you might ask, "do so many people keep fish?" There are at least as many reasons as there are fish species—which number more than twenty thousand. The extraordinary variety among those species and the diversity of the environments they call home offer limitless opportunities to hobbyists. Even if everyone you know decided to set up an aquarium, they could all collect completely different fishes and plants, and replicate totally different underwater scenes in their tanks. Even if all your friends kept twenty tanks in their basements, those tanks together could hold just a tiny fraction of the world's fishes.

Fish come in all colors of the rainbow, from brilliant red and orange to vibrant blue and green. Their body shapes range from "typical" fish profiles to silhouettes that resemble birds, butterflies, dinner plates, or even leaves and rocks. Fish behaviors are just as varied; some are timid, others affectionate, and still others aggressive or even fierce. Many form structured societies whose members communicate through silent languages of dips, quivers, and flourishes as graceful as those of Balinese temple dancers.

In the right environment, many fishes breed readily, disclosing courtship and mating strategies that put soap-opera scriptwriters to shame. Some fishes mate for life, some battle through brief and torrid affairs, while others are embarrassingly promiscuous. They build nests, stake out and defend their home turf, and—to the occasional distress of their keepers—beat the living daylights out of one another if they don't get along.

In practical terms, carefully chosen fish in properly maintained tanks can make perfect pets for people of all ages, incomes, and lifestyles. Many are both inexpensive and easy to keep, so they are within the means of those on limited budgets and can be ideal pets for busy professionals and growing families. Other species are sufficiently rare, exotic, expensive, and demanding to serve both as perpetual challenges to advanced hobbyists and as "status pets" for those whose BMWs and objets d'art no longer impress their friends. To fishes' further credit, they don't bark, howl, chew furniture, dirty carpets, or beg to be walked during ice storms. They inflame no allergies, upset no landlords, and stretch no co-op or condominium regulations. Most fare perfectly well with no care over vacation weekends or business trips, and many will survive perfectly well for a week or more without feeding.

## HOW TO USE THIS BOOK

I hope you're reading this book either before setting up your first tank or at a time when you want to expand your collection. In either case, spend time planning your tank before you make any final decisions about fishes. Consider the project an ongoing artistic and creative process, rather than a single afternoon's buying spree. Designing an aquarium—like planning a garden or renovating your home—can be as much fun as keeping the fish. What's more, careful design can avoid many problems, not to mention lots of unnecessary work and expense.

Read the entire book before buying anything. After familiarizing yourself with fishes' general requirements (Chapter 1) and learning the rudiments of water chemistry (Chapter 2), buy a test kit and analyze your tapwater. (This step alone may save you both the trauma and the cost of repeated trips to the store for replacement fish.) Select a tank that suits your taste and that fits your budget (Chapter 3).

Then, for the path of least resistance, determine the kinds of fishes and plants that will

be happy in the kind of water you can most easily provide for them (Chapters 4, 5, and 6). Look over the suggestions for types of tanks in Chapter 7, and choose a community whose personality and maintenance requirements appeal

to you. Follow the start-up schedule in Chapter 8, being careful to keep the recommended log. Be certain to follow proper quarantine procedures for new acquisitions and learn how to handle the most common fish diseases *before*

they occur (Chapter 9). Along the way, read some of the other books recommended, subscribe to a magazine or two, and talk to other hobbyists in person or via the FISHNET forum. From then on, Best Fishes!

# CHAPTER 1

# WHAT IS A FISH, ANYWAY?
# (AND WHY SHOULD I CARE?)

When you adopt a puppy, you have a lot to learn, but it is all familiar stuff. Like humans, dogs are mammals, and as such have familiar needs. Puppies need affection, some discipline, food, water, housebreaking, some shots, and a deworming now and then. Not much that's unfamiliar at all, especially if you've raised any kids.

But from the moment your first fish is bagged at the pet store, it thrusts you into the alien world of life underwater. Suddenly, you have to worry about aspects of water chemistry that put most of us to sleep in science class. You are bombarded with conflicting information about what fishes need to eat. And worst of all, you can't depend on fishes to whimper or cry when they're sick or unhappy; they just seem to go belly-up without warning.

Don't worry. Your wet pets will be a lot less mysterious in a short while, especially if you take the time to ask two basic questions: What is a fish, anyway? And how are fishes different from other animals?

## IT'S A FISH'S WORLD

Our planet is a fish's world. Oceans cover more than two thirds of the earth's surface. Lakes, ponds, and marshes dot the continents, fed by streams and linked by rivers with the sea. These water bodies vary wildly, from frigid Arctic streams to tepid tropical rivers, and from sunlit coral reefs to pitch-black underground lakes. And in virtually all of these places, there are fishes—beautiful, bizarre, and curious creatures that revel in the challenges of life on the water planet.

In the shallows of Asian mangrove swamps, mudskippers with bulging eyes hop from root to root as archer fish knock insects from the air with expertly aimed jets of water. In subfreezing water beneath the North Pole, ice fish survive thanks to biological antifreeze that keeps their blood from freezing. And in desert streams of the American Southwest, pupfish live in water that would boil almost any other animal alive.

Fishes manage all this not because they are "better" at adapting to their environments than other animals but because they've been at it a lot longer than the rest of us. Life on Earth began in water, and the earliest fishes—which happened to be the first animals with backbones—appeared at least 500 million years ago. (True mammals didn't appear until 250 million years later.) And ever since fishes appeared, they have been evolving, adapting their structures, behaviors, and body functions to different environments.

Although the first fishes vanished eons ago, their living aquatic descendants number more than twenty thousand species. This staggering diversity offers hobbyists both opportunities and challenges. On the positive side, no matter how long you remain a hobbyist, you'll never run out of new fishes. Furthermore, no matter what your tapwater is like, and no matter what size tank you choose, there are dozens of fishes that will do well for you. And if you decide to coordinate your pets with your slipcovers, have no fear; there are fishes to match every color scheme.

If, on the other hand, you are the sort of person who insists on having "one of everything," all those fishes saddle you with a Sisyphean task. Even world-class public aquaria, with buildings the size of football fields and operating budgets in the millions of dollars, can't house all the world's fishes.

In spite of that reality, the urge to collect surfaces in most of us any time we walk into a pet shop. Not wanting to seem self-righteous, I freely admit that I've had as much trouble with overcollecting as anyone else. Every other week, allowance in hand, I'd trundle off to the closest pet store for another fish. I knew little or nothing about where my pets came from. I understood less about the water conditions they needed. And I hadn't a clue about fish personalities that allowed some to coexist but condemned others to perpetual warfare. I just kept thinking, "That little guy is *so* cute! I know my tank is full, but what harm could it do to take just one more fish home?"

Over time, though, I discovered what experienced aquarists knew all along—that stuffing "just one more" fish into an aquarium that already resembled a sardine can is not the same as squeezing another curio onto a crowded knickknack shelf. In fact, overcrowded and improperly planned tanks are the major causes of distress to both fishes and aquarists. So moderating our desires to collect is a constant challenge, but is the key to successful tanks.

# OF NAMES AND FAMILY RELATIONS

The diversity of fishes also poses a practical problem for all of us who keep, study, or write about them.

For a start, we've got to figure out what to call them, because the simple English names we'd like to use have serious limitations. Talk about a sea robin or a striper in New England,

## Fish vs. Fishes

In this book, I subscribe to the convention among professional ichthyologists in choosing between the words "fish" and "fishes." I use the word "fish" to describe one or more animals belonging to the same species (a school of royal angelfish) or as an adjective (fish physiology). When talking about a number of individuals belonging to two or more species, the proper plural is "fishes"—as in the title of the great reference work *Fishes of the Gulf of Maine.*

and everyone knows just what you mean. And a guppy is a guppy, after all. But go farther afield or deal with even slightly more exotic species and the muddle begins.

Sport fishermen in Ontario, for example, love to eat a fish they call pickerel. To Americans south of the Great Lakes, though, "pickerel" are trash fish—not because of differences in taste, but because the same name is applied to two completely different fishes. One popular Caribbean reef fish is called "fairy basslet" by some and "royal gramma" by others. A Pacific beauty Americans call the "Koran angelfish" has been christened *ange de mer royal* ("royal sea angel") by the French and *Königsfisch* ("king fish") by Germans. Even more confusing, "angelfish" is also used for a completely different group of freshwater fishes from the Amazon basin!

This dilemma is neither new nor restricted to fishes. Back in medieval times, naturalists chatting across national borders decided to give organisms scholarly names based on Latin or Greek roots. All educated people studied Latin,

after all, so these names required no translation from one country to another. The first of these official names were cumbersome, as they could be up to fifteen words long. But the system was revised and simplified during the 1700s, and the resulting standard is used everywhere.

The rules in force today are simple. Each organism is assigned a unique, two-part name that often (though not always) describes its important features. The most important thing in dealing with these names is not to let their length and unfamiliar appearance intimidate you. Most are pronounced phonetically, and figuring out exactly what they mean can be fun. (You can often find the original roots in a good dictionary.) The scientific name for a large Pacific sea horse, for example, is *Hippocampus ingens. Hippos* is Greek for "horse," *kampos* means "sea monster," and *ingens* means "large," so the name, though unfamiliar at first glance, means "large, horselike sea monster"!

In this case, *Hippocampus* is the *genus* name, given to all animals we call sea horses. The next word, *ingens* is the *species* name, given to one and only one type of animal. (Note that both names are italicized, but that only the genus is capitalized.) Sometimes a genus contains only a single species, but more often many similar-looking, related species are placed in the same genus. Our Koran angelfish, for example, is *Pomacanthus semicirculatus;* its genus name describes the spine on its cheek (*akantho* means "spine"), and its species name refers to the bold arcs of blue and white on its flanks. Among its close relatives are *Pomacanthus annularis* (*annulus* means "ring"), and *Pomacanthus maculosus* (*macula* means "blotch" or "spot").

For convenience, we group related genera

into larger units called *families*. Sea horses are placed with pipefish into the family Sygnathidae. Marine angelfish and butterfly fish form the family Chaetodontidae. And freshwater angelfish, together with the regal discus and many other popular aquarium species, are placed in the family Cichlidae.

Why bother with all this stuff? At first, you may in fact find it easier to ignore scientific names. You can talk and learn about guppies, mollies, swordtails, and platies with little confusion and no need for Latin. So to make the first part of this book as user-friendly as possible, I'll use common names wherever I can. But as we move on to cichlids and other challenging species, Latin names become unavoidable, and I'll sneak them in with greater frequency. If you stick with fishkeeping, you'll soon find that being able to handle scientific names will come in mighty handy. Once you're comfortable with this system, you'll be able to read books and articles written anywhere and exchange information with fish people around the world.

## WHAT MAKES FISHES TICK?

Fishes all share many common features (that is, after all, why they are classified together as fishes). Because those characteristics often explain fishes' needs in captivity, the rest of this chapter surveys the features that make fishes what they are.

## Fins

Fins—and the ways fishes use them—are part of each species' unique personality. Fins de-

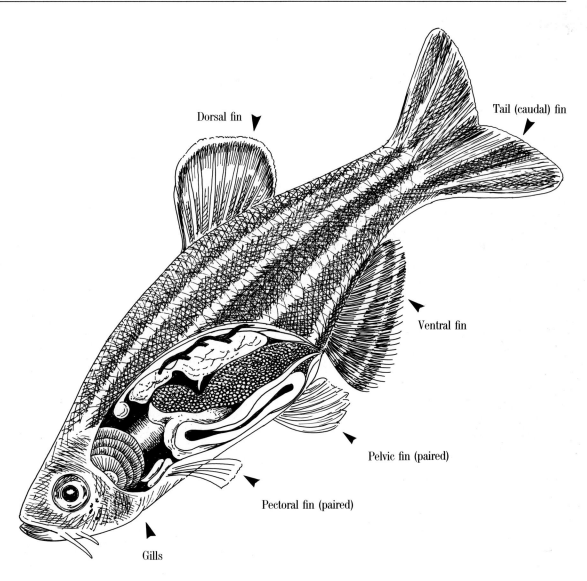

Dorsal fin

Tail (caudal) fin

Ventral fin

Pelvic fin (paired)

Pectoral fin (paired)

Gills

termine whether a fish darts through the water or glides, hovers like a helicopter or slithers like an eel. Although fins vary enormously in shape from species to species, all are constructed out of basically the same parts.

Most aquarium fishes belong to a huge group called the "ray-finned" fishes that includes everything from guppies to groupers, salmon, and eels. All these fishes' fins are built from slender rays connected to one another by a thin layer of skin. Although the size, position, and shape of fins varies enormously from fish to fish, once you understand the basic "themes" of fin placement, you can easily figure out the variations. Virtually all fishes have a single caudal fin (tail), a pair of pectoral fins (located where "arms" might be), and a pair of pelvic fins (where "legs" might be). Many, though not all, species have one or two dorsal (top) and ventral (bottom) fins as well.

## Body Shapes

Fish bodies come in as many varieties as their fins, and reveal a great deal about their habits. Species such as tuna, which swim constantly at high speeds, have streamlined, torpedo-shaped bodies, long, curved tails, and stiff dorsal and ventral fins that act as stabilizers. These sorts of fishes need lots of room to swim, and are hard to keep even in giant tanks containing thousands of gallons. Barracuda, trumpetfish, and some freshwater needlefish, on the other hand, spend most of their time hovering in the water, but launch themselves at prey like the arrows they resemble. Still other species, such as cichlids and coral-reef angelfish, can stop suddenly, hover motionless, and turn on a dime to maneuver around rocks and coral. These

fishes are often deeper-bodied, usually have flexible dorsal and ventral fins, and sport versatile pectoral and pelvic fins that act both as brakes and as rudders.

## Swim Bladders

Because fish muscles and bones are slightly heavier than water, without assistance of some kind they would slowly sink to the bottom. To help them maintain their position in water with minimal effort, most species that swim in open water have a balloonlike sac called a swim bladder that balances their weight and keeps them suspended in midwater.

## Scales

The bodies of ray-finned fishes are covered with scales that overlap one another like shingles on the side of a house. Each scale is firmly attached to the deep layer of skin from which it grows, and each is covered by a thin, delicate layer of outer skin. That skin, in turn, is covered by protective mucus that is continually shed and replaced.

In healthy specimens, the scales, skin, and mucus coat form a seamless yet flexible body blanket that protects against predators and parasites. Missing or protruding scales mean trouble. If scales are pulled out or rubbed off, the underlying tissue is damaged and ripe for infection. Protruding scales are often a sign of serious disease. And any damage to the mucus coat—from either scuffles with tankmates or rough handling in a net—can open the door to fungus, bacteria, and other troublemakers.

## Gills: Vital, Yet Fragile

Fishes, like the rest of us, breathe by taking in oxygen ($O_2$) and giving off carbon dioxide ($CO_2$). To manage this underwater, most fishes have four pairs of soft, feathery gills on each side of their heads. Gills are wonders of evolutionary engineering whose countless tiny filaments bring the fish's blood into close contact with water flowing past. This arrangement allows $O_2$ to enter and $CO_2$ to leave with remarkable efficiency, but also makes gills very vulnerable to disease and trauma.

Fragile gill filaments are protected and supported on the inside by curved bones called gill arches, and on the outside by a pair of bony gill covers. These help shield gills from physical damage, either from particles the fish swallows or from objects the animal might brush up against. But delicate gill tissue is still in direct contact with the water, and is therefore extremely susceptible to the sorts of changes in water conditions you will learn about in Chapter 2. And gills' rich, accessible blood supply makes them act like magnets for a host of fish parasites, as you'll see in Chapter 9.

In addition to getting rid of $CO_2$, gills also discharge another waste product—ammonia—that is generated whenever an animal "burns" proteins for food. Because ammonia is poisonous to living tissue, it must be eliminated from the body as quickly as possible. We humans, like most land animals, change ammonia into less toxic urea and concentrate it in our bladders until we feel the need to get rid of it. Fishes, on the other hand, dump ammonia from their bloodstream directly into the surrounding water through their gills.

This is a vital fact for all aquarists to remember. In nature, ammonia excreted by fish poses no problem, because it is quickly diluted in large bodies of water. In small, closed aquaria, however, ammonia can accumulate until it damages the very same fragile gill tissues that try to get rid of it. You'll learn how to avoid this problem in Chapter 2.

Finally, gills are important parts of the system by which fishes balance water and dissolved salts in their bodies. Because of physical forces no organism can control, water and salts tend to seek their own level in soft tissues. In freshwater, this means that water enters fishes' bloodstreams through the gills, while salts tend to "leak" out by the same route. In saltwater, the problem is reversed; fish tend to lose water and gain salt.

Fish kidneys handle part of this problem by creating either very dilute urine (that helps freshwater fish get rid of excess water) or somewhat more concentrated urine (that helps saltwater fish retain water). But equally important are cells in the gills that actively pump salts into the blood (for freshwater fishes) or out of the blood (for saltwater fishes). Fishes that can move from freshwater to saltwater (as salmon do) are able to adjust the activity of both gill salt pumps and kidneys as needed.

## Immune Systems and Disease

Fishes, like humans, have immune systems that work to fight disease. The fact that healthy fishes *do* have immune systems is important to remember, for a glance at the racks of medications in fish stores or at "disease" chapters in fish books might give you the impression that fish are helpless victims of every parasite known to science. It is true that diseases are common in small aquaria, but it is also true that these diseases are far more common than they need to be. But why?

Fishes, like humans, are healthiest when well-nourished, housed under suitable conditions, and protected from chronic anxiety. Overcrowd them, feed them improperly, or fail to take care of their environment, and you stress their body processes in ways that disable their immune systems. And once an individual's immune system is disabled, he or she can fall prey to scores of diseases and parasites that never bother healthy animals.

The problem is that unwitting aquarists often subject their pets to just about every stressful condition an aquatic animal could encounter. And once a single stressed-out fish succumbs to parasites, disease spreads easily to one fish after another until the aquarist feels like a draftee in the aquatic Red Cross. But treat your fishes properly, and they'll survive for years in good health.

## Breeding

Part of the fun in fishkeeping, especially for children, is waking up to a tank filled with scores of baby fish. Advanced hobbyists often help support their pastime by breeding unusual species for sale. Getting some fish to spawn is as simple as putting a male and a female together. Other species require months of conditioning in specially designed breeding tanks. We'll take a closer look at techniques for breeding and raising fish later in the book, so we'll just mention here that aquarium fishes reproduce in two main ways.

Most fishes reproduce as you'd expect them to. Males and females court for a spell, the female lays eggs, the male fertilizes them, and sooner or later there are lots of little fishes. It is not too difficult to get some of these egg-laying species to spawn, but their newly hatched young are often so small that they require special foods. Some require care from their parents after hatching, too.

But lots of popular fishes—including guppies, platies, swordtails, and mollies—bear their young alive. In these species, the male's anal fin is modified into tubelike structure that delivers sperm to the female. After the eggs are fertilized inside the mother's body, they develop for a time and are born large enough to survive fairly well on their own. Many live-bearers reproduce regularly, whether you want them to or not. If you keep any of these, you'd be well-advised to make plans in advance to take care of some young'uns.

## Water Colors

Whether seen with the naked eye or under a microscope, the bodies of fishes explode with shifting colors and patterns. Early eighteenth-century explorers described tropical-reef fishes as covered with "polished scales of gold, encrusting lapis-lazuli, rubies, sapphires, emeralds, and amethysts." A bit of an exaggeration, perhaps, but not much of one; these living kaleidoscopes rank right up there with hummingbirds and butterflies when it comes to visual extravagance. In fact, many fish do their terrestrial counterparts one better, by changing color at a moment's notice.

The colors in fish skin are produced by several kinds of skin cells that absorb and reflect light of different wavelengths. Those fish that can change color quickly—such as certain cichlids—do so by changing the size or position of the colored pigments in those cells. When the pigment is spread throughout the cell, the skin darkens. When the pigment is concentrated in one central spot, the skin lightens.

But why do fishes paint their bodies so lavishly? Many use color and pattern to conceal their positions and even to "lie" about their identities. Ambush hunters pretend to be part of the scenery in a ploy to snare a meal, while other species hide to avoid being made into a meal by someone else. In contrast, some reef fishes and cichlids use patterns on their bodies like images on billboards to advertise their presence and identity. Scores of freshwater fishes don bright colors during courtship to attract the opposite sex. And many species—as turf-conscious as any human street gang—use color patterns the way gang members use insignia caps and jackets—to identify themselves and to proclaim, "This is my turf . . . keep out!"

Learning fish color language is both fun and useful. Lots of freshwater fishes, particularly cichlids, use color change to communicate "moods," so a knowledgeable aquarist can tell at a glance whether one of these animals is hungry, sexually aroused, ready to breed, or frightened.

Knowing what a species' colors *should* be can also be helpful in evaluating fish for purchase. Some fish, such as the red-tailed black shark (common name problems again; they aren't sharks at all) are easily "spooked" by activity around their tank, and rarely show their true colors in pet shops. Take one of these "pink-tailed, dull gray" animals home, however, and—assuming the fish is healthy and that it finds your tank comfortable—it will darken to

reveal its full ebony and scarlet beauty within a day or so. Other species, such as discus, should never be purchased if they are unusually dark.

Finally, several fish wholesalers in Asia have recently taken to "gilding the lily" in one way or another. Some treat immature fishes with extracts of sexual hormones to enhance their colors for sale. Others actually paint otherwise drab fishes—particularly a few species of tetras—with Day-Glo shades of orange or green. Not only are these treatments strictly temporary, they are an affront to the dignity of the fishes and a threat to their health. Learn to identify such frauds and avoid them like the plague.

## SENSES:
### Windows on the World

When we dive into fishes' world, we find it thoroughly foreign. Our eyes can't focus without diving masks, our ears play tricks on us, and our senses of taste and smell are completely disabled. That isn't surprising; we are terrestrial creatures, and our senses are ill-suited for operation underwater. There are odors we can't smell, sounds we can't hear, colors and patterns we can't see. And all aquatic animals emit minute electric currents that create electromagnetic auras as personal as fingerprints. But though these phenomena are totally beyond human sensory capabilities, they provide vital information to animals whose senses are tuned to them.

### Eyes

Most fishes have well-developed eyes that (contrary to popular opinion) provide clear, detailed

views of the underwater world. Reef fishes and cichlids, for example, can move their eyes around easily, and can focus on both near and distant objects. Almost all fish active during the daytime have color vision at least as good as our own. In fact, some species see color better than we can! Fish active only at night or in very cloudy water, on the other hand, have large eyes with big pupils to gather as much light as possible. These species usually do not see color well, but see in the dark as well as cats.

The vast majority of fishes don't, however, have either irises or eyelids, the structures we use to regulate the amount of light entering our eyes. This has two consequences of note for hobbyists. First, fishes that normally live in shade need dark places to hide in brightly lit aquaria, because they can't just "shut their eyes" in strong light. Second, fish eyes adapt to lighting changes at dawn and dusk rather slowly—over the course of fifteen minutes to half an hour. That's no problem in nature, where sunrise and sunset take time. In the home, however, tank lights switched on or off too suddenly can "spook" fishes and send them into a panic. Thoughtful hobbyists therefore turn room lights on for a while before turning on tank lights in the morning, and leave room lights on for a time after darkening the tank at night. This gives fishes a chance to adjust to changing light levels at their own speed.

### "Ears" and Lateral Line

Most fish have rudimentary "ears" inside their heads, but because they have no external ears to collect and amplify sound, they can't hear very well. The only exceptions are goldfish and their close relatives. In these species, ear structures deep within their heads are connected with their swim bladders through a chain of three bones like the bones in our own middle ears. Sounds traveling through water set the swim bladder in motion, just as sounds in air cause our eardrums to vibrate. The three bones then transfer the movements of the vibrating swim bladder to the ear, where sounds are detected.

Fishes are, however, adept at detecting subtle vibrations and gentle currents in the water through a system called the "lateral line." This network of tubes, located just beneath the scales, branches all over the animals' heads and runs down the sides of their bodies. Each tube is connected with the surface at regular intervals by small pores that look like pinholes in the fish's skin. You can easily see the lateral-line system on large fishes, but on smaller individuals you need a hand lens. Some species use this system to detect tiny shrimp swimming through the water or insects struggling on the surface. The lateral line also allows them to "feel" when other fish are swimming nearby.

## Smell and Taste

Many fish possess senses of taste and smell that put ours to shame. Although most species have nostrillike openings, contrary to the old joke, cutting off these noses will not keep fish from smelling. Many species, such as catfish, can also smell with their "whiskers," or barbels. At the same time, lots of fish have taste buds located not only in the mouth but all over the head and much of the rest of their bodies. These taste buds respond to tiny quantities of chemicals in the water around them.

Fishes use smell and taste in a variety of ways. Many depend on chemical cues for feeding; sharks have an almost legendary ability to detect blood in the water. Others depend on odors for clues during long-distance migrations; salmon can smell the difference between their home stream and water from other streams far out at sea. And just as important, many species use odor to communicate with one another.

Think, now, about what this means to fishes in small tanks. They are constantly smelling and tasting the water around them, not only with their noses but with their entire body surfaces. If that water carries bad-tasting or noxious chemicals from wastes or rotting food, fishes can't avoid them by holding their noses or keeping their mouths shut. Keep this in mind when the importance of keeping tank water clean is discussed later on in Chapter 2.

## Electroreception

Sharks and certain freshwater fishes have evolved a sense that is totally alien to human experience: the ability to detect weak electric fields in the water around them. Sharks use this electric sense both to locate prey and to navigate through featureless open seas using the earth's magnetic field as a guide. Freshwater species that have this sense use it both for navigating through turbid water (in which vision is nearly useless) and for communicating with one another.

The electric fishes most commonly seen in pet stores are often called "knifefish," "baby whales," or "elephant noses." (I won't include Latin names here, but you can see the obvious problems with common ones.) These fishes not only *detect* electric fields, they *create* electric fields, using modified muscles on either side of their bodies. They can then detect the presence of neighboring fish and objects by sensing changes in the shapes of their personal electric auras. They also "talk" with other members of their species by modulating changes in their personal fields.

The full story of electric fishes would fill an entire book, so I'll just point out what these talents mean in captivity. You may not realize that our homes are filled with low-level electromagnetic radiation that is absent in the wilds of Africa and the Amazon. High-tension wires and fluorescent lights broadcast electrical "noise" at sixty cycles/second, and many household appliances create measurable electric fields. Although this presents no problem for "normal" aquatic animals, it gives electric fishes a hard time. The solution? Instead of just offering a rock cave for these species to hide in, thoughtful aquarists provide each individual with a length of PVC tubing large enough to hover in. This insulating shelter provides an electrically quiet retreat for these generally shy species.

## EVERY FISH IS UNIQUE

If fishes were as alike as the first part of this chapter implies, I could offer you a few simple recipes for fishkeeping and be done with it. But though all fishes are alike in many ways, each species is also unique. Every species, because of its history and the habitat in which it lives, has evolved specific features that enable it to survive and reproduce. And those features, which range from feeding habits to social behaviors, give each species different requirements in captivity.

## Feeding Specializations

As part of fishes' struggle to survive, they have evolved a remarkable array of ways to feed themselves. As a group, ray-finned fish leave no source of food untouched, from the toughest algae to the tenderest eggs of other aquatic animals.

Many popular aquarium species are omnivores, which means that they—like humans—can live on just about anything that tastes good and supplies important nutrients and vitamins. These omnivores are easy to feed properly in captivity, though it is a challenge for beginners to stretch beyond convenient dried foods to provide a truly balanced diet (Chapter 2). Some other aquarium species are carnivorous, which means that they prefer meat in one form or another. And still others are herbivores, who thrive only when fed lots of vegetable matter.

Within these broad groupings, however, are numerous species that are experts at feeding on one and only one kind of food. In nature, specialization allows these animals to become masters at their task; mouth and tooth design, body and fin shapes, and the entire design of their digestive tracts evolves toward maximal efficiency in procuring and digesting the food of choice. But many highly specialized species can eat *only* the food or foods on which they normally depend in nature. If provided with other foods in captivity—even foods that they eagerly devour—such species slowly waste away, to the bewilderment and dismay of well-meaning keepers.

Some of the ultraspecialists among coral-reef species, for example, will eat almost anything in captivity, but survive only if fed on a particular species of sponge or coral, or on a certain type of alga. Such animals are condemned by their biology to lingering death from malnutrition in captivity. That they are regularly offered for sale in pet shops is, in my view, a criminal offense against nature. The ready availability of such species (often not distinguished from their easier-to-keep relatives) places a great burden on you as a hobbyist; you must be able to recognize them and avoid them. For even if you're already an experienced hobbyist, you'll make life a lot easier for yourself and your pets if you stick to species with more catholic tastes.

## Behaviors

People who have never had aquaria of their own usually scoff at the idea that fish have personalities. Such people may be dog or cat chauvinists. They may never have even visited a large public aquarium. Or they may think all fish act like goldfish, which, I admit, have about as much personality as cucumbers.

But anyone who really knows fish, knows better. There are shy fishes and sassy fishes. There are hermits that insist on privacy, and there are social tag-alongs that feel comfortable only in a school of their own kind. There are laid-back fishes that get along with anyone, and there are hell-raisers who harass any tankmates and shred even plastic plants the way dogs devour rawhide bones. And many fishes have ordered, instinctive behaviors relating to such important life functions as feeding, courtship, mating, and care of young.

Among most fishes, the traits that add up to "personality" characterize all members of a species. In other words, just about any male betta will fight with his own kind, but is intimidated by active tankmates of other species. Male guppies will hustle around, persistently searching for receptive females. Hatchetfish hover just beneath the water's surface, ready to jump into the air at the slightest provocation. Tangs skitter about as if nervous. Catfish bustle along the bottom, wiggle their "whiskers," and glance at you quizzically. And triggerfish behave like schoolyard bullies—nasty when they have the upper hand (or fin) and cowardly when they don't.

These species-specific character traits are endlessly amusing, and the variety of available personality types is a large part of the fun of fishkeeping. But, as you'll see in Chapter 7, it is vitally important to keep fishes' temperaments in mind when setting up any kind of community tank. For even the largest home aquarium is pitifully small compared to a lake or stream, and the animals you place together in a community tank had best get along. When they do, home aquaria are delightful and relaxing to watch and little or no trouble to maintain. If your pets don't hit it off well, on the other hand, they make life miserable for one another and for you, as the resulting injuries and long-term stress lead to disease outbreaks.

Fishes also differ dramatically in the way they interact with their keepers. Most beginner species, such as guppies and platies, are basically mindless. They will learn quickly enough that food appears in a particular corner of their tank, but will swarm indiscriminately to that corner when anyone approaches. Many marine and larger freshwater species, on the other hand, develop remarkable rapport with the particular humans who care for them.

I once had five marine tanks in my bedroom. Those fishes, despite the fact that they saw me clothed in everything from a birthday suit to black tie, "knew" me. As long as I didn't stick a net in their tank, I could creep quietly around the room or bounce off the walls and they just went about their business. And when they saw me reaching for the food drawer, they went into a feeding frenzy. But if anyone else entered the room, regardless of what clothes that person was wearing (including mine) or how slowly and carefully the stranger moved, the fish dived for cover among the coral heads. Several friends, in fact, thought I was indulging in an expensive joke by maintaining five beautifully decorated but empty tanks! Only if strangers sat absolutely still in front of the tank for at least fifteen minutes did the fishes timidly peek out from their hiding places.

Among larger, long-lived species, individuals often develop singular dispositions. Freshwater angelfish and discus form breeding pairs that stay together for years. Some of those pairs raise their young tenderly, time after time, while others spawn repeatedly only to devour their own eggs or neglect the hatchlings. Other large cichlids, such as oscars, recognize their keeper as an individual, rub affectionately against his or her arm, beg for food, and periodically "ask" to be rubbed gently between the eyes. (When upset, on the other hand, the same fish can aim a jet of water unerringly at an unsuspecting human through the smallest opening in a tank cover.) All of us who have lived with these animals have stories such as these, although non-fish folk often choose not to believe them, and we usually refrain from discussing them with academic colleagues.

## Aquatic Roots: The Waters They Call Home

The final thing to remember about fishes is that their diversity has been spawned by the variety of aquatic worlds they live in. And each of those aquatic habitats has its own distinctive, if not unique, type of water.

Half of the great Amazon Basin—the home of many aquarium species—is fed by streams that cascade down off the Andes and drain through peat-filled marshes and swamps. That water (in unpolluted areas, at least) is free-flowing, tea-colored, acid, and contains little more in the way of dissolved minerals than distilled water. Every year, seasonal rains dump far more water into the main body of the river than even its mile-wide channel can hold, and it rises more than ten meters above its lowest levels to flood at 70,000 km² of forest and discharges eleven times as much water as the Mississippi.

By contrast, Lake Malawi, one of the great lakes of Africa, is a landlocked sea in a basically arid land. Much of the water that flows into it evaporates, rather than flowing out, and the resultant buildup of dissolved minerals makes the water hard and alkaline, although it is usually quite clear and strikingly blue in color.

Coral reefs, for their part, are bathed in warm, clear water that is saline, alkaline, and seasoned with a whole range of common and trace elements. The water around tropical reefs is constantly refreshed by breaking waves and ocean currents and varies little, if at all, in either temperature or chemical composition from one time of year to another.

For humans, terrestrial creatures that we are, these differences in water quality are at best interesting curiosities. For fishes, on the other hand, they are critical. Expecting a fish from the Amazon's Rio Negro to survive in Lake Malawi or in seawater is not very different from presuming that a human would be happy breathing the atmosphere of Venus. For this reason, a primary rule in setting up home aquaria is to know where your fishes come from and what water conditions they require. Then, as you'll see in the next chapter, you can select your pets according to the type of water you can most easily give them, and group together only those species whose basic requirements don't conflict. And that alone will be a giant step toward a successful aquarium.

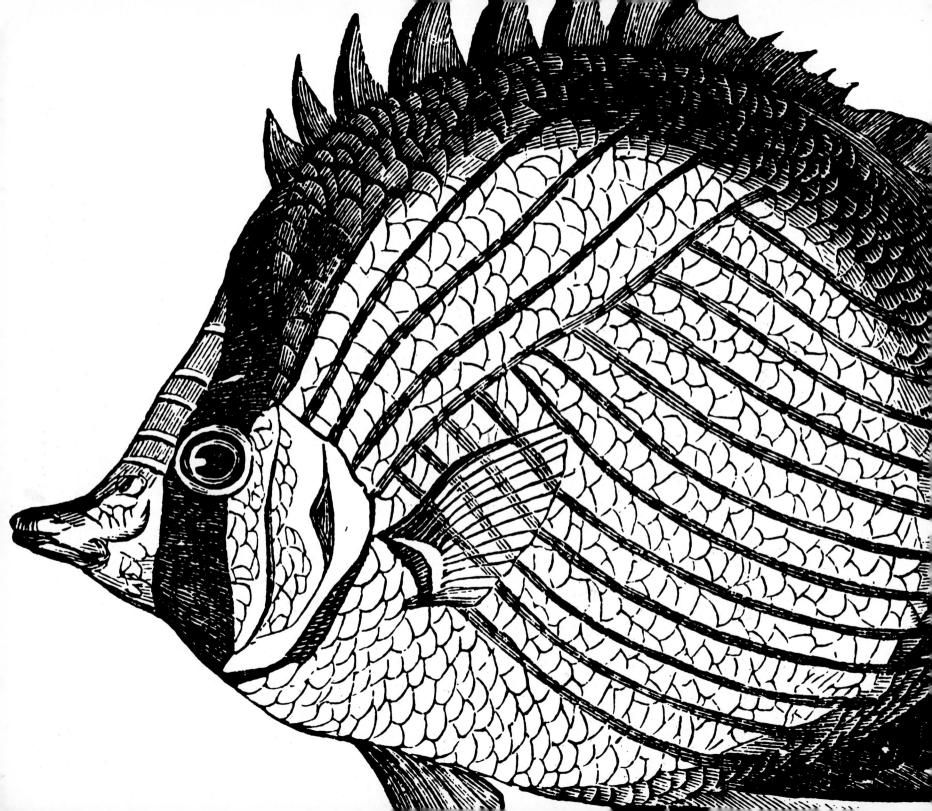

# WHAT FISHES NEED
# TO BE HAPPY

The Buddha, it is said, once cried out in pity for a yogi he met by a river. The unfortunate adept had delighted in showing the great teacher that after twenty years of study and meditation he had learned to walk on water. The Enlightened One, however, was sad that the fellow had invested so much time in trying to walk across the river. The ferryman a few yards downstream, after all, would have gladly taken him across for a small fee!

That fable comes to mind when I hear stories from beginning aquarists. Newcomers often succeed only after spending lots of time and money on elaborate solutions to simple problems. My job, rather than either teaching you how to walk on water or pretending to be enlightened myself, is to act as ferryman; to make your way easier by offering a straightforward, practical approach to the fundamentals of fishkeeping.

Another Eastern strategy applies here. It is said that Zen master wood-carvers accomplish tasks with very few strokes, and rarely need to sharpen their blades. They manage this by "tuning in" to both their blocks of wood and their tools to reveal the path of least resistance.

In the same way, master aquarists rarely reach for medications, seldom lose pets except to the ravages of age, and enjoy their hobby a great deal. To let you advance to that stage, I'll help you learn to observe your fishes carefully. You'll be surprised at how much they can tell you when you know how to listen.

## ON STRESS, HEALTH, AND HAPPINESS
### (Yours and Your Fishes')

The main subject of this chapter is stress—what it does to fish and aquarists, and how it can be avoided. Before getting into specifics, though, let's review a few terms. My dictionary defines "stress" as "a physical, chemical, or emotional factor that causes bodily or mental tension and may be a factor in disease causation." It describes "hobby" as "a pursuit outside one's regular occupation, engaged in primarily for pleasure or relaxation." And it defines "pet" as "an animal kept for amusement, pleasure, or companionship, rather than utility."

Notice that the definitions of "pet" and

"hobby" go together well, while the definition of "stress" is diametrically opposed to both. As a member of the "good times" school of aquarium maintenance, I couldn't agree more. Fishkeeping should be fun!

Fine. Great philosophy. No arguments. But as soon as you buy a tank, reality rears its head. How can you maximize enjoyment while minimizing work and stress? What makes the difference between a bucolic aquatic scene and a tank whose dead and dying fishes make their owners feel like the perpetrators of the Spanish Inquisition?

The simplest answer really *is* simple. Although fishes as a group are quite hardy, even the toughest are weakened by stress. In fishes (as in humans), low-level stress rarely causes visible harm right away, so it is easy to ignore—for a while. But chronic stress invariably takes its toll. Psychological stress alters the amounts of important hormones circulating through the body, and adversely affects the immune system. Physical stress affects heart rate and other body processes. Both kinds of stress affect digestion.

Fishes under stress are less likely to exhibit

good color, and rarely breed. In extreme cases, stress can slow growth or even stop it altogether. And weakened individuals are the first to fall prey to disease. Hence, the cardinal rule of fish-keeping: *Minimize stress on your fishes, and they'll reward you with good health and vigor.* That, in turn, will minimize stress on you and everyone else involved with the tank.

Many beginners ignore this rule, either through ignorance or derring-do. They mix incompatible fishes, ignore water quality, overcrowd tanks, or fail to provide proper foods. The results are familiar: Tank conditions deteriorate rapidly, and there is soon as much angst in the household as there is among the fish. One fish fancier I know had executive office meetings regularly interrupted by frantic phone calls from home—"Mommy, the water is cloudy, the angelfish is breathing hard, and the molly is upside down!" Such mishaps prompt many would-be aquarists to banish their tanks to the attic after a few months.

But you can avoid most of those calamities. Easily. Simply. All you need to do is to understand "the right stuff" to keep both you and your fishes as free from stress as possible.

# THE RIGHT WATER TO START WITH

As terrestrial creatures, we tend to think about water in superficial ways. To us, water either looks "clean" or "cloudy," smells "fresh" or "musty," tastes "good" or "a little funny," and either allows soap to lather or leaves sludge in the bottoms of teakettles.

To fish, subtleties of water quality matter a great deal. Remember that fishes' delicate gills are in intimate contact with the water, and that they constantly smell and taste with most of their body surfaces. For both these reasons, committed hobbyists want to do more than just make sure that water won't kill fishes; we want to make our pets feel at home. And to do that, we pay close attention to the liquid upon which all life depends.

Water rarely sits still for long. In the sea, currents rise from the ocean floor to the surface, sweep from poles to equator, and flow from Asia to the California coast. When water evaporates, winds buffet it around the globe. As it condenses into droplets, its weight pulls it back to the ground. If it stays on the surface of continents, it trickles through streams, plummets over precipices, and meanders through marshes on its way back to the sea. If it sinks underground, it may percolate through limestone rocks and mineral deposits.

Because of the many paths it takes, water's characteristics vary a great deal. In rain-forest streams, it may be nearly as pure as rain. In marshes, it may end up as acidic organic tea. Where it emerges from a subterranean journey, it may act like an alkaline cocktail charged with dissolved minerals.

Because all these water types house at least some fishes, few sets of water conditions can be called "good" or "bad" in an absolute sense. Peat-stained, acid water is fine for some species, but would make life miserable for others. Your success with fishes, therefore, doesn't depend just on the water that comes out of your tap, but on the way you either match that water with appropriate fishes or doctor it to suit your pets.

In order to understand water quality, we have to cover a few basics of water chemistry. But relax. You can handle it, even if you did fall asleep in chemistry class. One convention you should note from the beginning: Whenever I describe substances dissolved in water, I will use the term *"parts per million"* which is abbreviated as ppm. This measure is equivalent to the number of milligrams of compound in each liter of water (mg/l).

## pH and Alkalinity

With all the current talk about acid rain, many people know more about pH than they did a few years ago. Yet the pH scale, which describes the acidity or alkalinity of a liquid, can still be confusing. The units on the scale run from zero, which is extremely acidic, through 14, which is very alkaline. In the middle, around pH 7, is "neutral," neither acidic nor alkaline.

The numbers on the pH scale measure the concentrations of hydrogen ions ($H^+$) in the water. More precisely, pH represents the *negative logarithm* of the concentration of hydrogen ions. Thus, the *higher* the pH (the more alkaline the solution), the *lower* the concentration of hydrogen ions. For example, a solution of pH 8 has a $H^+$ concentration of $10^{-8}$ ($1 \times 10^{-8}$ = .00000001). A solution of pH 6 has a $H^+$ concentration of $10^{-6}$ or .000001. Note that the second solution contains *one hundred times* more $H^+$ ions than the first. Acids, which release hydrogen ions into solution, lower pH. Bases, which react with (and hence remove) hydrogen ions from solution, raise pH.

To view pH from a fish's perspective, unpolluted rainwater—if such still falls in North America—is mildly acidic, with a pH of between 5 and 5.6. When rain percolates over and through many types of soil, its pH is raised slightly by soil minerals to between 6.5 and 6.8. That's roughly the "slightly acid" range preferred by many egg-laying freshwater fishes. The pH in some tributaries of the Amazon, however, can be as low as 3; the relatively few species that live in this type of water are clearly used to much more acidic conditions than most fishes.

The ocean and Africa's Great Lakes, on the other hand, are alkaline, with a pH around 8.3. Thus, it shouldn't surprise you to find that cichlids from those lakes require alkaline water, with a pH range of between 7.5 and 8. Marine fishes *prefer* a pH of close to 8.2, but the hardier among them can usually *tolerate* pH as low as 7.7. Most marine invertebrates, on the other hand, do poorly in water much below 8.0.

Filling your tank with water of the right pH, though, is only the first step, because the presence of living organisms in your tank causes its pH to drop steadily. Remember that most of your pets will give off ammonia as a waste product. As beneficial bacteria in the tank change ammonia into less toxic materials (see below), they release hydrogen ions. Furthermore, if the tank is overcrowded (or underaer-

## pH PREFERENCES OF COMMON AQUARIUM FISH GROUPS

| GENERAL FISH CATEGORY | ACCEPTABLE pH RANGE |
|---|---|
| Live-bearers (guppies, swordtails, etc.) | 7.0–7.4 |
| Typical egg-layers (such as tetras and catfish) | 6.5–7.2 |
| African cichlids (from lakes Malawi and Tanganyika) | 7.6–8.4 |
| Saltwater fishes | 8.0–8.4 |
| Most marine invertebrates | 8.2–8.4 |

ated), carbon dioxide given off by both fishes and bacteria will build up in solution and acidify the water. For these reasons, periodic pH checks and adjustments (Chapters 3 and 9) are essential.

Another factor also affects your tank's pH. Several compounds, including familiar sodium bicarbonate (baking soda), can either release or remove $H^+$ ions from solution. These *buffers* help stabilize pH if present in sufficient quantity. What that means in practical terms is that water containing a buffering compound can ab-

sorb a certain amount of acid without changing its pH. The amount of buffer present affects water's *buffering capacity*—the amount of acid that can be added to it before the pH drops. Because the buffering capacity of aquarium water is often used to slow or prevent tank water from becoming too acid, buffering capacity is often also referred to as *alkalinity,* or *alkaline reserve*, measured in parts per million.

Many (though not all) bodies of freshwater pick up carbonates from rocks and soil, and thus acquire some ability to resist changes in pH. That natural buffering capacity can be useful in aquaria, as it protects your pets from sudden changes in water conditions. If your choice of fishes dictates a pH around neutral (a good place to position a beginner's community tank), a total alkalinity value somewhere around 100–200 ppm will help keep your tank water from becoming acid too quickly. Your municipal water supplier can tell you about your water supply's alkalinity, or you can use a commercially available kit to test the water yourself, as you'll learn in Chapter 3.

What can you expect your tapwater's alkalinity to be? If you live along the Eastern Seaboard from Maine to South Carolina, your water probably has little or no buffering capacity. (That's why bodies of water in this region are so susceptible to acid rain; the water in Boston, where I live, has an alkalinity of only about 10 ppm.) In such cases, you can add ordinary baking soda to act as a buffer, using a test kit to guide you. In other areas, such as parts of California, your water's total alkalinity may be just about right for aquaria. (Santa Barbara's city water has an alkalinity of about 190 ppm.) And in still other areas—particularly parts of Iowa, South Dakota, and Illinois—water supplies may have such high alkalinities that it can be difficult to lower pH below 7.

## Hardness

Does your water foam as it pours from your tap? Or do you have to double recommended amounts of laundry soap to get your clothes clean? These situations indicate opposite extremes in the quantity of certain salts in your water, a condition known as "hardness". Water with very little of these compounds is said to be "soft," and water with high concentrations is said to be "hard."

If your water presents neither extreme phenomenon described above, don't worry, because most beginners' fishes aren't sensitive to moderate variations in hardness. But if your water is exceptionally soft or hard, if you intend to work up quickly to pickier species, or if you plan to include plants in your aquarium, hardness can become an issue.

Unfortunately, working with hardness is more complicated than adjusting pH. First, total hardness results from a mixture of several dissolved compounds, predominantly (but not exclusively) calcium and magnesium carbonates and bicarbonates. Second, there is no single, universal scale for measuring hardness; at least two are in common use in the United States, while a third is more popular in Europe. The most common systems are the German degrees of hardness scale—written as °DH—and the system that describes carbonate concentrations in parts per million. To convert ppm to °DH, divide the first measurement by 18. (So an alkalinity of 18 ppm is equivalent to 1 °DH.)

### MEASURING WATER HARDNESS

| HARDNESS (PPM) | GERMAN HARDNESS | VERBAL DESCRIPTION |
|---|---|---|
| 18–90 ppm | 1–5° DH | very soft |
| 90–180 ppm | 5–10° DH | soft |
| 180–360 ppm | 10–20° DH | moderately hard |
| 360–540 ppm | 20–30° DH | hard |
| over 540 ppm | over 30° DH | very hard |

It is easy to increase water hardness, but it is difficult to soften hard water, and it may also be difficult to change its pH. Because very hard water is often alkaline, and because the same carbonates that create hardness also confer resistance to pH changes, doctoring such water to make it soft and acid can be tough. Standard water softeners used to treat hard well water should not be used for aquaria. These devices, though they make dishwashing and laundering easier, simply replace calcium and magnesium ions with sodium, which your fishes may not appreciate.

If you have extremely hard water and insist on keeping fishes that don't like it, you can try a combination of water-softening resins and filtering through sphagnum peat moss (see below). If that doesn't work, consider installing a water-purification system based on a process called reverse osmosis. RO systems, however, are expensive to install and maintain. Personally, if I were in a region with such water, I

would take the much easier route of specializing in either African cichlids or fancy live-bearers that enjoy those conditions.

## Temperature

Most fishes cannot regulate body temperature as humans can. For that reason, their body temperatures are completely dependent on water temperature. Most home-aquarium fishes come from tropical rivers and lakes with temperatures between 72° and 76° F. A few, such as discus, prefer warmer water (82° F or even a little higher), and others, such as goldfish and koi, like it cooler.

*As long as your tank is not overcrowded,* most species won't mind temperatures a little above their favored range during the hottest part of the summer, although water temperatures above 86° F can be stressful. Because fishes use more oxygen in warmer water, and because warmer water holds less oxygen, crowded tanks are particularly susceptible to oxygen shortages from overheating. During cooler weather, you'll need an aquarium heater to keep your tanks at the right temperature (Chapter 3).

Sudden temperature changes can seriously stress tropical fishes. When introducing new fish or moving fish from tank to tank, either be certain that tank temperatures are equal or bag the fish in plastic and float them in their new tank until temperatures equilibrate. When you're carrying fish outdoors during cold weather, a plastic bag inside a paper bag is *not* sufficient protection. When I buy fish during our New England winters, I drive from door to door (rather than walking or taking public transportation) and shield my pets from chills inside a Styrofoam picnic cooler pre-warmed to room temperature. When outside temperatures drop below about 20° F, I also preheat my car. During the worst of the unmentionably frigid weather in the Midwest, I'd forget about transporting fish altogether.

## TAPWATER IN YOUR AQUARIUM

Tapwater varies greatly, both because of where it comes from and because of things we do to it. Depending on where you live, your water may come from rivers, lakes, reservoirs, or wells. If you draw from your own well, you probably know a reasonable amount about your water. If your needs are met by a municipal supply, on the other hand, you may have left things in the hands of your water department. In either case, fishkeeping requires that you pay close attention to your water.

Learning all these details about your tapwater may seem like a lot of bother, but it will tell you in advance which fishes will be easy for you to keep and which will require a lot of fiddling with water chemistry. If your water is neutral and of moderate hardness, you're golden. All hardy species can tolerate those conditions, so you can take your pick from a very large pool.

If your water conditions are extreme, on the other hand, they'll make some fishes very unhappy. But don't despair. Just remember the joys of fish diversity; you can't possibly keep them all. So you might just as well choose species that will be happy in your tapwater. For very soft, slightly acid conditions, try South American tetras, angelfish, and some of the dwarf cichlids. If your water is hard and alkaline, the path of least resistance leads toward livebearers (such as mollies and swordtails), or to African cichlids.

Some advanced aquarists revel in the challenge of keeping fishes no one else in their area can handle. These enthusiasts often completely change their tapwater to suit their chosen fishes. Some install elaborate water-purification systems for their pets, while others buy pounds of water-treatment chemicals or set up cisterns to collect rainwater. To each his/her own!

### Chlorine and Chloramine

Check with your water suppliers about compounds they add to water for sanitary reasons. Back when I started keeping fishes, water was disinfected with chlorine, and chlorine alone. If chlorine is still all your town uses, don't worry about it, and don't waste money on the chemical chlorine removers pushed in pet shops. Just let your water stand a while in a clean container (overnight if you bubble air through it using an air pump and air stone; twenty-four hours if you don't), and enough chlorine will be driven off to make the water safe for your fishes.

Over the last several years, however, cities have begun switching from chlorine to *chloramine,* a compound produced by treating ammonia with chlorine. Compared to chlorine alone, chloramine is as harmless to humans, more effective against bacteria and other microorganisms, longer-lasting in the water mains, and cheaper. That's good news for public health and city budgets. Because of these advantages, chloramine is becoming the method of choice in more cities all the time.

For aquarists, though, chloramine is bad news, because it is toxic to fishes and more difficult to remove than chlorine. To find out if your local water-treatment plant uses chloramine, check with your municipal waterworks. *If your tapwater contains chloramine, letting it sit overnight will* not *make it safe for fishes.* If there is chloramine in your water, you'll need to use one of the commercially available chloramine-removing preparations, such as Kordon's AmQuel. If you have several tanks or one large tank, buy the stuff in gallon-sized jars, because you'll need to use it on a regular basis.

### Heavy Metals

Lead, mercury, copper, and some other metals that may be carried in tapwater can be harmful in aquaria, although the problems they pose vary greatly from one situation to another. Because of safe drinking-water legislation in most parts of the country, concentrations of dissolved metals in municipal water are rarely high enough to trouble either humans or fishes.

Copper and lead, however, can find their way into city tapwater from old pipes (see below), and a variety of metals may be present in high concentrations in private well water. Small amounts of dissolved copper are no problem for either freshwater or saltwater fishes, but can cause difficulties for other aquatic organisms, as you'll see later on.

## Tapwater: One City's Story

To give you a specific example of the information you can uncover with a little detective work, I conducted my own investigation of Boston tapwater. First, I called my local water department. City bureaucracies being what they are, it took six phone calls to find the right person. But once I found him, he was sympathetic and full of useful information. In addition to the data he offered over the phone, he was happy to mail me a detailed analysis of Boston water before and after treatment.

The most important thing he told me was that Boston periodically (though not constantly) treats water with both chlorine and chloramine. So to be safe, I now use a chloramine remover on any water I add to my tanks.

Additionally, I found that Boston, like many cities, uses water collected in reservoirs. That water is soft, free of metal ions, and runs from slightly acid to slightly basic (pH 6.9–7.3). Taken straight from the source, such water would be ideal for many fishes.

But today's Boston, like many other older cities, has inherited yesterday's water system and housing stock, complete with lead water pipes. Although the city has struggled valiantly to replace as many lead pipes as possible, some still remain. And our handsome but antiquated houses hide mazes of copper pipes joined with lead solder.

Unfortunately, soft, slightly acid water tends to dissolve metal pipes and carry metal ions along with it—into our bodies, if we drink it, and into our fish tanks as well. The longer water sits in the pipes, the more copper and lead it picks up. And whenever a run on the fire hydrants in the neighborhood riles the mains, clouds of rust pour out of our taps. Three consequences of this common situation are worth noting.

First, our water authority tries to minimize the risk from lead pipes by raising the water's pH to somewhere between 8 and 9. This reduces the number of metal ions picked up by water sitting in the pipes. That pH is fine as far as humans are concerned. It's also no problem for my African cichlids, who assure me that Boston water is almost as good as the stuff they get back home in Malawi. But I have to drag the pH down toward neutral before pouring it into my Amazonian tanks.

Second, because even neutral water picks up some metal ions sitting in pipes, water drawn first thing in the morning may carry more lead and copper than we want in our tanks (or in our bodies, for that matter). But there are simple solutions to this problem. If you find (or fear) that dissolved metals are a problem, use water for other purposes before taking any for drinking or adding to your aquarium. Some books advise letting water run for a bit in the morning, but in this era of water shortages I can't practice or recommend waste. Instead, I draw drinking and fish-tank water immediately after I've used water for other purposes: showering, running a washing machine, doing dishes, or the like. If you live in a large apartment complex, you might want to draw tank water on weekday mornings when most people in the building are also using water.

Finally, I use a commercially available mechanical filter to remove rust. The rust alone wouldn't hurt the fishes, but in excessive amounts it can stain the water and gravel reddish brown.

## Water Pollutants

Dangerous pollutants that may show up in tapwater are troublesome enough to humans that you should hear about them in local news before they affect your tanks. In some places, for example, tapwater carries high concentrations of dissolved sodium or nitrate because of runoff from road salt or agricultural chemicals. And in many sites across the country, insidious industrial pollutants—such as PCBs and TCE—have leaked out of toxic-waste dumps into private and municipal wells. If any of these compounds show up in your water, you may want to switch both your family and your fishes to bottled water immediately.

Although the levels of such compounds necessary to harm fish are rather higher than most states allow in drinking water, be aware that dissolved substances steadily accumulate in aquaria over time. When water evaporates, only pure water exits your tank; it leaves behind any salts and similar compounds it once carried. As you add more tapwater to replace that which has disappeared, you steadily add more dissolved compounds. Thus, even if levels of certain compounds in your water are acceptable to begin with, they can accrue over time. This is one reason for the regular water changes described below.

## THE RIGHT TECHNIQUES TO KEEP WATER CLEAN

The instant you add animals to an aquarium, however, your perfect water begins to deteriorate. Fishes add wastes including ammonia, carbon dioxide, proteins, amino acids, phenolic compounds, and a variety of hormonelike substances used in chemical communication. High concentrations of any of these compounds can stress your pets. Keeping water clean enough to stay within fishes' comfort range is not difficult, but it does require certain equipment and simple but periodic maintenance.

In this chapter, I'll concentrate on the "philosophy" of aquarium maintenance, explaining what needs to be done and why. The next chapter will handle the "nuts and bolts" of what equipment to use in your tank and why.

## Mechanical Filtration

To keep your aquarium free of debris and safe from dangers posed by solid wastes and uneaten food, you'll need a mechanical filter. No matter how complicated mechanical filters are, their goal is the same; to pass water through a filter medium that traps dirt particles and can be removed and replaced regularly. That's all there is to it—in the abstract. In reality, the best (and most economical) way to filter your water depends on the size of your tank and the number of fishes you keep.

The old standby—the inside box filter—is simplicity itself. A clear plastic box with slots for water to enter holds a fluffy white filter medium called filter floss. An airstream pumped into the filter base rises through a tube in the center like smoke through a chimney, pulling water up with it. Although there are many high-tech filters and a bewildering variety of filter media on the market today, the basic box filter works fine for uncrowded freshwater tanks less than twenty gallons in size.

Large tanks and tanks stuffed with fishes, however, need higher filtration rates. Enter the assortment of motor-powered filters now available: rectangular filters that hang on the backs of tanks, canister filters that sit under tanks, and custom assemblies built right into tanks. Many manufacturers make extravagant claims for their products, and some are better than others. But many filters and filter media are grossly overpriced and offer few advantages over simpler materials. Remember that all you need for mechanical filtration is a device that pulls (or pushes) water through a medium that traps dirt. We'll return to discuss the specifics of mechanical filters in the next chapter.

## Chemical Filtration

Chemical filtration removes what mechanical filter media cannot—dissolved organic compounds (abbreviated as DOCs) that are either released from bits of uneaten food or dumped into the water by fishes themselves. Chemical filter media are usually placed inside the same device that provides water flow for mechanical filtration, and—like mechanical media—need to be changed regularly. Commercially available chemical filter media vary greatly in price, quality, and usefulness. Only one I can think of is essential, another is optional and applicable only in certain cases, and most are virtually useless.

### Granular Activated Carbon or (GAC)

The most reliable and most cost-effective chemical filter medium, GAC is charcoal that has been "activated" by heating to high temperatures in the presence of oxygen. This process cleans minute surface pores, increasing the granules' effective surface area and their ability to remove DOC from water. Not all brands of filter carbon are activated, so read labels carefully. The best grades of GAC (the only ones worth using) are outrageously expensive in small amounts. Because I use lots of GAC, I buy it in bulk, either from pet stores or by mail order.

Whatever type of filter you use, place your carbon so that the mechanical medium can clear the water of floating particles before it hits the GAC. Otherwise, your chemical medium acts as a mechanical medium, quickly gets coated with "muck," and rapidly becomes useless for the work you want it to do. Experts in chemical filtration currently recommend using between four and ten grams (roughly ¹⁄₁₀–¹⁄₃ oz) of GAC per gallon, and replacing it each month. I've never actually weighed the carbon I use; for my fifty-five-gallon freshwater tanks I just pour a one- to two-inch layer into a typical outside power filter box and change it every three to five weeks.

### Assorted Chemical Filter Media

Several companies market formulations purported to eliminate ammonia or remove other harmful compounds. Most of these products are more hype than substance. Because they become chemically exhausted within a week or so in typical aquaria, and because biological filters (see below) remove ammonia for free, filtering your tank with these preparations is expensive and unnecessary. Put your hard-earned dollars into a good brand of GAC and forget these.

Peat   When I was a kid, I was fond of using a concoction in my tank called "blackwater tonic," a tea-colored liquid extracted from peat-like substances from the bottoms of streams and rivers. I didn't know enough about fishes to base my opinion on rational grounds; it just made sense. I didn't like the flat, metallic taste of our tapwater, and didn't imagine my fishes would like it, either. Why not furnish them with a little "taste of home"?

Think about it. Outfit your fish with distilled water and a sterile tank, and I'd wager they feel the way you might in a squeaky-clean, disinfected hospital room. You could certainly survive, but chances are you wouldn't feel very much at home.

So although I haven't bought blackwater tonic in decades, I "flavor" city tapwater for my Amazonian fishes by filtering it through peat moss. Peat treatment softens and slightly acidifies my water, while giving it the russet color that characterizes many tropical rivers. Although it might take a while for you to get used to water that color, fishes native to it appear to glow in that soft light.

Depending on my mood, I either add a layer of peat to my mechanical filter (behind the GAC in the water path) or hang a mesh bag of moss in the carboys I use to age water added during water changes. As you'll see in Chapter 4, I also wrap sphagnum peat around the roots of my plants. You can buy peat moss at any garden supply store for a *tiny* fraction of the cost charged for peat packaged specially for the aquarium trade.

### Biological Filtration: The Nitrogen Cycle

Ammonia released by fishes and other aquatic animals can quickly build up to toxic concentrations in the confines of an aquarium. Because well-stocked tanks constantly generate large amounts of ammonia, the chemical ammonia removers just discussed are temporary (and expensive) emergency solutions at best.

Luckily for fish fanciers, it is easy to set up a biological filter in which beneficial bacteria solve the ammonia problem. They manage that feat by duplicating in miniature several stages of the nitrogen cycle that operates in the world at large.

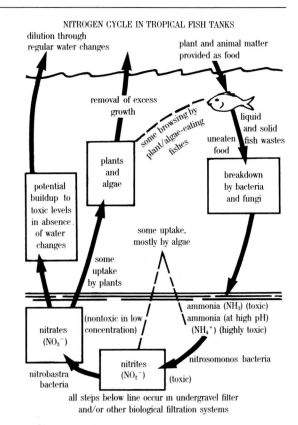

NITROGEN CYCLE IN TROPICAL FISH TANKS

dilution through regular water changes

removal of excess growth

plant and animal matter provided as food

some browsing by plant/algae-eating fishes

plants and algae

liquid and solid fish wastes

uneaten food

breakdown by bacteria and fungi

potential buildup to toxic levels in absence of water changes

some uptake, mostly by algae

some uptake by plants

nitrates (NO₃⁻)

(nontoxic in low concentration)

ammonia (NH₃) (toxic)
ammonia (at high pH) (NH₄⁺) (highly toxic)

nitrobastra bacteria

nitrites (NO₂⁻)

(toxic)

nitrosomonos bacteria

all steps below line occur in undergravel filter and/or other biological filtration systems

A simplified version of the nitrogen cycle in aquaria is shown above. We continually add nitrogen to the aquarium in the form of protein-containing fish foods. Our pets eliminate nitrogen-containing waste in the form of ammonia. That ammonia is taken up by beneficial bacteria and transformed into nitrite, which, unfortunately, is also toxic. In a properly established tank, though, nitrite is converted to relatively harmless nitrate. In planted aquaria, both ammonia and nitrate are taken up as fertilizer by plants that can either be eaten by fishes or removed when they grow too large. Extra nitrate is diluted by periodic water changes (see page 32).

**Undergravel Filters**  Biological filtration sounds almost too good to be true, doesn't it? Sort of like a free ride? Well, it is, when managed properly. All you need to do to encourage beneficial bacteria is to set up an undergravel filter. This simple device consists of slotted plastic filter plates connected to clear uplift tubes and covered with gravel between two and four inches deep. This gravel bed provides many square feet of surface area on which beneficial bacteria can live.

To keep those bacteria healthy, you must provide steady supplies of oxygen and ammonia. Undergravel filters do that by moving water through the bed and back into the tank at a slow but steady pace. In most freshwater aquaria, more than adequate water flow is provided by air stones supplied with the filter. In marine aquaria—where dissolved oxygen levels are lower and demands for bacterial efficiency are higher—electric pumps are sometimes used to power the lift tubes.

Because this flow pattern can pull solid wastes down into the gravel bed (essentially using the gravel as a mechanical filter medium), undergravel filters are usually used together with other mechanical filters. Additionally, some aquarists prefer what is called a reverse-flow configuration, in which the undergravel lift tubes are connected to the output of an outside power filter. In such setups, water is removed from the tank into a canister filter, where it is mechanically and chemically filtered. It is then pushed down through the airlift tubes and forced upward through the gravel bed. This setup, a little tidier in the long term, is not necessary in most freshwater tanks, but is preferred by many marine hobbyists.

Many sources will tell you that it is difficult or impossible to grow plants in an aquarium with an undergravel filter, theoretically because the plants don't like water flow past their roots. Rubbish! Many plants grow in riverbanks where continual seepage of water through the sand is a fact of life. What's more, some tropical plants prefer places where groundwater comes seeping in around their feet. And undergravel filters, by maintaining a steady flow of heated tank water through the gravel, prevent "cold spots" from developing near the bottom of the gravel bed. This can be especially important to ensure healthy plant growth in tanks kept in cool rooms. I've grown perfectly healthy plants in undergravel filters—in both regular and reverse flow configurations—for years.

**Wet-Dry or Trickle Filtration**  In marine aquaria, where even minute amounts of ammonia or nitrates can cause problems, many aquarists prefer souped-up filtration systems referred to as "wet-dry" or "tickle filter" systems. The philosophy behind these systems is simple; water is siphoned from the tank, mechanically and chemically filtered, and then trickled over a deep bed of gravel or artificial filter medium that houses beneficial bacteria. Because most of this filter bed is wet, but not underwater, bacteria on it are exposed to more oxygen and ostensibly do their job more efficiently as a result. The biologically cleaned water is collected in a tray at the bottom of the filter and returned to the tank by a submersible pump.

Most marine aquarists swear by these filters, and I like them a great deal. The only problem I have with them is that most are ludicrously overpriced for a simple collection of plastic tubes, acrylic containers, and a water pump. If you're concerned only with freshwater tanks, ignore trickle filters for now. If you're setting up a marine tank, see the more detailed filtration discussion in Chapter 7.

**Some Final Warnings on Ammonia**  Although biological filters do a remarkable job, there are a few potential problems involving ammonia to keep in mind.

First, getting bacteria established in a new tank can be tricky. Until the system is working well, ammonia and nitrite can rise to toxic levels, a problem often called "new tank syndrome." We'll examine this phenomenon in detail in Chapter 8.

Second, biological filters can't handle an infinite amount of waste, so you still need to restrict the number of fish in your tank. Remember, too, that no matter how long your tank has been set up, you must add new animals slowly to allow the biological filter time to adjust to the added load.

Third, ammonia vapors given off by household cleansers and floor-care products dissolve readily in tank water, so you should avoid using products containing ammonia in rooms where tanks are located. If that isn't possible, make sure the tank is covered and either place the air pump in another room or keep the room as well-ventilated as possible until all traces of ammonia have cleared out.

Finally, dissolved ammonia interacts with free hydrogen ions in water, and is much more toxic to fishes in alkaline water than in acid water. Thus, if you'll be keeping an alkaline pH in your tank (for either freshwater or marine animals), you must be especially careful to keep ammonia levels at a minimum.

## WATER CHANGES

All the mechanical, biological, and chemical filtration in the world won't keep your water in perfect condition forever. The steady addition of nitrogen to the system ultimately leads to a buildup of nitrates. Organic compounds not removed by GAC accumulate over time. And as you replace water that evaporates, you concentrate whatever minerals, metals, and other dissolved compounds your tapwater contains.

For all these reasons, you must regularly remove and replace a portion of your aquarium water. Although there is no "magic schedule" that works in all situations, a general rule of thumb is to replace roughly 20 percent of your tank water at least once every two weeks (once a week if the tank is heavily stocked).

Because water changes mean doing a little work instead of simply adding magic tablets or pushing a button, beginning aquarists often overlook them. That's a pity, because regular water changes are the simplest, cheapest, and most effective way to minimize stress from poor water quality. They offer an opportunity to siphon debris from the tank bottom. And they insure that you periodically look closely at your tank, a good way to spot problems before they get out of hand.

Chances are, though, that regardless of best intentions, you will sooner or later go too long between water changes. (I go through periods where water changes are the last thing on my mind, so I know you will.) And if that's the case, you are apt to discover someday that the tank's pH, hardness, and nitrate levels are way out of whack. The normal, immediate response is to try to correct the problems as quickly as possible. Don't. Do begin changing water again,

but be careful to make any other major changes slowly over a period of several days. Changes in pH, for example, should be made no more quickly than 0.1 units per day.

The importance of water changes reinforces the benefit of matching fishes' preferences with your tapwater. If your pets want soft, acid water and that's what you've got, changing water will be simple. Just draw the water, eliminate chlorine and chloramine, adjust its temperature, and you're set. But if the fishes you covet need soft, acid water and you draw yours from a limestone well, someone is in for trouble. Either you've got to spend time fiddling with pH and hardness every time you do a water change, or the fish will suffer.

## THE RIGHT FOOD

Fishes' diets in nature vary as much as other aspects of their biology. Some are strict vegetarians, others eat only insects, and some prey exclusively on snails or smaller fishes. A few are real gastronomic oddities; certain African cichlids dine only on the eyeballs of other fishes, several Amazonian species crack open seeds as hard as walnuts, and at least one giant fish species snags birds off low-lying branches!

It is morally indefensible to keep species with diets so specialized that they cannot survive in captivity. Luckily, although it may not be feasible to provide your charges with a supply of caterpillars, tropical ants, or planktonic shrimp, hundreds of fish species can thrive on readily available foods. The best approach is to familiarize yourself with your pets' natural food preferences, come up with some standbys that

require little fussing, and vary their diet every once in a while.

### Feeding and Overfeeding

Feed your fishes regularly—several times a day, if you like—but *give them only as much food at each feeding as they can completely consume in five minutes*. If, by accident, you drop too much food in, wait until your fishes have finished eating and remove the excess with either a siphon or aquarium vacuum.

Unfortunately, fishes can't stick their heads out of the tank and say, "Thanks folks, but I've had enough." And most of us seem to feel about feeding fishes the way my grandparents felt about feeding us: "If enough is good, too much is better." But excess food in your tank encourages the growth of undesirable bacteria that consume valuable oxygen and add extra dissolved organic carbon to the water.

### Dried Foods

The aquarium industry has done a splendid job of formulating prepared foods that cover the important nutritional bases. Such foods are available in flake form for small- to medium-sized fishes and in pellet form for larger individuals. While some fishes prefer to feed at the surface, others like to eat off the bottom, so manufacturers have provided both foods that float and those that sink. There are even freeze-dried meats and special vegetarian flake-food diets.

Basic beginners' fishes—guppies, goldfish, and the like—fare perfectly well on a menu of several prepared foods. But though the labels on cans of processed foods promise that each has all the right stuff in the right proportions, most experienced hobbyists agree that a single prepared food is not an adequate diet. To get the best growth and color out of your pets, and to maximize the chances for successful breeding, vary their diet regularly. The easiest way is to alternate feedings of two or three different dried foods, but the *best* way is to vary the diet with frozen, fresh, and live foods.

## Frozen Foods

If you haven't looked in a pet-shop freezer yet, you'll be amazed at the variety of frozen fish foods. Though these treats are not 100 percent odorless, they give off virtually no noticeable odor while frozen, and are conveniently packaged in plastic containers for easy freezer storage. Standard frozen foods include small saltwater creatures called brine shrimp; open-water marine shrimp called krill; tiny freshwater animals called daphnia; small, bright red worms called bloodworms; chopped squid, and several others.

Fishes devour frozen foods with the gusto most of us reserve for ice cream or chocolate. Unfortunately, some frozen foods aren't much closer to a balanced diet for fishes than popcorn and chocolate are for humans. Even brine shrimp, which are nearly perfect food when alive, undergo chemical and physical changes during freezing that decrease their food value. Brine shrimp often burst open when frozen, spilling their innards into the water, so what's left for fish to swallow may be little more than empty skeletons. Furthermore, some valuable compounds are altered in subtle ways by freezing. Thus, even though frozen foods are a welcome addition to aquarium menus, they aren't the final answer.

## Fresh Foods from Your Kitchen

Don't restrict your notion of fish foods to things you buy in a pet store. Many entrées on your own menu are equally good for fishes, and allow you to provide high-quality fresh food without going out of your way. Many big fish eat little fish, don't forget, so scraps of fresh (uncooked) fish will be eagerly devoured by many species. Fresh scallops, mussels, squid, any type of caviar or fish roe, and shrimp are also ideal treats for your pets, as long as you rinse them thoroughly and chop them into very fine pieces. As a second choice, frozen seafood is at least as good as—and invariably cheaper than—frozen fish foods. For vegetarian species, periodically anchor a carefully washed lettuce or spinach leaf on the bottom of the tank.

## Live Food

I grew up with an intuitive feeling that there was something "special" about live foods. Maybe it was an outgrowth of my days as an eco-groovy-brown-rice child during the late sixties. But much later, at the aquaculture lab where I earned my master's degree, we performed experiments to prove that this "factor X" existed. We had often discussed a "special something" that live foods seemed to contain. We didn't know what this mysterious substance was, but drying, freezing, or even freeze-drying seemed to destroy it.

So we set up a series of trials in which we fed baby fishes and lobsters nutritionally equivalent amounts of live, frozen, and dried foods. We cultured the food ourselves (organically, no less) so we knew that all portions started out with the same nutrient content. Yet the test animals receiving live food always grew faster and had better color and vigor than the other two groups. In fact, if we raised our subjects on a diet overwhelmingly composed of processed foods but added even a tiny percentage of live food, the animals grew nearly as well as those fed entirely on live-food diets!

We never did identify factor X precisely, but we did make educated guesses about its nature. (Or, more correctly, *their* nature*s*, because several substances were probably involved.) Because they worked in vanishingly small quantities, they weren't major nutrients like proteins or fats. Instead, they acted more like vitamins. (A vitamin is any compound required by an organism in small amounts that the animal cannot manufacture on its own.) Further experiments indicated that, at least in some cases, "factor Xs" were plant compounds called carotenoids that animals use in a variety of ways.

Because of these and other data, many aquarists agree that periodic feedings of live food are more than worth the extra effort, especially since that effort is really minimal. All the types of live food listed below are available either from pet stores or by mail order.

**Brine Shrimp**  One of the most popular and convenient live foods is *Artemia salina*, the brine shrimp. (You may remember these fuzzy-looking aquatic acrobats advertised in the backs of comic books under the misleading name of "sea monkeys.") Although none of our pets encounter brine shrimp in nature, nearly all feast eagerly on mature shrimp, and baby fishes devour tiny brine shrimp just as eagerly.

*Artemia* live in nature only in very salty bodies of water where few fish survive. There, *Artemia* feed on tiny, single-celled plants called phytoplankton. When mature, brine shrimp produce "eggs" (more properly called cysts) that can either hatch in a few days or withstand drying out completely for prolonged periods of time. These resting cysts are the key to the convenience of brine shrimp as fish food; you can keep them viable in a dry, sealed container for months, or even years. To produce live animals on short notice, just add saltwater and stir! Within a short time, the eggs hatch to release tiny shrimp that are just the right size for feeding to baby fish.

Brine shrimp in nature filter algae from the water around them. Thus, although they are continuously digesting food, their guts are always full. For this reason, fish that eat freshly collected living *Artemia* benefit from healthy doses of vegetable matter chock-full of carotenoids and other nutritional goodies. And newly hatched baby brine shrimp still carry with them many of the nutrients that sustained them through hatching.

*Artemia* held for long periods after collection, however, digest what they have eaten, swim around with empty guts, and steadily lose their nutritional value. And although the shrimp can be kept alive (even raised) on common baker's yeast, they don't have the full nutritional value of algae-fed shrimp.

**Daphnia**  Animals sold in the aquarium trade as *Daphnia* are usually species of small, free-swimming freshwater shrimp. *Daphnia* are common in ponds and lakes, and are readily available during seasons when local bodies of water are not frozen. As far as fish are concerned, *Daphnia* are the freshwater equivalent of brine shrimp. Though they lack the storable cyst of *Artemia, Daphnia* are easier to maintain in culture. If you live near a pond, you can collect *Daphnia* yourself during spring, summer, and fall. All you need is a net and some caution about collecting potential fish predators along with fish food.

**Mosquito Larvae**  Mosquito larvae are relished by fishes large enough to swallow them whole. These wrigglers are easy to collect; you probably don't have to go any farther afield than a water-filled trough or barrel in your own backyard. Of course, you don't want to keep mosquito larvae around for too long, or they'll mature and fly off to make a meal of you!

***Tubifex* Worms**  *Tubifex* worms are thin red aquatic worms that usually live in areas inundated by large quantities of organic matter. (That's a polite way of saying that they are most commonly found in open sewers.) For that reason, though excellent food for your fishes, they are also a potential source of disease. *Tubifex,* among the favorite foods of tropical catfish, are relished by many other fishes as well, but should not be fed too often.

If you buy *Tubifex* to feed your fishes, make certain that the worms are bright red, actively wriggling, and cling to one another in tight clumps. Worms that are grayish in color, lethargic, or stringy-looking are dying and should not be fed to fishes. When you get the worms home, place them in a deep container under a stream of cold running water strong enough to break up the clump. Discard any that float up to the surface. Rinse the worms two or three times until the only ones left are active and healthy-looking. Feed them to your fishes slowly, adding no more than your fish can eat at once; you don't want *Tubifex* escaping into the gravel, where they will probably die. Keep *Tubifex* in a closed container in a refrigerator or other cold place, and rinse them vigorously on a daily basis. *Tubifex* are not suitable for home culture.

**White Worms**  White worms, members of the genus *Enchytraeus,* are inexpensive, innocuous, and are good supplemental food for many small fishes. Although not usually stocked by pet shops, white worms are often available from fellow hobbyists locally, can be purchased through the mail, and can be easily cultured.

**Wingless Fruit Flies**  Many medium- to large-sized fishes eagerly devour fruit flies. The availability of mutant fruit flies that lack functional wings makes their culture nearly foolproof, and makes feeding them a snap. All you need to do is remove the cover of the culture container, tilt the bottle over the aquarium, and tap it to send the flies rolling into the aquarium.

**Tank-Raised Live Foods**  Don't overlook live foods that you can raise easily, right in the tank with your fishes. Nearly all fishes enjoy nibbling at green algae or at the tender parts of floating plants such as duckweed and *Riccia* (Chapter 4). Snails, too, are excellent food; some fishes devour small snails shell and all, and nearly any fish will enjoy eating larger snails if they are removed from their protective shells.

## THE RIGHT KINDS OF SPACE

"How many fishes can I keep in my aquarium?" is the most common beginners' question. Many books recommend "one inch of fish per gallon of water without aeration; two inches of fish per gallon of water with aeration." That formula has caused more grief to more fishes than any other bit of misinformation. In truth, such formulae all fall short, because stocking density depends on sizes and personalities of fishes, filters used, tank shape, and water temperature.

Furthermore, you should realize that there are two ways to approach this question. Usually, beginners are really asking, "How many fishes can I stuff in my tank without them all turning belly-up by morning?" It makes more sense to ask, "How many fishes can coexist comfortably in my tank, in a way that allows me to keep things running with minimal effort?"

The answer is not necessarily straightforward. No matter how large your tank, it is infinitesimally small compared to natural habitats. On a reef or in a pond, individuals of aggressive species have plenty of room in which to avoid one another once a contest between them has been decided. But even a fifty-five-gallon tank—which most of us think of as quite large—offers little refuge for the vanquished, who can be continually harassed by the victor.

And even generally peaceable fishes may harass one another if crowded into too small a space.

For these reasons, it is particularly important to observe warnings about species that do not get along with others of their own kind. Nearly everyone knows that male Siamese fighting fish won't tolerate one another, but there are many other, less flamboyant species that fight just as intensely. In nature, their aggressive behavior spaces them out with many yards between them; in tanks, without that room to roam, they fight both more frequently and more intensely.

There are also some fishes—such as the giant danio (*Danio malabaricus*)—that are peaceable but very active swimmers. Such species fare well in ten-gallon tanks when small, but need much more room to swim when three or four inches long.

That's why experienced aquarists stock tanks more by intuition than by calculation. Two dozen large cardinal tetras in a twenty-gallon tank, for example, present an entirely different—and far more peaceful—situation than two dozen half-grown cichlids of the same size. But because everyone needs a rough guide to start with, I'll offer my version of a formula, assuming that you equip the tank with full mechanical and biological filtration, and that you perform regular water changes.

## The Formula

The major physical limitation on fish density is not the volume of the tank in gallons, but its surface area. This is true because the exchange of oxygen and carbon dioxide between tank water and the atmosphere occurs mainly at the tank surface, so the greater a tank's surface area, the more oxygen it can supply to your fishes. Because the processing of nitrogenous wastes occurs mostly in the filter bed that covers the bottom, the larger the tank's footprint, the more fish wastes it can handle. A long, low tank thus has a greater carrying capacity than a shorter, taller one that holds the same amount of water.

**Sizing the Tank** Measure your tank's length and width (in inches) and multiply them to obtain surface area in square inches. We'll use that value as a "master number" in our calculations.

**Sizing the Fishes** Group your chosen fishes into three rough size classes based on their length from front end to the base (not the end) of their tails. The reason for this rough (and arbitrary) three-tiered system is that longer fish (with the exception of eels) are "beefier" than smaller ones. Because they carry more flesh per inch of body length, they require more oxygen and produce more waste per inch than smaller fishes.

*Small (less than two inches):* This range encompasses mature guppies, young platies and swordtails, most tetras, some damselfishes, and gobies.

*Medium (two to four inches):* Into this category fall mature platies and swordtails, dwarf cichlids, *Corydoras* catfish, and juvenile cichlids, rainbowfish, and sailfin mollies. This range also includes mature clownfish, dwarf marine angelfish, and dwarf lionfish.

*Large (more than four inches):* This includes full-sized cichlids, rainbowfish, and sailfin mollies, along with larger marine angelfish, butterfly fish, groupers, and moray eels.

**Estimating Fishes' Needs**   Calculate a stocking-density index for your fishes using the following guidelines.

TROPICAL FRESHWATER FISHES: For small fishes two inches in length or less, allow six square inches for each inch of fish length. For medium fishes between two and four inches, allow nine square inches per inch of fish. For large fishes over four inches, allow twelve square inches per inch.

TEMPERATE FRESHWATER FISHES (such as goldfish):   Double the above space requirements to twelve, eighteen, and twenty-four square inches for small, medium, and large-sized fishes, respectively.

TROPICAL MARINE FISHES:   For these animals, space requirements are still higher, both because saltwater holds less dissolved oxygen than freshwater and because marine fishes are less tolerant of poor water conditions. I'd recommend figuring as much as eighteen square inches per linear fish-inch for small specimens, twenty-four square inches for each inch of medium-size fishes, and thirty-six square inches for each inch of larger specimens.

**Sample Calculations**   How does this formula translate into specifics?

For simplicity, assume that all your fishes are roughly the same size. To determine how many of those fishes the tank can hold, first divide the tank's surface area by the index number above. Then divide the resulting number by the length of the fishes in inches. The final answer will be the number of fishes of that size your tank will hold comfortably.

Let's walk through that example step by step in one particular case, and then look at the results for slightly different cases. Assume that you have a twenty-gallon "long" tank that is twelve inches wide and twenty-four inches long. The tank's surface area is $12 \times 24$ or 288 square inches.

For a tropical freshwater tank stocked with full-grown guppies or good-sized cardinal tetras, roughly one-and-a-half inches in length, divide the tank's surface area by the index number for fishes of that size.

$$\frac{\substack{288 \text{ sq. in.} \\ \text{in your tank}}}{\substack{6 \text{ sq. in.} \\ \text{per in. of fish-body length}}} = \substack{48 \text{ in. of} \\ \text{fish-body length} \\ \text{in your tank}}$$

Now, divide that number by the length of your fishes in inches.

$$\frac{\substack{48 \text{ in. of fish-body length} \\ \text{in your tank}}}{\substack{1.5 \text{ in. of fish-body length} \\ \text{per fish}}} = \substack{32 \text{ fishes} \\ \text{in your tank}}$$

Following the formula, you could comfortably stock that tank with thirty-two large cardinal tetras or guppies ($288 \div 6 \div 1.5 = 32$).

If you perform the same calculations for larger fish, you'll find that your tank can hold eleven medium-sized platies, swordtails, *Corydoras* catfish, or good-sized barbs ($288 \div 9 \div 3 = 10.6$), or five full-grown mollies, African cichlids, or *Synodontis* catfish ($288 \div 12 \div 5 = 4.8$).

TEMPERATE FRESHWATER FISHES: The same twenty-gallon tank holds fewer specimens. A comfortable stocking density for cold-water fishes allows for twenty-four small (1.5–2 inch) goldfish, or five medium-sized (2–4 inch) goldfish, or two or three large (5–6-inch) show goldfish or medium-sized koi.

TROPICAL MARINE FISHES:   The formula immediately warns you that you can't safely stock many marine fishes in a twenty-gallon tank, perhaps five small clownfish or damsels, or three to four medium-sized damsels, dwarf angels, or blennies.

Although the formula would allow one five-to six-inch specimen in a tank this size, I wouldn't recommend it; marine fishes that large need more room to swim than a two-foot tank provides. Very few of us would keep a dog or cat in a cage barely big enough for it to turn around in. Yet many aquarists blithely dump twelve-inch fish into fifteen-inch tanks. Please don't.

## Why Less Is More

If you compare my recommended stocking densities with those you may see elsewhere (which I encourage you to do), you'll find that I've been very conservative; I recommend what some people might consider "understocking." I do this for several reasons.

Fishes in tanks are always more crowded than they would be in nature. As you crowd them further, you place them under more and more psychological stress. Beyond a certain point, that stress can become a major factor in causing disease.

The larger the biological load in your tanks, the faster both particulate and dissolved organic wastes accumulate. Thus, the more fish you cram into a tank, the more often you have to clean your filter and change water. Assuming that you'd like your tank to run with minimal work on your part, the less crowded, the better.

Many fishes (with the exception of certain smaller tetras) grow rapidly when happy. You may start your tank with young fishes an inch or so in length. But if those fishes happen to be angelfish, oscars, groupers, or triggerfish, they will soon be twice their original size. So if you start out with a full tank, it will become seriously overcrowded within six months. Alternatively, if you're keeping live-bearers, you'll soon have their offspring on your hands. To keep them, you must either leave room in the original tank or be prepared to buy another. Finally, it is nearly impossible to resist the urge to buy certain fishes when you see them. That's another reason to leave a little "slack" in the tank when you first start out; you'll have some space when you encounter that "must have" fish on a routine visit to a pet shop.

## Places to Hide

Many fishes need places to hide—from each other, from other fishes, from light, and from you. Some fishes are simply shy, and feel more comfortable knowing they have a place where they can duck out of sight when they want to.

Zookeepers and aquarists at large public aquaria know this phenomenon well; give animals a place to run to, and once they know it is there, they rarely use it. Fail to provide the hiding spot, though, and the animal ends up

as a nervous wreck. Exactly what sort of refuge you provide depends on the fishes involved. Many species that hang out in the middle of the tank will be happy with a dense group of plants in a back corner. Bottom-dwellers, on the other hand, often prefer the security of a small, dark cave among rocks, beneath an upside-down flowerpot, or under half of a coconut shell.

Many fishes, particularly reef fishes and cichlids, are territorial, which means that each male instinctively selects an area to protect from all other males as his private turf. Give these fishes enough room, and they'll stake out territories with no problem. Crowd them too much, and they'll battle with one another constantly, even in a tank with plenty of swimming room. This constant fighting causes long-term stress, especially for the loser of the battle. Once again, the trick is to know your fishes well enough to avoid such problems before they start.

## The Right Neighbors

As hard as we might try to avoid ascribing human personality traits to fishes, there are certain labels that stick. Most triggerfish and certain cichlids are bullies. Some cichlids are so nasty that they can scarcely be kept in mated pairs; they make fishburgers out of anything else in the tank, regardless of available space and the size of the interloper. Other species, such as the magnificent male *Betta splendens,* or Siamese fighting fish, are fierce only when faced with males of their own species. In the company of other species, they are timid hermits, easily intimidated and picked on. Still other species, such as many tetras, are highly

social species that are most comfortable—and hence show their best and brightest colors—only in the company of their own kind.

## HEALTHY FISHES TO START WITH

Although some fish diseases can be recognized and treated reliably, other aspects of aquatic medicine are closer to witchcraft than they are to science. We'll cover diseases and their treatment in Chapter 9, but by far the most important step in keeping your fish healthy is to *buy* them healthy.

There's no reason that freshwater fishes shouldn't be hale and hearty when you see them in dealers' tanks. Most (though not all) freshwater species sold these days are either bred in captivity or captured when small and reared under controlled conditions. Given proper husbandry, these animals should arrive at your neighborhood pet shop well-fed and disease free. But stresses during shipment, changes in water conditions, and overcrowding can add up to trouble, even for hardy fishes and even in the tanks of well-meaning retailers.

Spotting trouble can be frustrating to first-time hobbyists. While many signs of less than perfect health in fishes are obvious to experts, they can be nearly invisible to novices. Just recently, for example, I visited a friend who proudly pointed me toward his community tank. In an instant, I noted several serious problems: Fights in the tank had produced frayed fins, several fish were seriously stressed, and three of them had advanced fin rot. How could my friend ignore problems that screamed at me from across the room?

Judging fish health—like judging the health of kids or other pets—depends on knowing how healthy individuals act and how they should look. If you have children, for example, you know their bodies and behaviors in intimate detail—the way they hold their heads, the way they walk, the way they breathe, and even how their skin looks. So if one of them starts to sniffle or develop a rash, you instantly notice the change and take action. Assessing a fish's health requires similar skill.

But how can you tell when a fish has the sniffles? That's where time invested in fish-watching pays off. Once you've seen healthy specimens, you have a standard against which to compare others that may or may not be healthy. A few warning signs can be obvious to anyone: You should, for example, never buy apparently healthy specimens from a tank with dead fish floating in it. Other signs of disease or distress are more subtle and vary from species to species, but there are several specific problems to watch for.

### General Appearance and Demeanor
Fish should appear lively and alert, and should either hold their fins erect or move them in the typical manner for their species. You'll see for yourself that catfish and loaches hide in dark places, discus are shy and retiring, and most African cichlids are active and boisterous. Once you're familiar with such differences, if you see a discus dashing around or an African cichlid hiding, you'll know there's trouble afoot. Unless they have just been fed, healthy fish should be willing to feed for you in the dealer's tank. (Don't feel shy about asking the salesperson to toss in a little food so you can see what happens.)

### Body Shape
Bodies should be firm and well-rounded; a thin or depressed back, a twisted spine, or a shrunken belly is a sure sign of trouble.

### Swimming/Balance/Position
Fish should be swimming or hovering in the manner appropriate for their species. That means most species should be gliding or darting through the middle of the tank. As a rule, only catfish and other bottom dwellers rest on the bottom for long, and only hatchetfish and other surface dwellers linger at the surface. Deviations from these behaviors—catfish hanging around at the surface, for example, or tetras lying on the bottom—indicate stress or illness.

### Breathing Rate
Most fishes of similar size and activity have roughly similar breathing rates. Hyperventilation or gasping for air at the surface signifies problems, either with tank water or with the fish's gills.

### Eyes
They should be clear and mobile. Cloudy eyes or eyes protruding from their sockets indicate infections or other problems.

### Fins
They should be clear or cleanly colored, depending on species. They should not be cloudy, shredded, torn, or fraying at the ends. Most species (with some exceptions, such as bettas) normally hold fins erect; fins that are drooping or clamped along the body are a sign of trouble.

### Scales
They should be evenly lustrous and lie flat against the body. Missing scales signal fights or handling damage, while protruding scales indicate serious disease.

### Lateral-Line Pores
They should appear as small, clean "pinprick" holes in the scales. If they are enlarged, appear sunken or ragged, or are surrounded by areas where normal skin color has disappeared, the fish is in trouble.

### Coloration
Bit more difficult for novices to evaluate, for reasons discussed in Chapter 1, but in fishes you know well, it can offer important clues to health. When comfortable and well-cared-for, most fishes show full—though not necessarily breeding—colors; individuals whose colors are washed out are usually stressed out.

### Treatment for New Arrivals
Because many fish diseases involve invisible incubation periods, even healthy-looking fish can harbor disease. And, as you'll learn in Chapter 9, many parasites and diseases have life cycles that cause far more trouble in tanks than in the wild. For that reason, you should quarantine new purchases for a minimum of ten days to two weeks in a separate aquarium before adding them to an established tank.

Most hobbyists don't like quarantine because it involves keeping an extra tank (complete with heater and filter). But if you—like most of us—are constantly tempted by the urge to add "just one more fish" to your tank, quarantine can avoid disaster. I'd wager that nearly every aquarist has—at one point or another—destroyed a healthy community tank by failing to quarantine an invisibly infected addition.

Because virtually all marine fish are sold within weeks of capture in the wild, *quarantine is absolutely essential to protect established saltwater aquaria*. Virtually all wild-caught fishes—even those that appear healthy—harbor parasites or some sort of latent infection. Subject those fishes to the stresses of capture, transport, and life in captivity, and latent infections easily become life-threatening. Because of this near-certainty of infection, many experts advise not only quarantining newly acquired marine fishes, but medicating them as though they were infected. You'll find treatment details in Chapter 9.

# LIFE-SUPPORT SYSTEMS: TANKS AND EQUIPMENT

Back when I started with fishes, aquarium books dispensed with equipment in short chapters. Tanks, filters, air pumps, and aquarium lights came in a few standard sizes. That equipment had problems—tanks rusted, water heaters garbled TV reception, and air pumps sounded like jackhammers—but few alternatives were available. During the last decade, the aquarium industry has responded to a more sophisticated market by creating aquaria and accessories that are attractive and dependable.

The flip side of the industry's growth is that these options present an intimidating range of choices. Some manufacturers shroud products in advertising hype that would make Madison Avenue blush. And several "new and improved" products are simply *different* from (and more expensive than) their predecessors, without being any *better* from a fish's standpoint.

How should you find your way through this embarrassment of riches? Now that you know what fishes need, you should learn how different types of equipment can help you meet those needs. Then, once you settle on a tank size and decide on the fishes you want to keep, you can select the right equipment for the task at hand.

## ON FISHKEEPING AND FINANCES

The question that invariably comes up at this point is simple: "What's all this going to cost me?" The answer, typically, is not so simple.

I remember once asking a friend with two young children about the cost of living in his town. "Cost of living?" he replied. "There's no such thing as 'cost of living.' The cost of living is whatever you make!"

The same can be said of aquarium equipment if you let things get out of hand. Aquaria, like houses, boats, and other money pits, can theoretically be maintained on a shoestring but have an uncanny ability to swallow as much money as you throw at them. You estimate what your hobby will cost, inevitably overspend, and panic when faced with unexpected extra expenses. Three kinds of medication at ten bucks a shot? Sure. Fancy new filter for forty dollars? Of course. Anything to save Danny's guppies.

There's no way this book can guarantee to prevent these occurrences. The best I can hope for is to help you avoid the most common pitfalls. But before you trust me to recommend equipment, you should understand my perspective on fishkeeping finances. Although I treat my pets well, I have only a finite amount of money to spend on them. So whenever functionally equivalent options are available, I'll choose the one most reasonably priced. But my time and my pets' health are also valuable to me. So if a few extra dollars can either guarantee more dependable materials or eliminate maintenance work, I consider the better equipment a good investment.

The price/quality/design range for aquarium equipment parallels remarkably the situation with cars. At one end of the market are economically priced and dependable (if somewhat lackluster) domestic models. At the other end are high-styled, well-designed luxury imports (primarily from Germany) whose already high prices have risen steeply as foreign exchange rates have shifted. Somewhere in between are solidly engineered domestic and imported products that function perfectly well.

I generally recommend equipment in the upper-middle range. When you make your own decisions, inform your taste with common sense and knowledge of your limits. If you're a Mercedes/BMW kind of person, buy the best of the German products and enjoy! If you're like the rest of us, keep in mind that many models will do the same job for a lot less cash.

# CHOOSING YOUR FIRST TANK

## How Big?

You want to begin with a "starter" tank. Something small and manageable. A five-gallon model, perhaps. In the abstract, that makes sense. Starting small would seem to let you minimize your investment until you decide if you really like keeping fish. Right?

Wrong.

Ask experienced aquarists what tanks they recommend for beginners, and nearly all will respond, "The bigger, the better." Why? Because very small tanks are actually harder to maintain than bigger tanks. If that puzzles you, remember that constant water conditions are essential to keeping your fish stress free. The larger the body of water you're managing, the slower its character will change if anything goes wrong.

If the heater breaks down, for example, or if a nearby window is left open in cold weather, a twenty-gallon tank will take four times as long to cool down as a ten-gallon tank. The same is true for most water conditions; all other things being equal, pH, hardness, and levels of dissolved wastes change more gradually in larger tanks than in tiny ones. That gives you more time to notice problems and correct them before they harm your pets.

Next, remember about tank space. The bigger your tank, the more fishes you can keep in it. And from an aesthetic point of view, the larger the tank, the more numerous your options in creating attractive aquatic landscapes.

That's why I don't even *think* of setting up a tank that's less than fifty-five gallons, except for special purposes such as breeding. But don't panic. I would never advise you to shell out for that big a tank before you know what you're doing. I just want you to avoid two- to five-gallon "executive aquaria," "designer mini-aquaria," or "desktop aquaria" like the plague. Unless, that is, you plan to stock them not only with plastic plants, but with plastic fish as well. Minitanks do have their place; they make great toys for aquarists with enough experience to stay one jump ahead of trouble. They're just not the best things for beginners.

What's the smallest reasonable size? If you're certain that you want nothing more than a few guppies and platies, start with a ten-gallon tank. They're not much more expensive than five-gallon setups, they're easier to maintain, and they offer a lot more stocking possibilities. If you (or your kids) really take to fishes, you won't feel the need to run right out and buy a bigger tank. And down the line, if you do move up to a larger tank, a ten-gallon is always good to have for breeding, to quarantine new arrivals, or to treat sick specimens.

If you're really interested in fishes and want to give fishkeeping a serious try, start with a twenty-gallon tank. If financial constraints place a new setup that big out of reach, consider a used one (see Buying Used Equipment, page 56).

## What Shape?

Remember that a tank's shape affects its biological carrying capacity for several reasons. Furthermore, because most fishes swim back and forth rather than up and down, they utilize horizontal space more fully than vertical space. That's why long, shallow aquaria can hold more fish than tall, narrow tanks of the same volume. Many tanks, including twenty-gallon and thirty-gallon sizes, come in both "long" and "high" configurations. Unless you have to cram your tank into limited shelf space, opt for the long styles every time. Tall, hexagonal tanks may be impressive to look at, but they don't hold many fish.

## What Styles?

Assuming that you won't relegate your pets to either basement or attic, your tank should function as an element of design in your home. Tanks of old couldn't do that gracefully; clunky, bulky, and framed in rusting steel, they sat on rust-covered wrought-iron stands that exposed ungainly pumps, filters, and air tubes to full view.

Enter New Age aquaria: sleek, elegant, and built almost entirely from glass or acrylic and clear silicone sealer. Most tanks and accessories come in your choice of contemporary matte black or imitation wood grain. And many modern stands are designed (and priced) to function as serious pieces of furniture that suit any taste from American country to Eurostyle. Spacious cabinets contain and conceal equipment and supplies while complementing tank design and coordinating with room decor.

Glass and acrylic tanks each have advantages

and disadvantages. Glass is more scratch-resistant, a point to remember if you'll have young helpers scraping algae from inside surfaces. Glass tanks are available in most sizes (though typically only in rectangular shapes), and are usually less expensive than comparably sized acrylic models.

Acrylic tanks, on the other hand, are made in a wide range of configurations. (There are even double hexagon tanks joined by twin cylindrical tunnels.) Acrylic is a better insulator than glass, so it holds heat in (and out) more efficiently. Acrylic is also less susceptible to serious damage from a casual knock, though shoddily built models may leak for no apparent reason.

As far as stands go, don't feel restricted to pieces marketed specifically for that purpose; just keep in mind that even medium-sized tanks are heavier than you might expect. Water weighs roughly 8⅓ pounds a gallon. That means a twenty-gallon tank will weigh 166 pounds, even before you add 20 to 40 pounds of rocks and gravel. I can't stress strongly enough how important it is to provide solid support for your tank, because even the best models spring leaks if their stands settle unevenly. And a leaky tank is the last thing you want to deal with. You'd be amazed at how much floor the contents of a ten-gallon tank will cover.

With that caveat in mind, you can improvise a stand from any strong (and sufficiently water-proof) table or cabinet that suits your taste. I used my tank as the centerpiece of a Eurostyle living room several years before black-lacquered tank stands became available. So I hunted down a pair of good-quality Scandinavian lacquered chests to place side by side. Because a fifty-five-gallon tank covers them completely, I could

save a bundle by settling for a pair of floor models that were scratched on top. That top-quality lacquer has resisted spills and drips for five years now, and the cabinets haven't warped at all.

## EQUIPPING YOUR TANK

### Lights

Aquarium lights serve several functions; they let you see your fish, they let the fish see each other and their food, and they provide light to grow plants or live corals. Despite their importance, lights are often slighted in beginner aquarium "package deals." And if you compare notes among magazine articles and experienced hobbyists, you'll find more disagreement over lighting than nearly any other area of the hobby. Because of this honest confusion, you need know enough to choose your light source carefully.

Why should anything as apparently simple as choosing light bulbs be controversial? The problem is that light and its interactions with living things are so complex that explaining them in any detail would take a chapter by itself. But I'll do my best to set you on the right track without dragging you through a maze of physics and biophysics.

The energy carried in both sunlight and artificial light is spread out over a broad range of wavelengths, which we see as different colors. The part of that range our eyes respond to, called the visible spectrum, runs from violet light (wavelengths around four hundred nano-

meters (nm)), to red light (wavelengths around 700 nm). Wavelengths shorter than 400 nm we call "ultraviolet," and light of wavelengths longer than 700 nm we call "infrared." We use those names because we can't see light in those parts of the spectrum, not because they differ dramatically in physical properties from other wavelengths nearby.

Two things complicate efforts to describe the effects of light on living things. First, different light sources provide different amounts of energy at various wavelengths. Sunlight carries lots of energy all across the spectrum, and looks "white" under most conditions. Tungsten bulbs put out light that usually looks "white" to us, but carries far less blue light and a lot more red and infrared than you might expect. Cool White fluorescents emit mostly blue and green wavelengths and little or no energy in the red region of the spectrum.

Second, our eyes respond most strongly to light in different parts of the spectrum than do chlorophyll and other light-absorbing compounds in plants. Our eyes are most sensitive in the greenish-yellow region, around 550 nm. The chlorophylls of green plants, on the other hand, absorb light best in two narrow bands at opposite ends of the spectrum—one out in the red between 600 and 650 nm, and one down in the blue between 400 and 450 nm. Thus, the green and yellow wavelengths our eyes see best are precisely those wavelengths that are *least* useful to plants.

The upshot of all this is that light measurements used in photography (footcandles and lux, for example) relate to human vision, and have no predictable relationship to plants' needs. A green light, for example, can be bright to the human eye but virtually worthless to plants. And a light source that precisely duplicates the energy distribution of sunlight may provide less energy useful to plants than a source that concentrates its output in the red and blue parts of the spectrum.

It's no wonder that there's a great deal of confusion among aquarists about light and plants. To try to clear up some of the puzzles you're apt to come across, here's a list if the relative merits of the light sources commonly available.

## The Right Light for You

If, despite all my efforts to the contrary, you decide not to grow aquarium plants, choosing a light is simple. Buy a single-tube fluorescent reflector, select a bulb whose color appeals to you, and keep that bulb until it burns out, thousands of hours later.

If you do want to grow plants, select bulbs carefully, because most failures with plants can be blamed on insufficient light. Remember that no matter what type of bulb you choose, a single tube over a tank in a dark corner will not provide enough light for most aquatic plants. To ensure success, you'll need a reflector (or two reflectors) that hold at least two bulbs running the entire length of the tank. (Twenty-gallon "long" tanks take two-foot, twenty-watt fluorescents neatly; fifty-five-gallon tanks take four-foot, forty-watt bulbs.)

If you're handy enough to build a wooden enclosure above your tank, you can improvise with four-foot, two-bulb shop-light fixtures that cost little more than ten dollars. If you're starting with a ten- or twenty-gallon setup, the four-foot length leaves plenty of room for

houseplants on either end. (I've seen some beautiful aquarium and houseplant combinations set up this way.) If you've got a fifty-five-gallon tank, they'll be just the right size. Just be sure to protect the lights from spray with a glass tank cover.

If you choose commercial aquarium fixtures, steer clear of those with "push and hold"–type switches that have to be turned on manually. It is more convenient to control tank lights with a timer that provides regular light/dark cycles for your fish while leaving you with one less thing to remember in the morning. Set the timer to turn the light on ten to twenty minutes before your pets' morning feeding, so they will be "awake" and ready to eat. You can set the timer to keep lights on for twelve to sixteen hours each day, but can also turn them off earlier if you need to. Make certain your fixture has a grounded (three-prong) plug, and select a timer that is also grounded.

### Tungsten (Incandescent)
This is the easy part; stay away from incandescent bulbs. They get hot enough to overheat tanks in summer and to burn inquisitive young fingers year-round. Incandescents also burn out quickly, produce relatively little useful light for the electricity they consume, and don't put out enough blue light to support good plant growth.

### Fluorescents
Fluorescent lights are available in a bewildering variety. As a group, they put out more light than tungsten per unit of electricity consumed, and emit much less heat. Several produce light that not only displays plants and fish to good advantage, but also contains a good balance of wavelengths for plants.

Because the output of fluorescent bulbs drops off quickly during the second half of their rated life, it's better to buy cheaper bulbs and replace them more often rather than choose expensive bulbs and keep them until they burn out. (I know that I'm much more willing to replace bulbs twice a year if they cost three dollars rather than fifteen dollars apiece.) If you illuminate your tank for the recommended twelve to sixteen hours each day, replace your bulbs every six to eight months.

### Standard Warm White and Cool White Bulbs
Neither of these alone provides the perfect spectrum for optimal plant growth, although Cool White by itself measures up remarkably well against special plant bulbs that cost up to seven times as much. Unfortunately, neither type is very flattering to either fishes or plants.

### Regular Grolux or Aquarilux Bulbs
These were designed for maximum output in the red and blue regions of the spectrum absorbed most strongly by chlorophyll. They are relatively expensive and don't give off as much light as some other bulbs, but their pinkish light shows off the yellows, reds, and orange colors of freshwater fishes and the greens of live plant foliage spectacularly well. You could consider pairing one of these bulbs with a single Cool White for increased plant growth if plants aren't a major priority.

### Wide-Spectrum Grolux Bulbs
Wide-spectrum lamps are brighter, less strongly colored, and about half the price of standard Grolux tubes. They keep the high red output of regular Grolux and add more punch in the

blue end. Their attractive combination of price, appearance, and suitability for both houseplants and aquarium plants has made them my all-round favorites for years.

**Vita-Lite Bulbs**  Vita-lites are designed to duplicate the energy distribution of sunlight, and generate 15 percent more light than standard fluorescent bulbs of similar wattage. Combined with Cool White bulbs, Vita-lites produce impressively good growth in both freshwater and marine plants. Vita-lites run about the same price as standard Grolux tubes.

**Actinic Bulbs**  Actinic bulbs (specifically actinic 03 bulbs) are newcomers on the aquarium scene, though they've been used in copying machines and in certain medical applications for years. Actinics emit intense blue light with a maximum output at 420 nm, near chlorophyll's blue-absorption peak. Despite their intensity, they look dim to human eyes and are uncomfortable to look at, so they are rarely used alone. I don't recommend actinics for freshwater tanks, but in combination with daylight or wide-spectrum tubes they stimulate the growth of corals, sea anemones, and certain types of desirable marine algae. Their blue light (diluted a bit by an additional lamp of another sort) also looks "right" in marine tanks. Actinics are currently the rage among marine aquarists.

**Metal-Halide Lamps**  Metal-halide lamps, another recent addition to aquarium equipment, emit light of such high intensity that they are painful to look at. These lamps and their fixtures are expensive—a complete reflector to fit a fifty-five-gallon tank can run up to four hundred dollars—and emit a great deal of heat in addition to useful light. Carefully installed, they make it possible to maintain certain marine organisms and highlight freshwater plants, but improperly used they can "burn" even corals accustomed to tropical sunshine. Because of their expense and the uncertainties that remain in their use, I recommend them only to experienced hobbyists interested in experimenting.

## Covers and Hoods

Every aquarium needs a tight-fitting cover. You'll be amazed at how often fishes jump, and how frequently they manage to squeeze through impossibly small openings and end up on your floor. A cover also retards evaporation and helps retain heat during cooler months. Finally, tight-fitting covers protect lights, other equipment, and furniture from splashes. This is particularly crucial with saltwater, which is highly corrosive to metals and dries into annoying white specks on furniture.

Aquarium covers come in several styles. My favorite consists of two narrow pieces of glass, a set of heavy plastic end channels, and a lightweight plastic strip. The glass panels slide forward and backward in the channels to allow easy access to the tank, and the plastic strip fits along the back, where it can be cut to admit filter tubes and the like.

Equally functional (though not as convenient for access) are one-piece acrylic tank tops. Many aquarium stores also sell "full hoods" that combine tank covers with light fixtures, but most of these carry only a single fluorescent tube. That's fine for display, but, as discussed above, is insufficient for plants. Additionally, all full hoods I've seen in pet shops are finished in imitation wood grain, which is not to my taste at all.

## Heaters

As few of us heat our homes to 78° these days, keeping tanks in the right temperature range for tropical fishes requires an aquarium heater. The many brands of heaters commonly sold in this country fall into two categories, both of which combine heater and thermostat into one compact unit.

Traditional heaters clamp onto the aquarium frame so that an adjustable dial sits above the waterline while the thermostat and heating coil are submerged. Newer heaters, however, are completely waterproof, and are designed to be used totally submerged. I prefer submersible heaters for two reasons. First, once submersible heaters are properly adjusted, they can be placed almost anywhere in the aquarium. Second, because the controls are out of reach underwater, they are less likely to be tampered with by children or accidentally reset during tank maintenance. Although "dial-at-the-top" heaters come with covers to protect controls from accidental twists, some of them still make it too easy to cook your pets accidentally.

Until recently, aquarium-heater controls had only arbitrarily numbered dials that provided no relationship to actual temperature settings at all. To set them up, aquarists had to allow the heater to equilibrate with ambient water temperature and then boost the setting in gradual steps to raise the tank temperature on a trial-and-error basis. Thankfully, some manufacturers have begun calibrating heaters properly, and have provided them with accurate temperature settings. This welcome innovation simplifies tank setup and makes later temperature adjustments very easy.

What's the right size heater for your tank? Ideally, the heater should be powerful enough to keep the tank at the proper temperature without operating all the time. Oversized heaters in small tanks, however, switch on and off constantly, causing the thermostat contacts to wear out faster than necessary. Also, if an oversized heater should malfunction in the "on" position, it could rapidly overheat. So you do need to match heater size with the job to be done.

All brands of heaters come in standard sizes, usually 50, 75, 100, 125, 150, 200, and 300 watts. If your tank is in a room that is always kept at a comfortable temperature for humans, a heater of roughly four watts/gallon is a good rule of thumb. (Round up to the next-largest heater size when necessary.) Thus, a ten-gallon tank would take a fifty-watt heater, and a twenty-gallon tank would take a hundred-watt heater.

If you plan to put your tank in a cool room that you only heat to comfortable temperatures occasionally, increase that recommendation to ten watts/gallon. It's also a good idea in the such cases to use *two* heaters, each half the recommended wattage. That way, if one heater either quits altogether or fails to switch off when it should, your fish will neither freeze nor boil before you have a chance to correct the problem. In such a situation, a twenty-gallon tank would take a total of two hundred watts, split between two 100-watt units on opposite ends of the tank.

Because heaters are not attractive, it is tempting to stuff them into corners or—especially with submersible ones—to bury them

## Fine! Whodunnit?

I'd wager that many "mystery" fish deaths are caused by ammonia or other toxic fumes from paints, cleansers, and cigarettes. These fumes are nothing to fool around with; one brand of deck paint I used recently warned of brain damage from inhalation of vapors, and stressed the need for adequate ventilation during use and drying. Exposed to such vapors, humans can simply walk outside or open windows. But if noxious chemicals get into tank water, many will stay there until you do a water change. And your fish don't have the option of taking a stroll around the block until the room clears. So try not to use paints, varnishes, or ammonia-based cleaners in the same room as your tank. If you must, remember not only to cover the tank, but to open the windows and—if possible—use a long length of air tubing to place the pump in another room with cleaner air.

underneath rocks or gravel. *Don't!* Heaters should be situated so that water can circulate around them as freely as possible to distribute heat evenly. Unless heaters are placed properly, hot and cold spots can develop in the tank, to the detriment of both plants and fishes.

All submersible heaters come with suction-cup clips to attach them to aquarium glass. If you have a small tank and opt not to use an outside power filter, position the heater horizontally across the back of the tank a few inches above the gravel, to allow the heater water to rise on its own. If you use a power filter that keeps the tank well-stirred, you can place the

heater just about anywhere that water flows past it steadily. Feel free to "camouflage" the heater by judicious placement of plants and other ornaments, but don't box it in or cover it.

## Thermometers

A reliable thermometer is just as important as a heater. Thermometers made for aquaria come in a variety of styles; some clip on to the tank or float freely inside, while others attach to the outside of the glass. Simple interior clip-on types get my vote for simplicity and dependability. Murphy's Law insures that free-floating types will always face the wrong way. Liquid-crystal thermometer strips that stick to the outside glass are popular because they look sexy and high-tech, but they have some real problems. They are subject to misreading from cold drafts or sunlight, and are useless on acrylic tanks. (Plastic is such a good insulator that thermometers on the outside surface read closer to room temperature than to tank-water temperature.)

## Air Supply

Because tank water exchanges oxygen and carbon dioxide primarily at the water's surface, it is important to maintain a circulation pattern that mixes water thoroughly. You can do that using a source of compressed air to power either an air stone or an undergravel filter. (Other options are discussed under filtration.) There are many good air pumps on the market, and most manufacturers offer models with a wide range of outputs. Pumps are selected by the number of devices you want them to run, rather than by the size of your tank, so the size pump you buy will depend upon the filtration and aeration options you choose. Some stores offer tiny carbon cartridges that supposedly "clean" air before it enters the tank; in reality these quickly become saturated and worthless. Many pumps are equipped with useful dust filters that should be cleaned or replaced as needed.

## Undergravel (Biological) Filtration

The essential job of biological filtration can be handled by one of the simplest pieces of tank equipment—a slotted plastic plate with two or more air-powered lift tubes called an undergravel filter. Despite all sorts of hype, most brands available today are equally effective, as long as they completely cover the bottom of the tank. One useful feature on some models is a set of high collars around lift-tube openings that keep gravel from falling under the plate if the tubes come loose. Small cartridges of GAC designed to sit on top of the lift tubes for chemical filtration wear out so quickly as to be useless.

In most cases, the brisk, gentle flow provided by air stones is more than sufficient for biological filtration. Be aware, however, that air stones clog slowly over time, lose efficiency, and build up pressure in the airline that can damage your pump. Air stones are inexpensive enough that I replace them every couple of months.

There are some situations—notably in marine tanks and certain very crowded freshwater tanks—in which undergravel filters benefit from higher flow rates than air stone can provide. In these cases, you can greatly increase

filtration rates by adding submersible pumps called power heads. Most power heads offer optional controls that can inject air bubbles into the stream of water they pump to improve aeration.

Equipping an undergravel filter with power heads is not necessarily any more expensive than buying an air pump and the necessary valves, tubing, and air stones. But the high flow rates power heads produce are rarely necessary in freshwater tanks, and the strong currents they generate may be a liability to slow-moving or very small fishes. Additionally, pulling that much water through your undergravel filter greatly increases the degree to which it acts as a mechanical filter, and therefore also increases the need for regular gravel cleaning.

Another option is to set up the sort of reverse-flow undergravel filter mentioned in the last chapter. Because reverse-flow systems do not create the same sort of vigorous water circulation as power heads or standard power filters, however, I recommend using at least one air stone in such tanks.

## Mechanical and Chemical Filtration

There are enough different kinds of mechanical filters and filter materials on the market to drive a novice to distraction. Keep in mind while sorting through store displays that—advertising copy to the contrary—mechanical filtration is a simple process that can be accomplished in any number of ways.

**Inside Filters** Air-powered box filters that sit inside tanks are the old aquarist's stand-

bys, and they work as well today as they did twenty years ago. Such filters are fine for small tanks, although they do take up precious room that most of us would rather use for plants or fishes. If you use an inside filter, be sure to position it so that you can remove it easily for cleaning.

## Sponge Filters

One recent arrival on the inside filtration scene is the much-touted sponge filter. Sponge filters use the same airlift principle as box filters, but use a cylindrical piece of plastic foam that acts as both mechanical and biological filter. Because foam filters are simple and compact, and because they cannot trap baby fishes as most other filters can, they are ideal for tanks used to rear newly hatched fry, which are particularly susceptible to ammonia and nitrite poisoning.

The newest additions to this market are electrically powered inside filters. Although these look like they came out of *Star Wars,* I'm not convinced that they provide sufficient functional advantage to justify their expense. They will accept filter floss and GAC, but still take up interior tank space, and must be removed for cleaning.

**"Protein Skimming"** Many potentially harmful dissolved organic compounds can be removed from tank water by a device often called a "protein skimmer," but more properly referred to as a "foam fractionator." From whence the names? If you live near the sea, you may be familiar with the "foam" that forms where waves break on the shore. That foam appears because many dissolved organics form a persistent film at any surface where air and water meet. Crashing waves create countless bubbles, around which dissolved organics collect like soap bubbles. Aquarium foam fractionators do the same thing in miniature by sending a fine mist of air bubbles through a column of water in a tube. The slightly yellowish foam that results is collected for easy removal in a cup above the water's surface. Foam fractionators, though highly recommended for marine aquaria, are unnecessary in reasonably stocked freshwater tanks.

Outside Filters  Simple outside power filters provide the best all-around values for high filtration rate and ease of cleaning. The most reasonably priced are rectangular plastic boxes that hang on the back of the aquarium. Water is pulled into the filter through a pair of siphon tubes, passed through mechanical and chemical filter media, and pumped back into the tank. Several American-made models of this type are reasonably priced and admirably dependable. I had one Supreme "Aquamaster" filter in almost continuous use for at least fifteen years with no repairs.

Canister filters, used in major aquaria for years, are relatively new to home use. Many of these are "Mercedes" grade imports whose prices stagger even this jaded hobbyist. Designwise, they are attractive, and the "equipment freak" in me loves playing with the beautifully colored tubing and valves used to hook them up. But perhaps I've designed enough professional filtration systems to get the

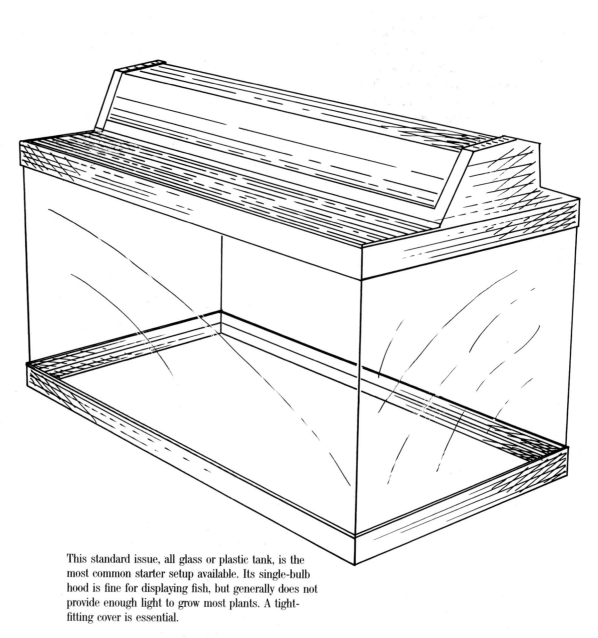

This standard issue, all glass or plastic tank, is the most common starter setup available. Its single-bulb hood is fine for displaying fish, but generally does not provide enough light to grow most plants. A tight-fitting cover is essential.

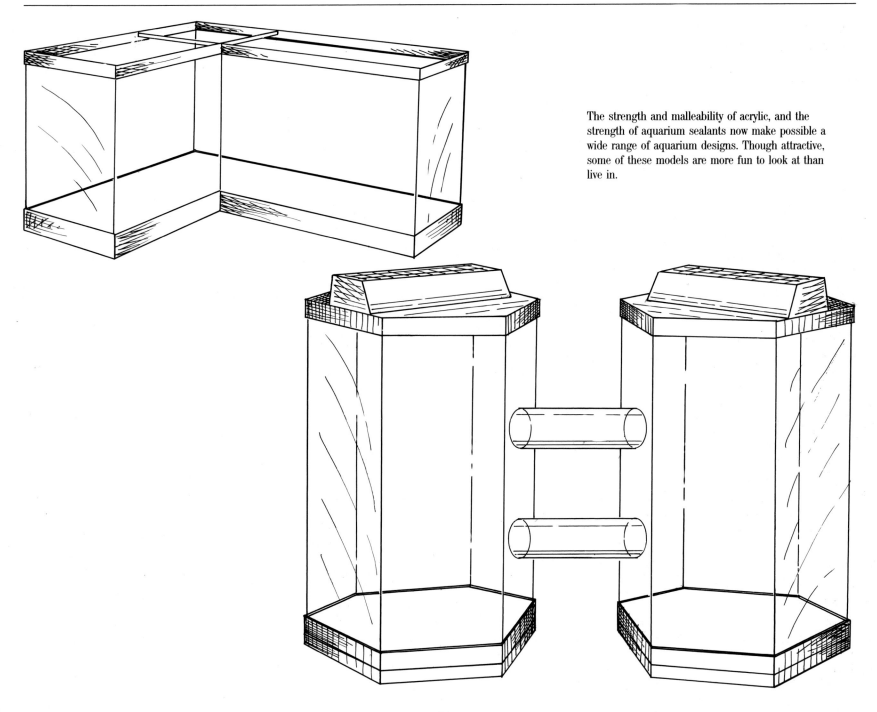

The strength and malleability of acrylic, and the strength of aquarium sealants now make possible a wide range of aquarium designs. Though attractive, some of these models are more fun to look at than live in.

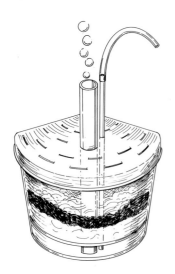

The corner box filter, an old standard but still dependable.

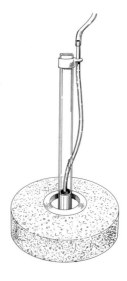

Sponge filter—a combination of mechanical and biological filtration ideal for small tanks containing newly hatched fishes.

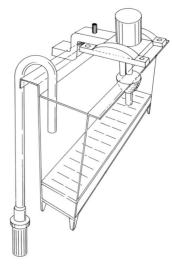

The outside power filter is simple, efficient, and reasonably priced.

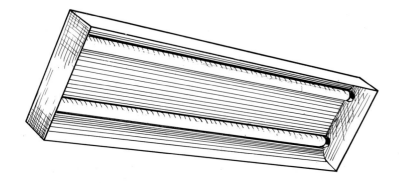

Full-length black acrylic enclosed hood with two fluorescent tubes.

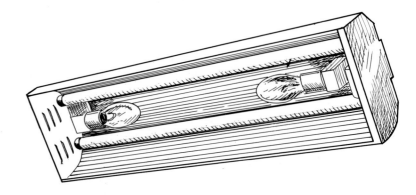

Full-length, fan-cooled enclosed hood with two metal halide bulbs and two actinic tubes.

Canister filter is the sophisticated choice of advanced hobbyists.

Protein skimmer," better called "foam fractionator," removes many dissolved organic compounds. Most useful in marine aquaria.

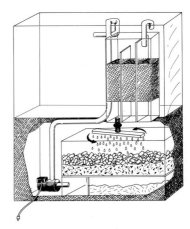

Trickle filters, sophisticated, expensive, and tricky to set up, are usually reserved for marine aquaria.

excitement of fiddling with tubes and valves out of my system, or maybe it's because most canister filters cost an arm and a leg. In any case, I don't see sufficient functional advantage in most of these models to justify their price for most home situations. Stick with the reasonably priced models described above, and put the extra money into a larger tank, more live plants, or more interesting fishes.

It is true, however, that modular canister systems—such as those of the Lifeguard line—are useful to advanced aquarists with several tanks, or with one really large tank. Canister models can also be functionally useful if you want to set up a reverse-flow undergravel filter. Alternatively, if you are using a large tank as room divider and want to keep both sides of the tank free from equipment, canister filters allow you to run tubing inconspicuously into a cabinet underneath.

Remember, however, that if your canister is located below your tanks, you must install

valves in the tubing to allow for easy, spill-proof cleaning. Also remember that if your electrical power goes off for any length of time, a canister filter—particularly one that has not been cleaned recently—will rapidly turn sour. Shortly after water flow stops, beneficial bacteria use up the available oxygen, and not-so-beneficial bacteria take over. Those bacteria synthesize a variety of compounds harmful to fishes that are pumped into the tank when power resumes unless you intervene.

## Trickle Filters

Some time ago, clever aquarists recognized that aquaria were not the only places where toxic animal wastes needed to be made less harmful to aquatic things. Delving into the literature and practices of sewage treatment, they discovered a process known as trickle filtration, in which ammonia-laden water is trickled slowly through enormous biological filters. The media for these

giant filter beds are plastic structures designed to offer the maximum possible surface area for beneficial bacteria without being dense enough to clog easily. Because the medium is not submerged in water, the bacteria have better access to oxygen, and the conversion of ammonia to nitrate proceeds rapidly and efficiently. Presto! The trickle filter (alias "wet-dry" filter) for the home aquarium was born.

The latest trickle filters combine the best aspects of mechanical, chemical, and biological filtration in a single system. Tank water is first mechanically filtered to remove particulate matter that could clog the biological filter bed. The water is then chemically filtered and trickled over one of several media before being returned to the tank. The best systems remove water not by siphon but by overflow, in order to carry off surface water and the accompanying film of organic matter. Three ways to accomplish this are shown.

Trickle filters must be carefully constructed,

because faulty joints can redirect a significant amount of water from your aquarium onto your floor. Because many configurations involve drilling a hole through your tank bottom and fitting it with a waterproof gasket, they require some skill to install. And because the pumps they use must operate continuously underwater, they must be chosen with care. For these reasons, I don't advise building your own unless you are both skilled with acrylic and willing to track down the right pumps and tubing.

Unfortunately, as they are still new to the market, most better trickle filters are ridiculously overpriced—between $200 and $400 a system. That's a lot of money for a water pump and a few clear plastic boxes! To date, trickle filters are used mostly by advanced saltwater aquarists interested in maintaining fishes and invertebrates that require the very best water conditions. For the sort of living-reef tank you will see at the end of Chapter 7, they are just what the doctor ordered. For other situations, they are strictly luxury items.

## Filter Media

The best, most reasonably priced mechanical and chemical filter media are filter floss and activated carbon (page 29). Some care must be taken when using floss in canister filters, as it can clog rapidly if packed too tightly, and it must be changed more regularly than other, coarser media. But its reasonable cost and ability to catch small particles are well worth the little extra effort.

The simplicity and utility of these media notwithstanding, pet shops and aquarium magazines are filled with promotions for an endless variety of alternatives. Most are outrageously priced, at best no better than floss and carbon, and at worst less effective. Several canister filter manufacturers in particular market mechanical filter media designed "exclusively" for use in their products. As a group, ignore them.

I cannot understand the reasoning behind the recent wave of "modular" filters whose media come in little prepackaged mesh bags. I suppose these are designed for beginning hobbyists afraid to dirty their hands when cleaning filters. For what these things cost, you could pay someone to clean the filter for you and still come out ahead! Some of the more poorly designed filter bags can even be counterproductive. Many contain insufficient GAC to function in a well-stocked tank for more than a few days. Others are placed in filters ahead of (instead of behind) the mechanical medium in the water path, cutting down on both their efficiency and their working life.

Finally, because flowing water takes the path of least resistance, bags that aren't filled with medium or that don't wedge tightly against the edges of the filter container may cause water to go *around* rather than *through* the filter material. Here's another place where sticking with old standbys will not only save money but assure you that your filter is working well.

Of all the high-tech filter media, the only ones worth their hefty price are several used in trickle filters. These plastic structures, including brands called Bio-Balls, Bio-Rings, and Tri-Packs, offer maximum surface area for bacterial growth and an open enough structure to minimize clogging.

## Test Kits and Aquarium Chemicals

To keep track of aquarium-water chemistry, every aquarist needs a good set of water-test kits. These come in many forms, from basic pH test kits for a few dollars to professional models that run one hundred dollars or more. All kits consist of one or more test tubes and a series of chemical reagents that change color when added to samples of tank water. The final color of the test sample is compared with a color chart to obtain a reading for the test. Most kits use liquid reagents measured by counting drops, while others use premeasured powders packaged in tiny plastic pillows. The most recent addition is a series of reagent-impregnated paper strips that perform several tests with a single dip in a tank-water sample.

Although few of these kits provide results that would be reliable enough for scientific purposes, most better ones are accurate enough to guide tank maintenance. One potential problem with even the best kits is that reagents have a finite half-life, and if they sit around on a dealer's shelves or in your home for too long, they lose accuracy. For this reason, most better kits carry expiration dates like meat and dairy products in your supermarket.

When making the color comparisons necessary for any of these kits, try to work in bright, indirect natural light near a window, rather than under tungsten or highly colored fluorescent light. Still, comparing the color of a liquid with colored ink printed on cardboard is not always easy. For that reason, some of the better kits provide either liquid color samples or translucent plastic standards.

If your tapwater chemistry is reasonable, and

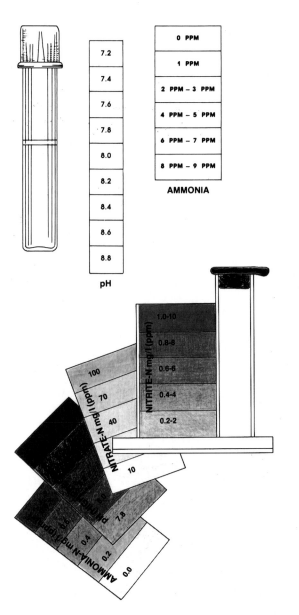

Modern water test kits are simple to use. Chemical indicator dyes are added to a sample of aquaria water and the resulting color is compared against a standard.

you plan to keep only beginners' fishes, you can get by with little more than a good pH kit. If your water is problematical, however, and if you want to move on to finicky fishes, I'd advise buying a complete kit that includes (in decreasing order of importance) tests for pH, ammonia, nitrite, nitrate, hardness, and alkalinity. You'll make things easier on yourself if you either buy individual kits made by the same manufacturer or pick up a "master" kit that contains all these tests in a single box. That way, the testing procedures and instructions will be relatively similar among all the tests.

## Some Frills: Convenience and Hype

In addition to all the essential equipment, large and small, pet-shop shelves are crammed with scores of accessories. Some of these are convenient, some are amusing, and others are either ridiculous or even dangerous for your fishes.

**Gravel Cleaners**  Several ingenious devices make gravel cleaning easier. Some of these are as simple as plastic attachments that fit onto the end of the siphon tube used to make water changes. Most have small openings that pick up both gravel and surface debris, and wide bodies in which gravel collects while dirt is removed. I'm partial to these because they are clever, inexpensive, and encourage regular water changes.

More amusing are electric-powered aquarium vacuum cleaners. These battery-powered devices separate gravel and dirt in the same way, but instead of removing the water, filter it through a mesh bag or some filter media and return it to the tank. There's nothing wrong with these devices, and they can be fun to use, but I don't like them as much as siphon cleaners. If the gravel bed has become *really* dirty, chances are its bacterial residents have produced unpleasant compounds that are best removed from the tank altogether. Also, relying on these devices can discourage the water changes so beneficial to aquarium health.

**Diatom Filters**  Every now and then, even the best aquarists are confronted either with tank water that just won't clear or with a new setup that they want to clear as quickly as possible. When cloudiness is caused by suspended particles too fine for ordinary filters to remove, the answer may be a diatom filter. I have owned one of these filters for at least fifteen years. It has always worked flawlessly and shows no signs of wear, but I rarely use it more than once or twice a year.

Diatom filters are designed primarily for occasional use to clear up cloudy tanks. They work by pulling water through a mesh bag coated with a layer of an ultrafine filter medium composed of the shells of minute aquatic plants. This "diatomaceous earth" removes vanishingly small particles from water, and can even filter out certain types of parasites. The manufacturers of these filters also make gravel-cleaning attachments for use while the filter is in operation.

**Automatic Feeders**  Automatic fish feeders are viewed by some aquarists as the ultimate convenience items. What could be sim-

53

pler or more delightful, after all, than programming a gizmo to feed your fishes for you? If you love gadgets, and just must have one of these, be my guest.

But I don't like automatic feeders, and have used them only once in my long history as an aquarist. That was when I was raising lobsters from eggs, and had to deliver brine shrimp to the babies every four hours around the clock without fail. But in both my laboratory and home tanks, I have always either fed the fishes myself, had someone else do the job, or have let them miss an occasional feeding.

Why? Theoretically, automatic feeders can be useful if you leave home for extended periods and can find no one to look after your pets. They could also ease your work load if you collect tanks the way philatelists collect stamps. But taking a few minutes to look over your tank each morning is a good idea on general principle, and feeding gives you that opportunity. On normal, and even four-day, weekends, most fishes (except newly hatched fry) will do better without food than they will if an automatic feeder dumps in more than they can eat. And if you go away for a week or more, you really want a warm body looking in on your charges. A daily (or even twice-weekly) visit helps ensure that heaters and filters are working properly and that no unattended deaths in the tank endanger other inhabitants.

**Automatic Water Changers** Another item gaining popularity is the automatic water changer. One end of this device attaches to your sink, while the other sits in your tank. Turn on the tap, adjust the temperature to match your tank's, and the water changer siphons out tank water and replaces it with tapwater.

Sound like a great idea? It can be, if you have a large tank within reach of a sink, and if your tapwater contains nothing any more dangerous than chlorine. But if your tank is smaller, or if your tapwater contains chloramine, this procedure can be dangerous. Particularly if your water contains chloramine, it's better to treat it with the appropriate chemicals in a separate container. Additionally, I could hardly believe my eyes when I saw one of these things—which consists of little more than a plastic tube and a siphon pump—retailing for more than seventy-five dollars! An extravagant waste of money in my book. Check Chapter 8 for a *far* cheaper way of changing water.

# WHERE TO PUT YOUR TANK

## Temperature

Because you want to keep tank temperature between 72° and 78° F, don't place it on top of radiators, or near windows or exit doors that will be open for long during cold weather. (Few things are more likely to produce an outbreak of disease than sudden chills.) With insurance in the form of a properly sized heater, tanks can be placed in cool (but not frigid) basement rooms. But because keeping tanks cool is far more trouble than keeping them warm, they should not be located in attic rooms that broil during normal summer weather for your area.

## Sunlight

Standard off-the-shelf aquarium wisdom says to keep your tank away from brightly lit windows. That's excellent advice for all small tanks, because their limited water volumes can heat up quickly in full sun. A dim location is also a good idea for freshwater tanks decorated only with plastic plants, and in marine tanks furnished only with dead coral. In these situations, minimizing light will help control undesirable algae.

But for those of you who opt for live plants in freshwater and "live rocks" in marine tanks, the situation is different. I can't help but chuckle when I read about aquarists who dutifully consign their tanks to dark corners and then bend over backward (and spend lots of money) providing high-intensity artificial illumination that duplicates sunlight as closely as possible!

Now I agree that it's not a good idea to place any tank directly in front of a south-facing picture window with no shades or curtains. And I'll admit that a tank near a window might need a bit more attention in the summer to avoid overheating. But intelligent use of sheer curtains or blinds will allow your tank to benefit from natural light for most of the year. Sunlight is not bad for most fishes, and those that dislike it will do just fine if your tank design offers dark hiding places. In fact, most freshwater fish are raised in shallow, sun-drenched ponds, and some of the most successful "living reef" marine tanks are kept in full tropical sun.

Study the areas around (not directly in front of) your windows. Watch the way the sun travels during the day and throughout the year, and use a little ingenuity to select the right location to make safe use of natural light. The fifty-five-gallon Amazonian tank in my home office, for example, is located in such a way that it receives two to three hours of direct sun around midday from fall through late spring, and bright indirect natural light the rest of the year. (As the sun's arc rises in late spring and summer, the light moves conveniently off the tank.) I do have to scrape algae off the side walls periodically, but my plants grow luxuriantly. I watch my water temperature carefully during the summer, and if I plan to be away from home on hot days, I simply pull down the shades.

## Electricity

Your tank must have an adequate and dependable supply of electricity as close by as possible. (You do not want to run extension cords over long distances where they can be tripped over.) If you plan to use your tank as a room divider or in some similarly dramatic location, be certain there's an outlet nearby.

*All outlets that supply aquaria should be fully grounded (equipped with three-prong outlets) with no exceptions.* From the wall outlet, run a heavy-duty power strip (with a minimum of four grounded outlets) to the area in back of your tank or inside your equipment cabinet. I prefer power strips with built-in fuses and "on-off" switches; they tend to be solidly built, hold up for years without malfunctioning, and allow you to turn tank power on and off quickly and easily. Be careful, though, not to position the strip under any outside filter boxes that might drip into it during cleaning.

When selecting timers for light fixtures, be aware that most appliance timers, while more than able to carry the minimal load imposed by aquarium lights, are not grounded. (For the life of me, I can't figure out why.) After much searching, I've found a heavy-duty Intermatic air-conditioner timer, which is no more expensive than most regular timers, is much safer for aquarium use, and can handle several fixtures at once.

It's also a good idea to protect your aquarium circuit with a Ground Fault Interrupt device (GFI), especially if the tank is near any plumbing (including metal baseboards or radiators) and *particularly* if there are kids around. GFI, now required in bathrooms and kitchens, protects you against serious electrical shock from improperly grounded electrical equipment.

GFI works by monitoring the amount of current entering and leaving its circuit. If more current is entering the circuit than is leaving through proper channels, some of it is leaving through another route—possibly through your fingers. When a GFI circuit detects that sort of discrepancy, it shuts off the power within one fortieth of a second. GFI devices are inexpensive (around ten dollars) and are available both as plug-in units and as replacement for existing wall sockets. I cannot recommend them highly enough.

A small tank (ten to twenty gallons) can easily share a circuit with other lights and small appliances, but tanks fifty-five gallons and up are best placed on an independent 15-amp circuit. That's not because the tank itself uses anywhere near that much power, but because you don't want to accidentally overload the circuit (and leave your tank without power) by using vacuum cleaners, power tools, or irons on another part of the same circuit.

Wiring in newer homes and condominiums usually supplies each room with two or more circuits. If that's your situation, existing wiring is fine if it is properly grounded. But in older houses (like mine) where both lights and wall sockets in three or four rooms are all on the same, ancient circuit, adding a large tank might cause trouble. In such cases, if you own your home, it may be worth the effort to install a dedicated circuit.

## Traffic

Don't forget to consider traffic patterns as you locate your tank. You'll naturally want your tank to be visible—in fact, you may want it to be the focal point of a room. But you don't want it to get knocked over or broken by rampaging children or adults overburdened with groceries.

Most beginners' fishes can handle a reasonable amount of activity around their tank, but if you plan to be keeping any shy fish—such as discus, certain killifish, and dwarf cichlids, tangs, etc.—you'd be well-advised to locate the tank away from hallways and other centers of activity.

## Aquaria, Children, and Other Pets

Aquaria and kids can either be delightful together or an absolute disaster. At best, aquaria can cultivate in young children a reverence for life. If you include children in such activities as feeding, changing filters, deciding on crowding limits, and so on, you can sneak in a touch of useful math. As your children mature, involving them in keeping track of tank progress over time through water testing and occasional applications of medication can cultivate habits of careful record-keeping and provide them with a sense of responsibility. Watching fish grow, breed, and die over time fosters an understanding of the basic processes of life, and can ultimately open doors into understanding ecology and other aspects of biology. You'd be surprised, in fact, at what this can lead to; at least one aquarist I know of has his six-year-old reciting Latin names of fishes to guests!

But mixing aquaria with small children does require common-sense precautions. Keep all tanks, wires, aquarium chemicals, foods, and test kits locked away or out of reach. Select only sturdy aquarium stands that are really tip-proof. The old-fashioned wrought-iron stands I remember—particularly those designed for small tanks—were unstable enough that an energetic three-year-old could easily pull one over. And although I would encourage situating your tank in a way that allows you to watch it with your child, it's a good idea to keep tanks well above the reach of an unaccompanied toddler. And above all, don't forget to make certain that all electrical circuits are properly grounded and protected by GFI.

## Buying Used Equipment

If, to follow my advice on minimum tank size, you'd like to save money by purchasing a used tank, check your local papers and want-ad publications. You're sure to find a wide variety of used aquaria, usually offered with an eclectic selection of equipment. Many people dive into fishkeeping with abandon, invest a fortune in a huge tank and apparatus, and discover a few weeks later that their spouse can't stand fishes or that they have to move to another state. Such "distress sales" can be gold mines for beginning hobbyists. Be certain, though, to inspect all merchandise carefully.

To start, don't buy any metal-frame tanks, for they are probably too old to be dependable. Look carefully at newer tanks as well, because even the best tank can be damaged if it is filled on an uneven surface or moved with too much water in it. If you have any doubt about the way your potential purchase was handled, ask the sellers to fill it for an on-site leak test. If they refuse, go elsewhere.

When inspecting used electrical equipment such as light fixtures, pumps, and filters, don't just plug them in to see if they work—inspect them for signs of rust or other deterioration. If the equipment was used for more than a few months, especially on a saltwater setup, look carefully for signs of heat damage. (If electrical connections become corroded, their resistance increases and they heat up during normal use, melting insulation and creating a potentially hazardous situation.)

Be especially careful of "home-made" aquaria, and investigate carefully the reputation of the builders of any custom tanks you find for sale. Water, you will recall, is extremely heavy, and places great stress on the seams of any except the smallest tanks. And it bears repeating that ten or twenty gallons is a *lot* of water when it is spread out all over your floor.

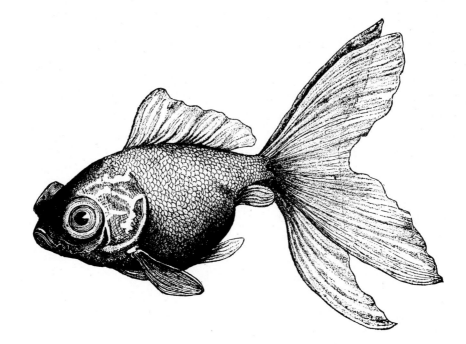

# THE INS AND OUTS OF AQUARIUM DESIGN

Aquarium decorating is potentially the most creative and enjoyable aspect of fishkeeping— a part of the hobby where those who are more intuitive and artistic and a bit less scientifically minded can *really* have a good time. It's your chance to have a go, not only at designing an underwater landscape, but at transforming a sterile, empty glass box into a glowing, living part of your personal environment. This process includes many activities, ranging from the collection of bits and pieces of underwater scenery to serious (and potentially expensive) decisions about furniture, lighting, and room arrangements.

But for some reason, American aquarists rarely have as much fun with this process as they should. Once people decide to buy a tank, their immediate goal is to fill it with fishes as soon as possible. Pet shops capitalize on this urge by selling absolutely-everything-you-need packages, including gravel and decorating accessories along with tanks and life-support equipment. At best, dealers throw in an eclectic mix of rocks and driftwood. At worst, they toss in painted ceramic mermaids, castles, and other garbage. Package deals that include all the se-

rious tank *equipment* you need are fine, and may save you money. Those that include the props for an underwater Disneyland are a waste.

What to do without recourse to prepackaged decorating kits? Spend time with this process. Please. Not only is aquarium decorating as much fun as collecting and keeping the fishes, but it involves decisions that have a major impact on the well-being of the tank for as long as you own it. Will the interior design of the tank suit both your tastes and the requirements of the fishes? Will its appearance and identity as part of your home environment please you and inspire you to keep it up? Will the pleasure it provides you be worth the time you need to take to maintain it? Now is the time—before you have a single fish in the bag—to think seriously about the *kind* of tank you want and how you want to place it in your home.

## THE CASE FOR LIVE PLANTS

To my mind, the difference between a *real* aquarium and an oversized goldfish bowl can be summed up in two words: living plants. A

lushly planted tank creates in your home an image of aquatic nature at her mythically tranquil best. Most important, live plants help your pets feel more at ease in their limited space. Fishes, according to their nature, shelter in swaying foliage, lie in ambush amid concealing stems, build nests among tangled roots, and spawn on supple leaves.

Plastic plants, on the other hand, are an affront to the senses and to a naturalist's soul. They are stiff, unyielding, and unchanging. They may be good for hiding unsightly pieces of equipment, but little else. Fishes don't avoid them, but don't embrace them, either. As for bubbling shipwrecks with skeletons at the helm, fetching plastic mermaids, and brightly painted ceramic castles, the less said about them, the better.

I hope to convince you that the work needed to maintain aquarium plants is more than worth the effort. In my fervent efforts to do so, however, I won't attempt to prove that live plants are *necessary* to keep fish healthy. Many professional breeders coax fishes to spawn on pieces of slate in bare-bottomed tanks. And some species—notably the larger cichlids—are destructive enough to make live plants (in some cases, even plastic plants) impossible. In fact, I've even included one idea for a totally artificial habitat in Chapter 7.

But there are several logical—though subjective—reasons behind my preference for live plants. As a biologist and scuba diver, I'm accustomed to observing fishes both in nature and in captivity. And, invariably, wherever there are fishes in nature, there are also plants. An occasional snack from a live plant is good for many fishes, even those that are not full-time plant-eaters. And, finally, plants absorb $CO_2$ and nitrogen-containing fish wastes, and release oxygen.

But there are also behavioral "intangibles" that recommend planted aquaria—intangibles whose importance I can most easily convey by analogy to more-familiar animals in zoos. If you can recall trips to the zoo as recently as the late sixties, you can probably remember large animals on display in exhibits as grand—and as artificial—as those I gawked at in the Victorian-style mammal houses at the Bronx Zoo.

Given the zoo's high standards of veterinary care, all animals were in good physical health. I remember, though, not just what the animals *looked* like, but what they *did* in those captive settings. Big cats paced—endlessly, tirelessly, repetitively—back and forth across their clean, tiled enclosures, or they slept. Monkeys squatted morosely, made faces at gawking humans, begged for food, or threw excrement around their cages. They were healthy, perhaps. Even psychologically sound enough that many (though not all) of them bred occasionally. But they were certainly not happy.

Visit the Bronx Zoo (or any other great zoo) today, and you'll see a world of difference. On an unobtrusively fenced, landscaped hillside in the Bronx, snow leopards cavort contentedly. Disarmingly at home (especially in winter), they frolic with their cubs, climb trees, cavort in the snow, stalk an errant bird or two, or curl up for naps. They *don't* pace. In Seattle's cool autumn mist, a troop of mountain gorillas relaxes by a trickling stream. The animals toy with (and occasionally eat) fallen leaves, stare at the sky, socialize with one another, and periodically play "king of the hill" on a pile of boulders. They *don't* sulk.

The snow-leopard and mountain-gorilla exhibits are just two examples of captive habitats that mimic natural habitats. While neither of these exhibits duplicates *precisely* the natural flora and landscape of the captive animals, they do provide *naturalistic* environments that achieve at least the general ambience that animals are used to in nature. By doing so, they ease the stress of captivity and encourage animals to behave more naturally. Results such as these have helped spark a revolution in captive-animal habitat design that is spreading from zoos to public aquaria.

For although fish behaviors are far more limited than those of apes and big cats, fishes do behave more normally in naturalistic settings. Damselfish stake out and guard territories on coral heads. Siamese fighting fish glue floating plants together with strings of sticky bubbles as they build nests in which to spawn. South American cichlids compulsively clean and then lay eggs upon the broad leaves of Amazon sword-plants. It is the chance to watch behaviors such as these in my living room—rather than just being able to keep fishes alive—that sustains my interest after nearly three decades in the hobby. Also remember that the sense of well-being fishes acquire in a properly landscaped tank will go a long way toward keeping them stress free and disease free.

The best way to explain this enthusiasm for the interactions between fishes and plants in aquaria is to convey some sense of the intricacy of their associations in nature. Because fishes are everywhere, there's no way this chapter could relate even a fraction of those relationships. But I can give you a glimpse of one aquatic system while introducing information that will help you understand the plant-husbandry advice that follows.

## THE AMAZON FLOOD:
### Heartbeat of the Jungle

Although you've probably heard of the world's endangered tropical forests, particularly the vanishing Amazonian jungle, you may not have realized that many of our prized aquarium fishes—not to mention aquarium plants and thousands of other magnificent species—are bound up with those rain forests in a complex and majestic web of life.

Our story begins as seasonal rains begin over the brow of the Peruvian Andes, swelling mountain streams that tumble toward the lowlands. At first, the runoff is contained in the peat-stained Rio Negro and the café-au-lait rios Madeira and Solimões—giant rivers themselves, but only tributaries of the Amazon. Then, inexorably, the rivers begin to rise. A meter . . . three meters . . . up to fifteen meters the waters climb, until they pour over the riverbanks to inundate thousands of square kilometers of tropical jungle.

Despite its awesome proportions, this great

Amazonian flood is no catastrophe, for its annual ebb and flow are as predictable as the seasons. Like the floods of the ancient Nile, those of the Amazon have become vital chapters in the lives of all plants and animals that live within their reach.

Each year, the flood sends land animals fleeing to higher ground or up into the trees. But hard on their heels come the fishes—some twenty-five hundred species of them—rising with the floodwaters to sweep over what had been terra firma. To these river creatures, the flooded forest spells freedom. Freedom to roam among the trunks of forest giants and the leaves and stems of shorter plants. Freedom to feed on leaves, buds, flowers, and fruits. Freedom to dine, too, on the endless rain of insects that lose their footing on the branches and tumble into the water below. And freedom to breed in an area far larger, far richer in food sources, and far less crowded with predators than the dry season's riverbanks.

And though experiences with overwatered houseplants might lead you to expect otherwise, many small plants of the riverbanks and forest floor thrive beneath the flood. While fishes cavort among their leaves, these seemingly drowned plants respond in their own ways, making dramatic adjustments to life underwater. In some cases, you'd never guess that underwater and aerial forms of these plants belong to the same species.

Those on fairly high ground that are only covered for a while slow down their growth and wait for the waters to recede. Others, fully adapted to an amphibious lifestyle, grow new leaves adapted to underwater life. Totally submerged, those leaves need no waxy coverings to shield them from drying out. Supported by

their buoyancy in water, they have no need for sturdy stems and veins to hold them erect. In fact, the best stems under these conditions are supple enough to allow flexible movements in changing water currents. Finally, in response to dark and turbid water, immersed leaves often stretch and broaden to obtain enough light for photosynthesis.

When the deluge reaches its peak, many flooded plants flower, either setting seeds or producing plantlets on their flower spikes. Both seeds and plantlets come to rest in the mud as waters recede, and, left emersed along the banks of lagoons and marshes, grow aerial leaves once again.

## OTHER TROPICAL RIVER SYSTEMS: Theme and Variations

Elsewhere, in the habitats of other aquarium fishes and plants, seasonal rains produce conditions that are broadly similar in nature, yet different in important specifics.

Across much of Southeast Asia, rains fall not only on the tributaries of great rivers, but across the lowlands as well. In some places, these rains are more evenly distributed across the seasons than they are in others. As a result, plants—depending on their precise locations—may be constantly underwater, flooded, and emersed on a regular basis, or half-covered, with their roots underwater but their leaves in air.

In parts of Africa, on the other hand, dry seasons are long enough that many wet-season ponds dry down to muddy depressions for part of the year. Many plants from these environ-

ments form bulbs or tubers that store food and enter a dormant state as water disappears. They begin growing vigorously when the rains regenerate their ponds once again.

Incidentally, many strikingly beautiful fish species from these habitats have life cycles that parallel those of their companion plants. Growing to maturity in a few months, these fishes spawn and die as their ponds dry down to mud. Their eggs remain dormant through the dry season, and hatch when the rains return. If you become interested in unusual fishes and plants as you gain experience in the hobby, you can use these species to create a fascinating seasonal fish tank. Buy eggs and dormant bulbs of these species, "plant" them together, add water, and stand back. At the proper time, condition the fish for spawning, allow the tank's water level to drop, and keep the resulting eggs and dormant bulbs cool and moist for several months to simulate the dry season. With proper care, you can repeat the cycle several times. (See Mail-Order Sources on page 226 for suggestions on obtaining these fish and plants.)

## WHERE HAVE ALL THE AQUARIUM PLANTS GONE?

If you find this natural history as fascinating as I do, you might wonder why don't we see more plants in American fish tanks. In large part, that's because aquarists here haven't been provided with either the right information or reliable sources.

I should know.

For at least a decade of my fishkeeping life,

I was in that situation. Time after time, I planted aquaria that stayed lush and green for a few weeks at most, and then disintegrated into mats of rotting, leafless roots and floating, rootless leaves. Frustration gave way to despair as I discarded handfuls of brown mush that had once been living plants. I sighed with envy each time I opened books written by Dutch or German aquarists. Those aquatic magicians managed—effortlessly, it seemed—to create landscaped underwater jungles so dense that nary a square inch of gravel was visible through the foliage. The accompanying text described the need to prune plants regularly to remove excess growth.

Pruning? Excess growth? I would have been happy if I could have kept my plants from decaying, even if they never put out a new leaf! What was I doing wrong?

Nearly everything. I hadn't chosen the right plants for my tanks. The plants I bought were in bad condition to begin with. I didn't plant them properly. And I didn't give them anywhere near enough light.

## The Wrong Plants

To put it bluntly, most plants sold in American pet shops are *not* aquatic plants. They are nothing more than a handful of attractive houseplants that tolerate drowning for varying lengths of time before giving up the ghost. If you browse pet stores with a plant person's eye, you'll quickly recognize that "underwater palms" are seedlings of *Chamaedorea elegans,* a plant grown in living rooms since Victorian times. Likewise, the attractively mottled "sanderana plants" are just tiny specimens of *Dracaena*

*sanderana,* the "corn plants" that loiter in hotel lobbies. And "underwater pines" turn out to be bunches of local *Lycopodium* (club moss) species collected among the pine needles of local woods. Several prayer plants of the genera *Maranta* and *Calathea,* several dumb canes of the genus *Dieffenbachia*, and several vining plants of the genera *Spathiphyllum* and *Syngonium* are other terrestrial plants often sold "wet."

This preponderance of nonaquatic plants in pet shops is a major stumbling block to aquarists. No matter *what* you do with these plants in your tank, they will deteriorate steadily. Any well-informed pet-store owner knows of this problem, though most won't volunteer the information unless pressed. I recently walked into one pet shop and asked (as I usually do) for aquarium plants. "You're in luck!" replied a clerk I'd known for some time. "We just got in a big shipment—ten tanks' worth." "No," I replied, "I mean *real* underwater plants." The employee checked to see if the boss was looking, lowered his voice, and pointed sheepishly toward a solitary tank in a corner. "There are a few of them in there."

## The Right Plants in Bad Condition

Even when real underwater plants are available, they are often in poor condition. Many retailers —who don't see a large market for aquarium plants—buy second-rate merchandise to go through the motions of offering live plants. They also mistreat these plants after arrival by handling them roughly, burying them too deeply, or leaving them to float across the tops of their tanks until they're sold. This treatment is guaranteed to send the plants into a downhill spiral.

The result is a supply and demand catch-22. Customers who buy poor-quality plants don't buy any more, so a mass market doesn't develop. The retailer sees only a limited market, and so doesn't bother to order good plants.

This scenario is not universally true, of course; one retailer I know took a risk and broke the self-defeating cycle. He began stocking only top-quality live plants, taking care of them correctly until sale, and instructing customers how to grow them properly. As a result, he created a strong local market for quality plants. Today, he asserts that plants are one of his most profitable items.

## The Right Plants in the Wrong Tanks

Aquatic plants—like fishes—are living things, rather than just decorative objects. Like fishes, they have cultural requirements shaped by conditions in their natural environments. But this simple fact is rarely—if ever—made clear to novices by pet-shop personnel. Either salesmen don't know that plants come from as many different places as fishes do, or they don't care. The results are predictable. Cold-water plants put in tropical tanks grow into leggy, unattractive misfits. Plants that like strong sun and hard, alkaline water turn to mush when relegated to a shaded tank with soft, acid water.

None of this is necessary. The fact that plants have specific cultural requirements doesn't mean that they're difficult to grow. In fact, just knowing that such requirements exist will make success with aquatic plants much easier. All you have to do is to learn the needs of the plants you fancy, match them appropriately with those of the fishes you want to keep, and you're off! Specific advice on how to select and buy plants can be found on page 76.

## THE RIGHT FRAME OF TANK AND MIND

If tank design is to be a significant process, where should you begin? The most important general piece of advice I can offer is to let the design period last as long as its nature and your schedule require. Decide where the tank will sit in your home, determine what fishes you want to keep, and start thinking about plants you want to grow.

From then on, whenever you hike through the woods, along lakes and streams, or by the seashore, put yourself on "aquascape alert." Linger over fallen trees, rocks, and sand to remind yourself how things really look in nature. Examine and reexamine proportions and relationships among plants, rocks, and driftwood. In what ways do logs get wedged into stream banks? What do exposed underwater roots of trees look like? In what sorts of patterns do algae and mosses cover stones in shallow ponds? How are sand and gravel arranged around rocks and driftwood?

If you spend your spare time in cities, browse pet stores and libraries. Peruse aquarium books and books on aquatic natural history. Meander through photo-essays about fishes and their habitats. Visit a public aquarium, if there's one near you, to get an idea of the way curators and exhibit designers lay out their tanks. Attend lectures at local museums to check out people's slide collections of aquatic life in the field.

Because you'll want to fine-tune your tank to the needs of the specific fishes you want to keep, you should begin with some idea of the animal community you want to end up with. Look over the descriptions of fishes in the next chapter, and look over the tank "recipes" in Chapter 7. It's also a good idea to spend some time looking over the fishes offered for sale in your local pet shop. You'll see that fishes have different personalities and that different species show different patterns of swimming behavior. Once you've reached that stage, you're ready to match tank design with fish psychology.

Some fishes, such as giant Danios *(Danio malabaricus),* are energetic, almost manic, and constantly rush back and forth over long distances near the top of the water. For this sort of species, you'd want to leave plenty of open space for swimming near the top of the tank.

Others, such as angelfish, move much more slowly, and pick their way through the water in the middle region of the tank. They hover, nearly motionless, among leaves and stems of plants, but do like some open space in which to swim around. Still others, such as neon tetras *(Cheirodon axelrodi),* dart back and forth in schools that wander to and fro, also in the middle of the water column. For both these species, ideal tank configurations would include both well-planted areas and places with more open space.

African cichlids, such as members of the genus *Pseudotropheus,* are tireless swimmers who constantly patrol the entire volume of their tank, side to side and top to bottom. These guys—as well as many other full-sized cichlids—are hell on daintily decorated tanks and delicate plants. Sometimes they're just hungry. Other times they seem to have their own ideas about how the tank should be arranged. But whatever their motivation, they can uproot plants, pile gravel up everywhere except where you want it, and even rearrange small rocks. To save yourself a lot of grief (and to make these fish comfortable), you'll want an aquascape with lots of open space that uses medium-large-sized rocks and only the hardiest, thickest-leaved, most solidly rooted plants.

Dwarf cichlids, such as members of the genus *Pelviachromis,* on the other hand, tend to be shy and retiring, and are most at home if they have the option of ducking into a clump of plants or under a sloping rock. Like their larger cousins, dwarf cichlids may choose to do a little "redecorating" here and there, but only where they decide to create a little personal retreat. And the magnificent red-tailed black shark *(Labeo bicolor)* lives on the bottom, where it likes to stake out territories. For these species, well-planted tanks, amply furnished with rocks and bogwood, work very well.

### Assembling Materials

This is another part of the process that can be fun and should take longer than most beginners allot to it. Because naturalistic aquascaping isn't yet the rage here, the right raw materials can be hard to come by. Many pet stores have only one "naturally" colored gravel, though they'll have an endless variety of Day-Glo colors. Stores often have an impressive selection of rocks and minerals safe for aquarium use, but few specimens that look natural underwater. Chunks of rose quartz, for example, aren't part of any real underwater habitat *I've* ever seen! So finding the right materials—whether you collect them from nature or buy them—may take a little ingenuity and patience.

## On Collecting

Whenever you take a nature hike, be on the lookout for rocks and driftwood whose shape and texture appeal to you. There are, of course, several things to remember if you'll be collecting your own decorations. Avoid rocks that have obvious veins of iron or other metals. You should also stay away from sandstones and limestones except for use in hard, alkaline tanks. Soluble elements in both these rocks can raise your pH and add dissolved minerals, hardening the water slowly but steadily. If you *want* your tank to be hard and alkaline (as you would for many African cichlids), that's fine. Otherwise, it's trouble. One way to test a rock is to pour some household vinegar on it; if it fizzles, it will make your water alkaline. My final advice to beginners on this subject: When in doubt, leave it out.

If you look around at natural environments, you'll notice that there are usually only one or two kinds of rocks in any single location. One place may have mostly black basalt, another gray granite, and a third red shale. In very few places will you see dramatically different rocks jumbled together. Take your clues from that reality, settle on a type of rock for your display, and stick with it. Remember, you want your aquarium to show off your collection of fishes and plants; it's not meant to be an underwater mineral show.

It is hard to maintain an accurate sense of perspective about the size of your aquarium when you're out in the woods. It is tricky, there-fore, to know exactly what sizes and shapes to take home. I've played this game two ways. When I'm very organized and efficient, I'll take with me a full-sized "footprint" of the tank on heavy paper. If I come across some likely rocks, I roll out the paper and start designing then and there. When I'm feeling less organized and more energetic, I intentionally overcollect rocks, making sure to take some that are too big and others that are too small. Invariably, I end up using some of all sizes in the final design.

Collecting wood requires similar caution and imagination. Only thoroughly aged, well-leached wood is safe for aquaria; newly fallen branches may contain resins and other compounds that cause problems in the confines of a tank. Avoid fresh pine branches at all cost. The best kinds of wood to look for are commonly referred to as "bogwood" and "driftwood." Bogwood is found either in real bogs or on the bottoms of lakes and streams where it has been soaking for a few years. Driftwood is bleached wood that has been floating in the sea and washing around on a beach for some time.

Both these kinds of wood should be thoroughly boiled, scrubbed (but *not* with soap), dried (in the sun, if possible), and soaked again to get them as waterlogged as possible. If they still won't sink, drill a hole in a flat piece of slate and attach the wood to it with a screw. By burying the plate in gravel, you can keep the wood where you want it.

## Buying Materials

Even I, ardent naturalist that I purport to be, occasionally buy tank decorations in pet shops.

The important thing to remember if you take the commercial route is that you are unlikely to find everything you want in a single trip to a single store. Living in a major metropolitan area with a wide selection of pet shops to choose from, I stop in at any pet shop I pass whenever I can spare the time.

Shopping around pays off in several ways. First, retail markups on decorating materials vary *wildly* from one pet shop to another. (We're talking 20 to 40 percent here!) So shopping around can save you a bundle. Aesthetically, shopping around also gives you the widest range of choices. Driftwood is a good example. Most pet shops in our area buy their driftwood from a single, Maine-based company called Driftwood Arts. Dealers like the stuff because it is cured for aquarium use and is carefully mounted on slate for easy installation. Unfortunately, part of the "art" practiced on this wood often involves drilling holes for fish to swim through, or sanding to achieve a smooth finish. Some look fine. Some even look spectacularly good; I've found several that evoke masterfully the lines and proportions of drowned roots and tree trunks. But many are patently artificial or cutesy—the underwater equivalent of country knickknacks sold around ski resorts. So I survey stock in each shop with a critical eye for those that look natural.

One thing you probably will want to buy, rather than collect, is gravel. You'll need plenty of it, and you may as well start off with it as clean and as well-graded as possible. Although standard neutral-colored aquarium gravel is fine, I'm bored with it. More substantively, standard gravel is significantly lighter in color than the bottoms of most habitats I've seen in nature. I prefer the hue of some of the more interesting—but naturalistically—colored varieties, such as "nutmeg" and "walnut." Needless to say, no Day-Glo orange gravel shows up in *my* tanks. Remember that you'll want a minimum of three inches of gravel to cover your undergravel filter. For big tanks with large rooted plants, you'll want to sculpt terraces and other raised areas that will need more gravel to fill them.

There is also the matter of what you see if you look *through* your tank. I try to place tanks in front of featureless walls painted in shades that complement—rather than clash with—the colors and shapes within the aquarium. Because I plant tanks heavily, I don't worry too much about seeing out the back. But many situations call for a background to screen out distracting or conflicting sights. The most naturalistic solution to this problem is to use silicone aquarium cement to create a wall of slate that screens the back of the tank. Be sure to use only silicone designed for aquarium use; other formulations —such as bathtub caulking—may harm fishes. If you change your mind about your arrangement, it's easy to scrape off the silicone and start again. Another option is to use cured, thin-sliced cork bark (not the sort of plain cork used for bulletin boards) in the same way.

An easier alternative is to screen the back of the tank with an opaque backdrop. Back when I started with aquaria, background paper was invariably bright blue- or orange-tinted metallic foil. People even suggested painting the outside of the tank with the sort of paint that forms crystals when it dries. Not for me, thanks.

Today, you can buy several naturalistic-looking backgrounds in several heights and lengths. One company supplies a background that's two-sided; a lushly planted, freshwater aquascape runs along one side, while a marine scene covers the other. I choose not to use such things, but they can be both useful and attractive in the right situations.

## Experimenting with Design

Once you've collected raw materials, arrange these nonliving props to see what effects you can create. Play around with rocks, gravel, and driftwood to create terraces, caves, nooks, and crannies for fish to hide in and swim around. Experiment with ways to use decorating elements to hide filter stems, heater tubes, and the like (keeping in mind that plants will help a great deal in that respect). If you want to build caves or terraces from rock and wood, but can't get your arrangements to stand up, glue them together using silicone aquarium cement. Just be wary of assembling things in flimsy configurations that look artificial.

We'll talk about specific aquascapes for particular fishes in Chapter 7. In the meantime, I'll offer only general aesthetic suggestions. The most important rule is to avoid centering anything precisely or arranging rocks and plants symmetrically. That doesn't happen in nature, and it won't look right in your tank. Try also to avoid straight rows of rocks and terraces built out of flat pieces of slate. Neither looks real.

As you experiment, keep in mind the shapes and growth habits of your chosen plants. You may want to arrange a spot to show off a large specimen plant or an understory ground cover. Or you may fancy a blanket of moss working its way over a curving piece of driftwood. Don't rush yourself—enjoy the process.

# DECORATING WITH AQUARIA

Now, we get down to the nitty-gritty. Just where, amid chairs, tables, and TV sets, are you going to put this collection of rocks, wood, plants, and fishes? Within the constraints of tank location discussed in Chapter 3, there are lots of options.

You can, for example, squirrel your tank away wherever you keep your kids; they'll probably be the last to complain about any noise the pump makes, and they might even help you take care of it. (Well, now and then, anyway.) That was one of the few real options for tank location when I was young. The tanks themselves were clunky-looking, and wrought-iron stands were as ugly as sin. Put one of those things in your living room? Not on your life.

But, as we discussed in Chapter 3, today's tanks are sleek and handsome, and stands, covers, and lights are available in a wide, endless variety of styles and finishes. Many contemporary stands are set at just the right height to position tanks vertically in rooms with standard ceiling heights. Really tall ceilings (above ten feet or so) might demand a tank position slightly higher off the floor to maintain aesthetically pleasant proportions. Around most major cities are custom fabricators who'll make anything you can't get off the shelf. The only things that really limit you are your imagination and your supply of cash.

As parts of room decor, fifty-five-gallon, all-glass tanks are just about the best. They are large enough to contain a varied and visually interesting collection of aquascape elements and fishes. They're large enough to provide a major visual focus for a room, and yet small enough that most rooms can contain them comfortably. Just as important, although they are unquestionably heavy, they do not present load problems for the floor in any decently constructed building. (Really large tanks, on the other hand, could be dangerous in shoddily built modern condos.)

But you're not restricted to my taste in tank shapes. There are squat and towering hexagonal tanks, trapezoidal tanks, semicircular tanks, and even tanks that fit neatly into the corner of a room. Just a reminder: If you find yourself captivated by an odd tank shape, look back over Chapter 3 to make certain you know what the tank's assets and limitations will be.

Finally, don't underestimate the impact a decent-sized tank will have on your living space. If you can't visualize the tank in place, throw together a simple three-dimensional mock-up of both stand and tank out of cardboard, and try placing them in various locations.

## Fish Tanks as Focal Points in Decor

Because of these stylistic options, aquaria can take their place in any home-decorating scheme. Because they are bright themselves and give off some extra light, they're perfect for windowless corners, dark rooms, and nooks in the walls or wall units (assuming, of course, that you supply enough artificial light to keep plants happy). Because they can be either frenetic or peaceful—depending on the personalities of the fishes you choose—aquaria can help set the psychological tone for a living room, family room, or dining room. (Although you might feel a little odd eating sushi in front of your pets, *they'll* never know the difference!)

To get up close and personal for a moment, I'll admit to strong feelings about television sets in living rooms—I hate them. I refuse to arrange my entertaining space around a TV. I'd consider it an insult to my guests to turn on a TV, and I'd feel the same way if they flicked it on while visiting. The tube goes in a bedroom, guest room, den, kitchen, or anywhere else. Not in the living room. To share that space with friends, I prefer plants, fish tanks, and art; they're lovely to look at, and visitors find them restful and interesting. Aquaria are visually animated but quiet, so they can draw attention without seducing people out of conversation into couch-potatoness.

In that respect, aquaria can be ideal decorating elements in town-house apartments—those long, narrow spaces with windows only in front and rear walls. One former Boston apartment of mine had a spectacular urban view out the front of the living room, and long, featureless walls on either side. Solution? Angle a contemporary couch toward the window, and set up an equally contemporary, fifty-five-gallon aquarium along the wall. Sprinkle in a few plants, a rug or two (coordinated with the colors of the fishes, of course), and the room comes pleasantly and vibrantly—but not belligerently—alive.

Aquaria are often employed as room dividers. My opinions on this practice are mixed. A tank can work as a divider, especially if it contains an abstract landscape such as the Study in Black and White listed in Chapter 7. Using more naturalistically landscaped tanks as room dividers, though, presents some problems.

For a start, unless the tank is built into a major piece of custom furniture (the equivalent of a freestanding wall/shelf unit) there's no place to hide filters, tubes, and power cords that must snake into and out of the tank somehow. The resulting clutter is far from aesthetic. Furthermore, most standard tanks are not wide enough to allow aquascaping that presents naturalistic pictures from both sides. At best you can include tall, wavy plants that offer vertical interest without blocking the view.

More substantively, because I think of tanks as windows onto an underwater world, I don't like seeing a piece of *my* world peering back at me through an aquarium. That problem can be avoided if the space on one side of the tank is darkened when the other is in use. I once used an aquarium as a room divider in a desperate attempt to partition living from working space in a cramped studio apartment. It worked. The tank separated home office from living/sleeping area well. The apartment, located on the ground floor, was dark unless I illuminated it. So, when I was "out of the office," relaxing or entertaining, I kept the office in shadow and allowed light from the tank to screen out work lurking on the other side. That configuration wouldn't work nearly so well (except at night, of course) in a skylit loft space.

Remember to consider the angles from which your tank will be visible, as well as the angles from which your fish will be able to see you. Be certain to take into account the psychology of the particular fishes you'll be keeping. Some of the more timid species will go belly-up if housed in a playroom with kids constantly bouncing off the walls. Others will do fine with the same degree of activity around them.

This freshwater setup, complete with multiple-tube hood, features a thriving community of aquatic plants and animals. The state-of-the-art life support system shown here is by no means *necessary* for a typical freshwater tank, but it is a delight for those that can afford it. This sophisticated system ensures near-optimum conditions automatically, requiring only infrequent maintenance.

◄ This custom marine installation proves that tank supports and equipment enclosures don't have to be homely to be utilitarian. The sleek, contemporary cabinet houses trickle filter, air and water pumps, and other life support equipment neatly and efficiently. The matching full hood provides enough light to sustain those organisms that must photosynthesize in order to survive.

The marine aquarium in this ► installation features similarly sophisticated life-support equipment, but is housed on a stand of more traditional design.

## Location, Location, Location

It really is worthwhile to plan your tank's location carefully. Believe me, you won't want to move a tank once you get it set up. For that reason, once you've made your decision on aesthetic grounds, run through the list of tank-placement considerations from Chapter 3 once again, and factor in these additional matters before you make up your mind.

Placing tanks near the gentle heat of full-length baseboard heating units is not usually a problem as long as you keep wires away from the heating element. But don't, under any circumstances, put tanks on top of metal covers used to hide steam or forced hot-water radiators!

Consider the pros and cons of locating tanks near windows discussed in Chapter 3. Remember that there are benefits to natural light, but be prepared to make necessary adjustments with curtains or shades when appropriate. If you'd rather not worry about such things, don't put tanks close to south or west windows.

Because fish are susceptible to fumes from oil-based paints, varnishes, strippers, floor finishes, and so on, it's best to fill your tank only *after* you've done any major refinishing in its vicinity. If you'll be building your tank into a room divider or other custom piece of furniture, place the tank and equipment wherever you need to during construction, but keep it covered and empty until all fumes have cleared away.

If you live in an area with frigid winters, be extra careful about drafts near your tank. In my old house, for instance, certain outside walls, because of their construction and exposure to prevailing winds, are colder than others. Luck-ily, they knew how to build houses back in the nineteenth century, so the north and east walls of this building are occupied by hallways, closets, kitchen, and pantry. The real living spaces are lined up along the south wall where there's usually more sunlight and natural warmth.

But the outside wall in the living room is cold on winter nights, and despite everything I can do to seal the window in that wall, it's drafty. This I discovered by placing a couch in front of it one autumn; the arrangement looked great, but guests were forever asking for lap blankets. I eventually moved the couch away from the wall, and my guests are much happier for the relocation.

Needless to say, I would hesitate to put an aquarium against that wall or near that window. If I had to, I'd choose an acrylic model, because acrylic is a better thermal insulator than glass. I'd make certain the tank had a draft-resistant cover, and that no external filters or tubing got pushed up directly against the cold wall. I'd also equip the tank with two heaters whose combined rating was 20–25 percent higher than standard recommendations, just to make certain that they could keep up on cold nights.

Finally, remember that while well-maintained aquaria make spectacular accents for important rooms, tanks require regular maintenance to keep them looking good. If you use one as a major focus in a popular room, therefore, be sure to budget the time to keep things ship-shape inside. If you've never kept an aquarium before, I'd recommend placing your first tank in a "medium exposure" zone, rather than in a place everyone sees constantly. That way, if you slip up on the maintenance now and then, you won't be so embarrassed about how the tank looks.

# THE LIVING LANDSCAPE

The plants that share our fishes' native haunts have a long and fascinating history. The first algae, like the earliest animals, evolved underwater, and modern algae never left; they've been evolving in aquatic habitats ever since. Others —mosses, liverworts, and ferns—moved onto land, but live only in wet places. Still others— conifers and flowering plants—live almost everywhere save for the driest deserts.

At least a few members of all these plant groups (except conifers) live underwater today. Having returned to water after a long sojourn on land, most bear telltale signs of their terrestrial ancestry. Just as dolphins can breathe only by coming to the surface, for example, most aquatic plants can flower or produce spores only when either floating or growing at least partially in air.

The world of aquatic plants is as unusual and exotic as the world of fishes. And like fishes, underwater plants vary greatly in hardiness and adaptability to life in home aquaria. Several are practically foolproof; because there's no way to overwater or underwater them, even "black thumbs" can triumph with these species. Other varieties—many of them strikingly beautiful— require a bit more care. From an aquarist's standpoint, there are four major ecological categories of tropical aquatic plants, each of which has adapted to a different set of conditions.

## Underwater Plants

True underwater plants grow in rivers, streams, lakes, and ponds that are relatively stable throughout the year. Temperature, sunlight, and the amount of dissolved nutrients in the water invariably change with the seasons, but the water in which these plants grow doesn't fluctuate greatly in depth. If conditions in one of these plants' native habitats happen to match those you'll be creating in your tank, they will do well for a long time.

These species grow roots and leaves completely adapted to underwater life and cannot grow on dry land. Some are shaped like typical houseplants, with well-developed root systems and leaves that radiate from a central crown. Others have strong roots and long, branching stems. Still others grow short roots (or none at all) and consist entirely of trailing leaves and stems. A few of them flower underwater, although many grow floating leaves and send flower stems up into the open air.

Because these plants grow permanently underwater, they can pick up nutrients either through their roots (as the majority of land plants do) or directly through their leaves. Although controversy exists as to which route is more important for particular species, it is clear that some species favor one method, while others switch back and forth depending on where the nutrients are available.

## Amphibious Plants

Many aquarium plants evolved in the seasonally flooded habitats discussed earlier. Some of these species need their natural rhythm of flooding and emersion to flourish, while others adapt well to long-term submersion. Many, if they thrive in a tank that is too small for them, will produce first floating, and then emergent,

leaves. Under certain conditions, this can provide an attractive display, but it can also be a nuisance.

## Floating Plants

Floating plants, which differ enormously in size, drift on the water's surface and rarely sink roots into anything. Some, such as duckweed, are tiny, and if kept under control can make interesting additions to home aquaria. Others, such as water hyacinths, are too large for most indoor tanks but make beautiful additions to outdoor pools.

## Terrestrial Visitors

Having insisted that terrestrial plants don't belong in aquaria, I'll backtrack a bit and allow that they can be treated as visitors. (After all, cut flowers on the dining-room table are pretty, even if they don't last forever.) Several of these plants—particularly prayer plants (species of *Maranta,* and *Calathea*), and "Chinese evergreens" (which belong to the genus *Aglaonema* and come from Malaysia and India, not China) have beautifully colored leaves that make striking accents. And some—notably a few *Aglaonema* species sold in florist shops—can survive for up to a year underwater.

Maybe I'm stuffy. Maybe I'm a purist. But I don't use these plants in fish tanks. Though they may *survive* in aquaria, most stop growing, so they don't participate in the life of the tank. Because they don't grow underwater, they must be prepared for tank life as houseplants. They must be planted in small pots—in a growing

mixture safe for tank use (see page 77)—allowed to reach the size you want, and then buried, pot and all, in the aquarium. This means that all leaves and stems displayed in the tank will have grown and developed in air. It may seem like a picky aesthetic point, but plants that grow in air look different from those that develop underwater; they are stiffer and are held at different angles. Thus, though these plants look fine in bog terraria, they look out of place in most fully aquatic circumstances. If their looks don't bother you, however, your fishes won't care, so feel free to use them.

## AN AQUATIC PLANT SAMPLER

Now that I've tantalized you with generalities, let's get down to specifics, with detailed descriptions of some mosses, liverworts, ferns, and a few flowering plants for freshwater tanks. While algae are often frowned upon in freshwater tanks, please consider my dissenting opinion.

## Mosses and Ferns

Several mosses and ferns are among the easiest plants to grow in home aquaria. They were the first plants that rewarded me with unqualified success, and I recommend them highly.

*Vesicularia dubyana,* commonly called Java moss, is rarely seen in pet stores, and I can't imagine why. It is not picky about pH, temperature, hardness, or light levels, though it does prefer soft, slightly acid water. It grows slowly at first, but rapidly once established. Be-

Subularia aquatica

Anubias nana

Nymphoides aquatica                    Cryptocoryne nevillii

cause it never roots (although it attaches itself to driftwood or stones), it can be moved without damage. It makes an ideal spawning medium for many egg-laying fishes, and an excellent "baby grass" for all kinds of fry. Because it does so well with such minimal care, it is an ideal starter plant for novices.

*Ceratopteris*, a group of underwater ferns collectively called "water sprite," are attractive and rapid-growing plants that are perfect for beginners. Given slightly acid water and moderate light, they grow luxuriantly. Fronds that float to the surface develop many new plants along their edges. If planted on the tank bottom, these pieces grow vigorously, and if left floating, they will produce stiff aerial fronds that bear spores. If kept in hostile water, however, fronds will deteriorate and plantlets will produce ever smaller plantlets until they gradually fade away.

*Microsorium* (also known as *Polypodium*) *pteropus*, the Java fern, is one of the most handsome of all underwater plants. It grows slowly but steadily, putting up a series of bright green swordlike leaves from a creeping rhizome that attaches readily to rocks or driftwood. I rarely see this plant in pet stores, perhaps because of its slow growth and relatively high price. But for those who can find it—either locally or through mail-order suppliers—I cannot recommend *Microsorium* highly enough. Like other ferns and mosses, it grows well in slightly acid, relatively soft water, and does well with limited light.

# FLOWERING PLANTS

## Floating Plants

*Lemna*, or duckweed, a floating species, is among the smallest of flowering plants. A favorite food of many plant-eating fishes, duckweed can reproduce so rapidly that if allowed to grow unchecked, it covers the surface of an aquarium in less than a week. A few of them, however, provide shade and psychological retreats for such surface-dwelling species as hatchetfish, and are often used by bubble-nest builders (such as bettas and gouramies).

## Rooted Plants

*Echinodorus*, the Amazon sword-plants, are the most familiar rooted aquarium plants. This genus embraces more than fifty relatively hardy and adaptable species, most of which are native to periodically flooded riverbanks of South America. As a group, they prefer water that is neutral or slightly acid and not too hard.

The varieties of *Echinodorus* commonly sold in pet shops are not quite foolproof, but are not too difficult, either. Although very hard water can make life difficult for them, these plants usually fail in home aquaria from lack of light. Intense artificial light and/or a few hours of sunlight are beneficial.

*Echinodorus* species are wildly diverse; some are midgets barely two inches tall, while others grow aerial leaves nearly ten feet long. Some medium-sized species—such as *E. bleheri* (the "broadleaf sword"), *E. maior* (incorrectly *E. martii*) and *E. osiris*—make spectacular specimens in tanks of twenty gallons or larger. Others, such as *E. tenellus* (the "micro sword" or "creeping sword"), spread like ground covers

to carpet tank bottoms. Some larger species, when grown well, can get out of hand and produce huge floating and aerial leaves. Most commonly available smaller species, however, live for long periods completely underwater.

*Aponogeton* is one of the few large, commonly seen genera that is completely aquatic. Ranging from Africa across India to Southeast Asia, many *Aponogeton* species are native to the wet-dry habitats described earlier. Several highly seasonal types are offered in aquarium stores as dry, resting bulbs. These plants—because they come with their own supply of stored food—are good choices for newly established tanks, where they will grow actively. But although these plants are easy to start from bulbs, they require a cool, dry rest period roughly once a year. Lacking that, they may either stop growing or die.

In the long run, it's easier to stick with the numerous hybrids made by crossing various species of *Aponogeton* artificially over the years. Although growth in these hybrids often slows or stops for a few months, they do not require the drastic seasonal changes required by many species.

Naturally, the most attractive species is the most difficult to grow. The Madagascar Lace Plant (*Aponogeton madagascariensis* or *A. fenestralis*) is well known among aquarists, both for the beauty of its lacy leaves and for the speed with which it rots if conditions are not to its liking. When grown with care in a rich planting medium, sufficient light, and frequent changes of soft, slightly acid water, it does well. Under more normal aquarium conditions, it lasts only for a single season.

*Cryptocoryne* is a large genus of small plants that are favorites among advanced hobbyists.

Most common species require slightly acid water (in fact, they tend to acidify the water themselves), and get by with less light than many other plants. As a group, *Cryptocorynes* like a nutrient-rich substrate and dislike transplanting intensely. These plants do particularly well when provided with "pockets" of good growing medium.

*Vallisneria* and *Sagittaria,* two popular, long-leaved plants, prefer harder water and more alkaline conditions. Both genera grow long, slender, upright leaves that make a handsome screen or backdrop. When growing actively, *Vallisneria* reproduces rapidly by means of runners. One commonly available cultivar, "corkscrew val," has particularly attractive, spiral leaves.

*Vallisneria* tends to make the water around it more alkaline. Because this activity resists the slow acidification common in aquaria, these plants are ideal for tanks with fish (such as livebearers and African cichlids) that prefer alkaline water. One warning, though: If these plants are placed in poorly lit tanks with acid water, they will languish and fall to pieces.

Both these genera require a moderately rich growing medium, and as much light as you can possibly give them. I've had best success with these genera in tanks lit either with a *four-bulb* fluorescent fixture, or by a more standard two-bulb reflector in a tank that received several hours of direct early morning or late afternoon sun.

## Bunch Plants

"Bunch" plants, as a group, tolerate a broad range of temperature, pH, and hardness. Most, however, require strong light to stay as attractive as they are when purchased. I recommend a minimum of two 40-watt fluorescent tubes, along with some added sunlight and bright indirect natural light. Several species of *Cabomba, Lobelia,* and *Rotala* come in all shades of green from emerald to chartreuse, and exhibit a wide variety of leaf shapes and textures when well-grown. Brightly colored cultivars of popular species such as *Ludwigia* and *Alternanthera* have leaves that are beautifully suffused with red or reddish purple, but must have intense light to maintain that color.

A few bunch plants—such as *Elodea*—grow most attractively in cool water, and as such are better suited to well-lit, unheated goldfish tanks. In tropical community tanks, even with the best light, *Elodea* tends to get spindly.

## Algae

Nearly everyone who has kept fishes has also —usually involuntarily—cultivated algae. Novices seem instinctively to hate algae, and their prejudice is reinforced by an assortment of algicides sold in pet shops. After all, if there are so many products made to kill algae, they must be bad, right?

Not necessarily.

Hobbyists usually lump together as algae several very different kinds of photosynthetic organisms. Some of these are good to have around, others do no harm, and only a few really present any problems.

### Green Algae
Green algae—and by that I mean the members of the plant division *Chlorophyta*—are viewed by knowledgeable aquarists as "good" algae. At least one variety invariably crops up in well-lit, well-stocked tanks. Some attach to aquarium walls, while others grow on gravel, rocks, or the leaves of real and plastic plants. Several grow in the form of short "hairs" or filaments; when these grow densely on a rock or piece of driftwood, they can be quite attractive. They also provide nutritious snacks for many fishes such as mollies and cichlids. And actively growing green algae—like higher plants—help remove excess nitrogen-containing wastes from aquarium water.

Why, then, do people dislike algae so much?

Part of the reason is that algae on aquarium glass make a tank look "dirty." The solution is simple: Remove the algae as part of regular aquarium maintenance. It takes less than five minutes a week. There are many commercial algae scrapers, most of which allow you to keep your hands dry. Some scrapers are on long handles, while others use a two-part magnet to hold a mildly abrasive pad against the glass. I just roll up my sleeves, grab a single-edged razor blade, and go at the stuff by hand. (Note that razor-blade scrapers work well on glass tanks but scratch acrylic; to clean algae off acrylic tanks, use the soft-scrub pads sold in pet stores and use them gently.)

Another cause of American "algaphobia" traces back to the artificial tanks many people here seem to prefer. Algae just don't look right in spotlessly clean tanks decorated with white and rose quartz crystals, orange gravel, plastic plants, and other ersatz objets d'art. In fact, even a little algal growth makes those tanks look pretty scuzzy.

The same algae, though, doesn't look halfbad on driftwood, dark stones, and the leaves of live plants in naturalistically designed tanks.

As a matter of fact, it makes the tanks look *more* natural; as anyone who's ever gone scuba diving in freshwater can attest, green algae are a part of most underwater environments. As long as your tank and its algae smell clean—like the smell of good soil after rain—you're in fine shape.

## Blue-Green Bacteria and Their Relatives

An entirely different matter are other photosynthetic organisms often called "blue-green algae," but which are actually bacteria. These nasty critters can grow with amazing speed, forming a noxious carpet that covers and smothers everything in sight. They also give off unpleasant compounds that smell bad, overload your chemical filtration system, and don't do your fishes any good.

A heavy growth of blue-greens, in addition to being bad for your tank, usually indicates less than ideal conditions for fishes. Your tank may not have sufficient water circulation. Your water chemistry may be off. You may have neglected to change water regularly, allowing nitrates to build up. Or your tank may be getting too much light, too little light, or the wrong kind of light to encourage the growth of the right photosynthetic organisms.

You can distinguish blue-greens from green algae by several criteria. Green algae that show up in tanks are often (though not always) filamentous or "fuzzy" in look and feel. All are bright green in color, and have nearly no odor. Blue-greens, on the other hand, are dark blue-green, slimy-looking and feeling, and have a distinctive, less-than-pleasant aroma. (Note that

some of the members of the blue-green bacterial group that invade marine tanks are actually reddish purple, but otherwise fit the same description.)

## Controlling Excess Algae and Blue-Greens

Once you understand that your tank will always have some algae in it, there are several things you can do to keep both beneficial algae and blue-greens under control. Actively growing live plants help, because they compete with algae for nutrients. Regular water changes and attention to aquarium chemistry will help tip the balance in favor of desirable plants and green algae. Certain catfish, notably several members of the genus *Plecostomus,* can devour astonishing amounts of the stuff on a daily basis. Many live-bearers, such as mollies, eagerly use green algae to supplement their diet. And tadpoles and certain snails will eat both green algae and blue-green bacteria.

Note that these methods will neither *eliminate* algae nor remove enough to keep your plants and aquarium glass spotlessly clean. A little manual maintenance is in order here; scrape the glass as suggested above and remove any heavy algal growth from plant leaves by rubbing gently between your fingers.

If you insist on keeping a tank completely free of both plants and algae, you can resort to commercially available algae-controlling chemicals. I haven't used algicides in more than fifteen years, and have no plant-free tanks in which to test the new ones on the market. Informed sources tell me, however, that they are reasonably—though far from completely—effective. Be aware, though, that if you don't cor-

rect the tank conditions that created the problem to begin with, the algae will be back as soon as the chemical wears off. Algicides won't hurt your fishes, but I can't promise the same for plants.

One final note about snails. One or two are attractive, but two can produce hundreds in a few months. Pulling excess snails out by hand is about as effective as trying to bail out the *Titanic* would have been, but there is another way. If snails get out of control, consider keeping one or more of the fishes that eat them. The best is the Clown Loach *(Botia macracantha),* a beautiful, even-tempered, and social species that does best in groups of three or more. Another snail-eater is the cichlid commonly called "jurupari" *(Geophagus jurupari).* This species, suitable for community tanks only when small, cannot be trusted with small live-bearers or tetras. Large specimens can be temperamental, and are best kept only with large, active fishes.

## Selecting and Buying Plants

Now, you're ready to choose your plants. If there's a pet store in your area that knows its plants, you're in luck (see Choosing a Pet Shop in Chapter 8). Check plant descriptions and cultural recommendations above, and pick out a few plants that will work in your tank. If you're seriously interested in plants, buy one of the aquatic plant books listed on page 228.

Inspect plants with care. Leaves should be firm and solidly green (or mottled with color if appropriate), not soft, yellowish or spotted heavily with brown. Stems and roots should be firm and healthy-looking. Rooted plants should be properly planted in the dealer's tanks with their crowns even with—not above or below—the level of the gravel. Sturdy, newly emerging leaves are a reassuring sign that plants are in good health. If you find a shop that stocks quality plants but doesn't care for them properly, find out when their shipments arrive and select yours as close to their arrival time as possible.

If there isn't a good source near you, contact the mail-order companies listed on page 226. Prepare a list of plants that appeal to you, and know in advance the water and lighting conditions in your tank. Tell the supplier that you want a few specimen plants and others to fill in around them. If you're not sure what plants will do well for you, describe your conditions and see what the person at the other end suggests. I've found several suppliers to be pleasant, well-informed, and helpful over the phone. Both as dedicated aquarists and as good businesspeople, they're eager to treat customers properly. The stock I've received over the years has varied in quality, but most of it has been much better than anything I can buy locally. The only real problem with buying plants through the mail is that tropical varieties don't ship well during the winter.

## Deciding on Your Growing Medium

Before your plants arrive, decide exactly how you want to grow them. There are two basic approaches to aquatic plant-growing media, though there are many variations on these themes.

**Clean Gravel** The safest, simplest medium—especially for first-timers—is straight aquarium gravel, as it minimizes both setup work and the number of variables involved in keeping your tank balanced. The problem with this approach is that the clean, washed gravel preferred as a biological filter medium is woefully lacking in plant nutrients. Nutrients will accumulate as your fish do what comes naturally, but that ultimate solution doesn't help plants get established in the beginning.

For this reason, when setting up a new tank with clean gravel, start with plants that depend minimally on outside nutrients. The best choices are bunch plants and rooted specimens that have either bulbous roots or thick rhizomes. Bunch plants don't have any roots to begin with anyway, and the others have reserves of stored food they can utilize for a while.

Another option is to add fertilizer to the tank water. Do *not* use garden or houseplant fertilizer. Many of these supply nitrogen as ammonia, which could be fatal to your fishes. Garden fertilizers are also often extremely acid. There are fertilizers designed specifically for aquaria, and though generally overpriced, they do their job.

When setting rooted plants into a gravel bed, be gentle. Don't drag the plant by its crown or jam roots into the gravel. Instead, make a shallow planting hole with your fingers, gently arrange the roots within the depression, and cover them with gravel. This will probably take two hands, and may take a couple of tries at first, but you'll get the hang of it. When you're finished, make certain that the crown is even with the surface.

**Planting in Richer Media** Once you've got the hang of fishkeeping and decide to have a go at aquascaping, you may want to provide a more varied and nutritious medium for your rooted plants. Having slogged through many aquatic habitats, I have a pretty good idea of the soil that underwater plants usually grow in. But covering your tank bottom with an oozing black mixture of sand, silt, clay, and muck would be disastrous. You want to keep most of your tank bottom covered with gravel that allows water to circulate freely through your undergravel filter. This not only encourages proper biological filtration, but prevents the growth of anaerobic bacteria that can release toxic substances.

So what can you do to enrich gravel for your plants? Some useful products are sold in better pet shops. Two companies offer blocks of treated peat fiber to place beneath your gravel. These blocks give your plants something other than gravel to root into, and as they decompose, they release some nutrients to the water and trap others passing through the filter. At least one company offers river soil from tropical Asia, carefully sterilized and packaged in neat little boxes. This soil is meant to be mixed with gravel before planting, and is said to supply a variety of trace elements and iron that support plant growth.

Both these products are useful and are not misrepresented in any way. They are, however, so expensive that most beginning hobbyists want nothing to do with them. But these specialty items aren't necessary, if you're willing to do some shopping around and a little horticultural work on your own.

My approach to planting aquatic plants borrows heavily from experience in my garden. Just as you might prepare a hole full of good topsoil to plant a tree or rosebush, offer aquarium plants little patches of soil in which to establish roots.

At your local garden center, pick up a batch of three-inch peat pots used to start plants from seed, and a small plant-misting bottle that you will never use for either soap or insecticide. Finally, buy a small bag of each of unmilled (long-fibered) sphagnum moss and any organic, sterilized potting soil that contains such ingredients as peat, humus, loam, and composted bark.

When choosing the potting soil, avoid mixes that contain either vermiculite or perlite. There's nothing dangerous to fishes about these ingredients, but they float, and will invariably end up coating your tank's surface. You can skim them off simply enough with a net, but they're an unnecessary nuisance. I've successfully used several planting mixes, a few of which are available from the mail-order suppliers on page 226.

To make the planting medium, mix equal parts of aquarium gravel, organic potting soil, the tufts from the tips of the unmilled sphagnum moss, and aquarium or horticultural charcoal. (NOTE: Ordinary charcoal will do here; the more expensive GAC isn't necessary.) Moisten the mix slowly by adding water with the misting bottle. The medium is moist enough when it has a loose and friable texture but just holds its shape if you squeeze it in the palm of your hand.

Next, moisten the peat pots with the spray bottle to make them easier to work with. If they're either too dry or too wet, they'll fall apart during handling, but you'll get the hang of this pretty quickly. Then use a small, sharp scissors to remove the bottom of the pot, and trim the remaining pot walls to a height of about two-and-a-half inches. Place the pot on a flat surface, and lay moistened, unmilled sphagnum

across the bottom to form a cup whose sides cling to the peat-pot walls.

Fill the peat pot about one-third full of potting mix and pat it lightly into the shape of a cone. Take a plant, gently spread its root out over that cone, and add more soil to cover them. As you work, adjust the height of the plant so that its crown ends up about one-quarter inch above the top of the peat-pot rim. Then, nearly fill the pot with soil, pressing it in gently (you don't want to compact it into cement by squeezing out all the air pockets). Top the pot off with a layer of aquarium gravel, and you're ready to place the pot in your aquascape. Be certain when you make the final arrangement in the tank that the crown of the plant is even with the top of the gravel.

Bunch plants don't really need this treatment, but you can pot them up, too, if you like. Just be sure to bury at least an inch and a half of stem to prevent the plant from floating free when the tank is filled.

## Planting Protocol

Whether you buy plants locally or through the mail, you will probably get them home wrapped in wet newspaper inside plastic bags. They will survive that way for some time, but can't photosynthesize in the dark and will be living on stored reserves. Because they'll depend on those reserves until they get established, you want to plant them as quickly as possible. Some tropical species are also susceptible to cold damage, so get them into your warm tank as soon as you can.

When you have your plants ready, set them in a place where you can keep them moist and

out of direct sun as you work. Once you begin planting, use the misting bottle to spray them regularly to keep them from drying out.

It's easiest to arrange rooted plants in a tank that's between half and two-thirds full of water (see detailed setup instructions in Chapter 8). That allows you to see how their leaves will float, but still lets you get up to your elbows in the tank without spilling water. Once the rooted plants and major pieces of driftwood and rockwork are in place, add enough water to fill the tank to within a few inches of the top. That'll give you nearly a full picture of how the tank looks and make it easy for you to arrange bunch plants in the best positions.

## Lighting

Remember that the most common reason for failure with aquarium plants is lack of light, so be certain to follow the lighting instructions from the last chapter. If you will be setting up a "high light" tank with three or more fluorescent bulbs, it's a good idea to wire your reflector in such a way that you can turn one of them on by itself. That way you can blast the tank with light for most of the day to keep them growing, and create more subdued "mood" lighting for viewing of your handiwork in the evening.

## Pruning

If your plants do well, you will need to prune them periodically. Decaying leaves of rooted plants should be carefully snipped (not pulled) from the crown with small, sharp scissors.

(Manicure scissors are best, although a pair of small, sharp desk scissors will do.) Even under ideal conditions, most bunch plants eventually become either leggy or too tall. When this happens, just cut off the top few inches, tie them together, and replant. If lower stems are still healthy, they should branch and produce dense masses of foliage quickly. If they don't, replace them with the cut tops.

# CHAPTER 5

# FRESHWATER FISHES FOR THE HOME

Walk into any well-stocked aquarium store, and you'll be impressed by the variety of fish on sale. Open any fish atlas that covers even a fraction of the tens of thousands of living species, and you will be overwhelmed. To spare you the angst of facing the entire fish world at once, I've assembled here a "Top 40" sampler that provides cultural information for a number of tried-and-tested freshwater favorites. It also includes a few particularly beautiful rarer and more difficult species.

If an interesting, stable, and peaceful freshwater community tank is your goal, the species covered here can keep you busy for years. If, on the other hand, you have an urge to collect dozens of exotic species, buy one of the fish encyclopedias recommended on page 228. Saltwater fishes, all of which I consider expert fishes by default, are discussed in the next chapter.

Here is where you'll finally see the value in fish taxonomy, for the only sensible way to organize a long list of fishes is to group them by family and genus. Because members of each family share numerous characteristics, many of their cultural requirements are also similar. Once you're familiar with the general habits and

habitats of the tetra family (family Characidae), for example, you can make reasonable guesses about many (though not all) tetras you've never seen before.

I have not arranged these families in the sequence usually chosen by ichthyologists. That sequence is based on the higher taxonomic categories to which families belong, and has little relevance to hobbyists. Instead, I've presented them in an arbitrary but coherent order from the most common and least demanding through those that are rarer and more difficult to care for. Each family section starts off with cultural information and helps you recognize most members of that family. Within each family, species are ordered by the criteria of availability and care.

## PRIDE, PREJUDICE, AND YOUR FISHES

Before diving into descriptions of individual species, I want to dispel a few misconceptions connected with labeling fishes as "easy" or "difficult." For too many hobbyists, calling a species easy robs it of cachet. There's an implicit as-

sumption that the most exotic and difficult fishes are both more beautiful and more "sophisticated" than those that are "common."

As a man who loves fishes, I disagree. Many "beginner" fishes are just as brightly colored and just as fascinating to watch as any exotic species. The main difference between easy and difficult species is that the former tolerate more deviations from ideal conditions before going belly-up. Easy species also tend to be catholic in feeding habits; most readily accept (and stay healthy on) simple diets that are easy to provide. The implications of their rugged constitutions are clear. If—despite your best intentions as a dedicated hobbyist—you find yourself juggling a new job, a new baby, and a winter flu, easy fishes will survive a reasonable amount of benign neglect. They also make it easy for you to disappear on a week's vacation without making special plans to have your tank cared for.

Difficult species are fussier all around. Neglect their water changes and special diets, and they're likely to start on a downward spiral. Subject them to changes in pH or hardness, or restrict them to food they don't like or can't digest, and they'll either embarrass you by dying overnight or make you feel even guiltier by taking weeks to fade away. And if you leave finicky fishes in the care of well-meaning but less-experienced aquarist acquaintances, you might be risking both your pets and your friendships.

So aside from the thrill that we "Type A" folks feel when we rise to a challenge that other (and perhaps more sensible) people avoid, there's nothing better about keeping difficult species. And as a person with respect for life in all its forms, I encourage hobbyists to start with less demanding species and work up. It's far more satisfying—and more humane—to keep easy fishes alive and thriving than it is to struggle with difficult fishes that teeter between life and death.

Keep in mind that even the easiest fishes present a series of graded challenges; once you've kept them alive and healthy, you might decide to breed them. Buy a few guppies or swordtails, and you'll soon have babies on your hands. Whether you'll succeed in raising those babies to maturity the first time around is another matter. Other, more difficult species present greater challenges. I kept Siamese fighting fish and dwarf cichlids healthy for years before I managed to raise their tiny fry. So there's plenty in the "easy" category to keep you occupied.

My own willingness to fuss with persnickety fishes waxes and wanes. At some points in my life, I've enjoyed breeding recalcitrant cichlids and maintaining a living-reef tank. But there have also been times (right now, for example) when I want nothing more than a beautiful, care-free aquarium. Right now, I look across my office to a fifty-five-gallon tank containing a jungle of plants (that could use a little pruning), schools of cardinal tetras and harlequin rasboras, a trio of clown loaches, a few assorted *Corydoras* catfish, and two *Plecostomus* cats. All "novice" fishes, but all attractive, peaceful, and easy to keep healthy while I maneuver through a hectic year. When I'm ready to invest more time in fishes, and can not only tolerate but enjoy the heady combination of anguish and challenge, I'll set up a living-reef tank and add discus to the freshwater tank.

## Adding to an Established Tank

Adding new fish to an established community tank can be trickier than you'd expect. In addition to following the quarantine procedure recommended in Chapter 9, it's also a good idea to know how your tank rates on the belligerence scale. Peaceful tanks populated by guppies, swordtails, and other inoffensive fish can usually absorb new members without any problems.

More belligerent communities of territorial cichlids or marine fishes, on the other hand, usually exist in a sort of uneasy truce that the addition of newcomers invariably disturbs. Most often, the new addition is attacked by all the resident fishes. Because long-term residents enjoy a psychological advantage over newcomers, the new fish usually suffers, and may die. Other times, a particularly aggressive new fish succeeds in routing a former inhabitant from its territory. This sets off a round of conflicts that involves all tank members.

To give everyone more of an equal chance in such a situation, you need to upset the existing dominance hierarchy in the tank, so that all fishes start from scratch in carving out new territories. To do this, either net out all the fish and put them back in as you add the new specimen, or rearrange the aquascape. Both of these procedures cause a ruckus in the tank, and the resulting squabble can be unnerving to both fishes and hobbyists. There is always the risk that some of the tank's original inhabitants will suffer some, but it's just about the only way to place both residents and new arrivals on an equal footing.

Assuming that your tank has space available, it's also a good idea to add several fish at once, rather than one at a time; this spreads the aggression against intruders over several individuals, instead of concentrating it on a single unfortunate.

# SELECTED FRESHWATER FISHES

"So many fishes, so little time!" That could be the motto of this chapter. Without spending half the book listing fishes, it's hard to provide a representative sample of the freshwater fishes available today. So it's only fair to warn you that in selecting a few dozen species from among tens of thousands, I've invoked personal bias. There are many aquarium-worthy fishes—both common and rare—that may appeal to you more than those I have chosen.

But I recommend strongly that new hobbyists spend a while sampling from the menu I've provided, to get firsthand experience with the requirements and personalities of fishes. Later, if you decide to specialize in one or another family, you will likely find that there is a national or international organization devoted to your favorites. From the American Catfish and Loach Association to the International Panchax Association, these organizations exist to distribute information about "their" fishes, and are filled with friendly and experienced hobbyists. I encourage you to check the listing of these societies on page 228 and contact them for detailed information on care and availability of unusual species.

# GUPPIES AND THEIR KIN:

## Family Poeciliidae

Guppies and their live-bearing kin have brought more joy to more beginning hobbyists than any other fishes. Members of this family are colorful, active, peaceful, and able to survive in a variety of water types. As an added bonus, they breed constantly and bear their young alive, providing a steady stream of baby fishes to entertain both children and parents. (See Maternity Leave, page 89.) Because males of several species (other than guppies) may squabble, poeciliids are often sold in trios consisting of a single male and two females, a combination that keeps everyone (including the fish) amused and contented.

The fact that poeciliids are hardy and adaptable, however, shouldn't be taken as a license for careless husbandry. These fishes look their best under proper conditions, and suffer from adverse circumstances or sudden changes in their environment. As a group, poeciliids prefer a pH not too far from neutral, and water that is moderately hard. These preferences make poeciliids ideal fishes in areas of the country where tapwater is naturally hard and alkaline.

Because many poeciliids wander from streams into brackish-water coastal marshes, as a group they not only tolerate but stay healthier and freer of fungal diseases in water to which some salt has been added. All popular live-bearers —mollies in particular—appreciate the addition of a tablespoon of either uniodized kosher salt or artificial sea salts for every five gallons of aquarium water. (NOTE: Salt should be added only *once,* and replaced only with water changes; because dissolved salts are left behind when water evaporates, water added to replace evaporation loss should be fresh.)

Poeciliids as a family are omnivorous, which means they will eat nearly any fish food you give them. Most require vegetable matter in their diet, however, and mollies are almost entirely herbivorous. In home aquaria, all these fishes like to nibble at such small plants as duckweed, and they graze eagerly on green algae. To keep these fishes at their best, alternate daily between general-purpose dried foods and foods designed for plant-eaters. Even better, spice the diet with live brine shrimp and a piece or two of lettuce or spinach weighted down with a rock so that it stays submerged. You can provide a real treat for mollies by growing a crop of filamentous green algae (not blue-green bacteria) on rocks kept in a jar on a sunny windowsill. Rotate the algae-covered rocks through the tank now and then and watch your fish give them haircuts!

Although I've listed these fishes under scientific names, most varieties offered for sale have been produced by intensive hybridization that blurs scientific identity. Swordtails and platies, for example, all members of the genus *Xiphophorus,* breed freely with one another, and many have been interbred commercially. For this reason, it is often impossible to assign modern varieties to any particular wild species.

## Poecilia reticulata:
## THE GUPPY

Guppies, while easy enough to keep to make them perfect fishes for rank amateurs, are beautiful enough to keep many aquarists fascinated for life. Because guppies are small, more of them can live more comfortably in smaller tanks than most other aquarium fishes. The objects of intensive selective breeding for many years, guppies now come in nearly every color of the rainbow, and with a wide variety of fin shapes and sizes.

In nature, male guppies use their colors to attract females; the most colorful males get the most chances to breed. But because those "peacock" males are also eaten most regularly by predators, natural selection keeps wild fish from getting *too* colorful. Guppy breeders, however, have exploited the fishes' flamboyant tendency to the fullest, and have produced dozens of spectacular varieties, several of which are illustrated here.

SIZE:   Males, 1½ inches; females, 2½ inches.

TEMPERAMENT/COMPATIBILITY: Extremely peaceful, highly desirable in community tanks; avoid keeping veiltail varieties with other species (such as tiger barbs) that are potential fin-nippers.

TEMPERATURE:   60–90°; ideal temperature 72°.

WATER CONDITIONS:   pH: Neutral to slightly alkaline; hardness: medium-hard (but tolerates soft water well); in soft water, add 1 tbs of salt/5 gallons.

FOOD:   Accepts wide variety of dried and live foods; regular diet should alternate between general-purpose flake food and vegetarian flakes; offer live foods occasionally as treats.

SPECIAL NOTES:   Many strains of championship-quality fancy guppies are available. If you intend to keep your strain going for a long time, or if you want to raise fish for sale or trade with other hobbyists, keep only members of a single strain in each tank. Indiscriminate crosses between desirable varieties often lose the best characteristics of both parents. Full-grown healthy guppy females can have broods ranging in size from a handful to several dozen.

Guppy

Guppy

# Xiphophorus maculatus and X. variatus:

## THE PLATIES

Platies, the next step up from guppies on many beginners' lists, are hardy, colorful animals, and welcome additions to any community tank. Swordtail and platy breeders are producing an assortment of striking hybrids in an ever-increasing variety of colors. Several strains have long, graceful fins.

I list these species together because hybrid platies are the result of so much creative interbreeding that it is difficult or impossible to determine their ancestry. There are dozens of beautiful platy strains that range in color from almost black through reds, oranges, yellows, and blues.

Larger and more agile than guppies, platies are active swimmers that enjoy well-planted tanks but require substantial open space to move around in. Include vegetable matter in their diets and a little salt in their water, and they will grace your tank for a long time.

**SIZE:** Males, about 2 inches; females, up to 3 inches.

**TEMPERAMENT/COMPATIBILITY:** Extremely peaceful and highly desirable in the community tank.

**TEMPERATURE:** 70–80°; ideal temperature 72–74°.

**WATER CONDITIONS:** pH: Neutral to slightly alkaline; hardness: medium-hard (but tolerates soft water well); in soft water, add 1 tbs of salt/5 gallons.

**FOOD:** Accepts wide variety of foods; supplement diet with vegetarian flakes and fresh spinach, lettuce, and green algae if possible.

Platy

Sunburst Platy

85

# Xiphophorus helleri:
## SWORDTAIL

Closely related to platies, swordtails share their peaceful dispositions and color combinations. Males are distinguished by the swordlike extension of their tail fins. General cultural requirements are the same as those for platies.

One variety of this fish was a high point of my second year of fishkeeping. Allowance in hand, I raced to the local pet shop for my very first trio of albino swordtails. Brand new to the trade back then, they cost ten dollars, a fortune to me at that age. Although the male jumped out of the tank after a few months, the females blessed me with several broods, and they remained my favorite fishes for a long time. They are hardy, prolific, and long-lived, providing you can prevent them from jumping.

SIZE:   Males and females, 4–5 inches.

TEMPERAMENT/COMPATIBILITY: Peaceful and desirable in a community tank; if kept with more aggressive species, provide hiding places for occasionally skittish swordtails.

TEMPERATURE:   70–80°; ideal temperature 74°.

WATER CONDITIONS:   pH: Neutral to slightly alkaline; hardness: medium-hard (but tolerates soft water well); in soft water, add 1 tbs of salt/5 gallons.

FOOD:   Accepts wide variety of foods; supplement diet with vegetarian flakes and fresh spinach, lettuce, and green algae if possible.

SPECIAL NOTES:   Swordtails are fast swimmers, so don't keep even a single pair in any tank smaller than 10 gallons. Regardless of tank size, swordtails are also champion jumpers; keep their tank *tightly* covered to prevent them from ending up dead on the floor. These fishes seem to find even the smallest opening in a tank cover, so don't leave any!

Red Swordtail

Longfin Swordtail

## Poecilia latipinna and P. velifera:

## SAILFIN MOLLIES

Sailfin mollies are among the most dramatic of all poeciliids. They are also the largest and the most difficult to maintain. Mollies normally inhabit brackish environments, and do best in captivity in hard, alkaline water with added salt. In nature they are nearly exclusively plant-eaters, so feed them accordingly. Full-grown mollies should have at least a twenty-gallon "long" tank to swim around in.

Sailfin mollies are available in several color varieties, ranging from olive speckled with black to jet, velvet black. Only in males does the dorsal fin grow into an impressive "sail." Although these fishes breed readily, young raised in tanks do not normally develop the full dorsal fin; that usually requires a full season in a spacious outdoor pool.

SIZE:   Pool-grown specimens 4–5 inches; tank-raised individuals 3–4 inches.

TEMPERAMENT/COMPATIBILITY: Active, but peaceful and a striking addition to a good-sized community tank.

TEMPERATURE:   *P. latipinna* (most commonly seen), 50–85°, ideal 75° *P. velifera* 75–82°.

WATER CONDITIONS:   pH: Neutral to slightly alkaline; hardness: medium to hard; can manage with salt levels recommended for other poeciliids, but does best with as much as 1 tbs of salt/gallon; in very soft water, add 1 tsp Epsom salts and 2 tsp salt for each gallon.

Black Sailfin Molly

Silver Sailfin Molly

FOOD:   Mollies accept all foods, but do best long term when given vegetarian flakes and plenty of live plant material in the form of lettuce, spinach, or green algae.

SPECIAL NOTES:   Velvety black strains are particularly susceptible to body fungus if not fed properly and kept in water with high enough salt content.

## Poecilia sphenops Hybrids:

## BLACK MOLLIES

The black molly, nearly the only variety of this species offered for sale these days, looks nothing like its wild ancestors. Usually seen in pet shops at between two and three inches in length, these velvety black fish make striking additions to any community tank containing poeciliids or other species that enjoy salt in their water.

SIZE:  4–5 inches.

TEMPERAMENT/COMPATIBILITY: Peaceful; good with any other even-tempered, salt-loving freshwater fish.

TEMPERATURE:  55–80°; does well at 70–74°.

WATER CONDITIONS:  pH: Neutral to slightly alkaline; hardness: medium to hard; can manage with salt levels recommended for other poeciliids, but does best with as much as 1 tbs of salt/gallon; in very soft water, add 1 tsp Epsom salts and 2 tsp salt for each gallon.

FOOD:  Though mollies accept all foods, they do best long term when given vegetarian flakes and plenty of live plant material in the form of lettuce, spinach, or green algae.

SPECIAL NOTES:  Like sailfin mollies, this species needs salt in its water and plenty of vegetable matter in its diet to stay healthy.

Black Sphenops Molly, male

Black Sphenops Molly, female

## Maternity Leave

Keep your poeciliids alive and healthy, and they will invariably present you with babies. For that reason, particularly if you've got young'uns of your own, you'd be well-advised to know what to do when the blessed event occurs.

The path of least resistance is to let nature take its course. In even a peaceful and well-planted community tank, most newborns end up as live food for tankmates. If you haven't additional space for the babies, and especially if your tank is already full, no action may be the best action of all. But if you want to raise the babies, you'll have to protect them from their parents and larger tankmates. (Yes, most poeciliids will cannibalize their own young if given the chance.)

The simplest procedure is to remove gravid females to a separate small tank densely planted with Java moss or other fine plants. Watch her carefully, and remove her as soon as she has dropped her brood. From then on, care for the young as described below.

If a separate tank doesn't appeal to you, buy a breeding trap; a clear plastic container that hangs inside your community tank. These devices hold the gravid female above a V-shaped false bottom with a narrow groove at its base. When the babies are released, they fall through this groove into the safety of another compartment below. Breeding traps come in several sizes; guppies do fine in the smallest ones, while mollies, platies, and swordtails need larger sizes with more slots for water movement.

After a day or so, *gently* transfer the young to a baby net, a five-sided cube of fine mesh held open by a plastic frame. These nets allow water circulation around the fry while affording protection from baby-eaters. At first, feed your babies lightly, but several times a day, with any of the commercially available baby foods designed for live-bearers. As time passes, vary the diet with finely ground flake food. In a week or so—when the young are old enough to swallow them—try newly hatched brine shrimp. When the young are large enough to be safe in the tank, release them a short while *after* feeding their larger tankmates. If you're not *sure* the young fishes are big enough to be safe, release a few at a time to test the waters.

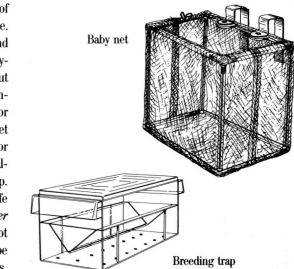

Baby net

Breeding trap

Swordtail platy with one-day-old fry

# GOLDFISH, KOI, AND BARBS:

## Family Cyprinidae

The family Cyprinidae has members around the globe, from the Far East to North America, and from southern Canada to equatorial Asia. The temperate branch includes goldfish and koi, which have been cultivated in China and Japan for centuries. These fishes, which can be kept in aquaria or outdoor pools as far north as central New England, are enjoying a resurgence as pets. Tropical cyprinids include some of the most peaceful, beautiful, and undemanding fishes for the home aquarium.

Common Goldfish

## Carassius auratus:
## THE GOLDFISH

The Chinese began cultivating goldfish hundreds of years ago, when they fashioned what we now call the common goldfish from a nondescript wild species. From there, various breeders took off on extended flights of fancy, shaping over the years an extraordinary variety of beautiful and unusual forms.

SIZE: 3 inches to over a foot, depending on variety and size of container in which animals are grown.

TEMPERAMENT/COMPATIBILITY: Most goldfish varieties are compatible with one another, with the exception of certain bizarre bubble-eyed varieties, especially those called celestials. These animals have fragile, fleshy globes around their protruding eyes and are slow swimmers; they are easily damaged by rough tankmates and often have trouble competing for food. Keep these only with their own kind.

TEMPERATURE: 45–70°; require ample space and aeration in summer if water warms further; most varieties should be kept indoors during prolonged periods of subfreezing weather.

WATER CONDITIONS: pH and hardness not critical; maintain, however, a good biological filtration system to avoid buildup of toxic biological wastes. Avoid the temptation to overcrowd either tanks or ponds.

FOOD: Dried food formulated for goldfish is widely available; supplement indoors with occasional feedings of live or frozen foods.

SPECIAL NOTES: Goldfish are not truly compatible with most tropical fishes because these temperate fishes prefer cooler water. To my taste, goldfish are best displayed with one another; somehow, their shapes and their movements don't make aesthetically pleasing counterparts to most tropical fishes.

Lionhead Goldfish

Bubble-Eye Goldfish

Lionhead Oranda, also known as Chinese Lionhead Goldfish

Red and White Veiltail

Calico Oranda Goldfish

Ranchu Goldfish

Lionhead Goldfish

# Cyprinus carpio:

## KOI

Koi, molded over the centuries by Japanese breeders from wild carp, are gems of the fish breeder's art. In a masterful aesthetic judgment, the Japanese bred koi—which are kept as pool fish in Japan—to look their best when seen from above. The best of these fish, therefore, have broad backs and striking color patterns on their top surfaces; what is seen from the side is considered less important. (You can invariably tell whether or not a koi photograph has been taken by someone who knows these fishes' history; neophyte Western photographers take pictures from the side, while cognoscenti show them from above.)

Happily, many koi are beautiful when viewed from the side as well. Small specimens do well in aquaria, but full-grown koi can be three feet long, and need a sizable pool.

Koi range in price from less than five dollars to several thousand dollars apiece, depending on size and the degree to which they meet established criteria for their breed. To an outsider such as myself, many inexpensive koi are just as handsome as those costing several months' salary.

SIZE: Up to 3 feet.

TEMPERAMENT/COMPATIBILITY: Peaceful.

TEMPERATURE: 32–70°; provide plenty of aeration if temperature rises higher in summer.

WATER CONDITIONS: pH and hardness not critical; maintain good biological filtration to avoid buildup of toxic biological wastes. Avoid the temptation to overcrowd.

FOOD: Omnivorous; any prepared koi or goldfish food will do.

SPECIAL NOTES: Koi larger than 6 inches or so should be kept in either indoor or outdoor pools where they have plenty of oxygenated water and ample room to swim. In areas where subfreezing temperatures prevail during winter, outdoor pools should be a minimum of 5 to 6 feet deep to keep them from freezing solid. Animals in outdoor pools should not be fed during the winter; resume feeding when water temperature reaches the low 50s in spring.

Yellow Veiltail Koi

Black Veiltail Koi

A pool of Koi

# Brachydanio rerio:
## ZEBRA DANIO

The "guppy" of egg-laying fishes, the zebra danio is handsome, easy to maintain, and among the easiest of all egg-layers to breed. These active swimmers look best in small schools that require open space in which to swim. Darting back and forth, and constantly changing places with one another within the school, they are fascinating to watch.

Several recently developed strains carry long, flowing fins, making them even more graceful and intriguing in community tanks.

SIZE: 1½–2 inches.

TEMPERAMENT/COMPATIBILITY:
Very peaceful, and highly desirable in the community tank. Keep in schools of at least half a dozen.

TEMPERATURE: 70–85°.

WATER CONDITIONS: pH: neutral to slightly acid; hardness: soft to medium.

FOOD: Omnivorous; vary diet to maintain best health.

SPECIAL NOTES: Keep a tight lid on your tank to prevent this highly active species from jumping out.

Zebra Danio

## Brachydanio albolineatus:
# PEARL DANIO

Photographs of this lovely fish rarely do it justice, for the interplay between its pearly pink background color and the blue-green iridescence of its scales is hard to capture on film. Slightly larger than the zebra, it is an active swimmer that likes to be kept with others of its own kind.

SIZE: 2½ inches.

TEMPERAMENT/COMPATIBILITY:
Very peaceful and highly desirable in the community tank. Does best in schools of at least half a dozen.

TEMPERATURE: 70–85°.

WATER CONDITIONS: pH: neutral to slightly acid; hardness: soft to medium.

FOOD: Omnivorous; vary diet to maintain best health.

SPECIAL NOTES: Keep a tight lid on your tank to prevent this active species from jumping out.

Pearl Danio

## Danio malabaricus:
# GIANT DANIO

This handsome, active species is a welcome addition to any community tank large enough to offer sufficient room to swim. Like other members of its genus, the giant danio does best in small schools. Photographs rarely do this fish justice; when properly maintained in the home, its body is covered with striking patterns of pink, blue, and yellow.

SIZE: 4–6 inches; tank-raised specimens at the lower end.

TEMPERAMENT/COMPATIBILITY:
Very peaceful, and highly desirable in the community tank, even with smaller species. Does best in groups of at least three.

TEMPERATURE: 70–80°; ideal temperature 75°.

WATER CONDITIONS: pH: neutral to slightly acid; hardness: soft to medium-hard.

FOOD: Omnivorous; accepts prepared foods readily but does best if offered live or frozen foods periodically.

SPECIAL NOTES: Larger than the *Brachydanio* species and equally active, giant danios require ample room to swim; a 20-gallon-long tank is a minimum requirement for a small school.

Giant Danio

## Tanichthys albonubes:
# WHITE CLOUD

Another beautiful, nearly foolproof fish, this species survives both in tropical tanks and in unheated indoor tanks with goldfish. Its attractive coloration and easy disposition make it a favorite for low-maintenance tanks.

SIZE: 1–1½ inches.

TEMPERAMENT/COMPATIBILITY: Extremely peaceful, a good addition to any community tank, looks best in schools.

TEMPERATURE: 40–85°; optimum in tropical tank 70–74°.

WATER CONDITIONS: (Not at all fussy, but prefers) pH: neutral to slightly acid; hardness: soft to medium.

FOOD: Easily raised on any well-rounded diet.

White Cloud *(Mountain Minnow)*

## Barbus tetrazona:
# TIGER BARB

This active species, striped like its feline namesake, is one of the most colorful and easy-to-care-for members of its genus. Albino and "green" varieties have been bred, but to my eyes they are not as attractive as wild-type fish in good condition.

Although generally peaceful with active fishes of its own size, tiger barbs will eagerly swallow baby fishes, and may nip the long, trailing fins of more placid species such as angels, bettas, and veiltailed guppies. Barbs are most comfortable (and probably less aggressive) when kept in schools, rather than as isolated individuals or in pairs.

SIZE: 2–3 inches.

TEMPERAMENT/COMPATIBILITY: Active, but generally peaceful; good for community tanks with other active species, but may nip the long fins of slow-moving species. Best kept in schools of at least 3–6 individuals.

TEMPERATURE: 70–85°; ideal temperature 74–76°.

WATER CONDITIONS: pH: neutral to slightly acid; hardness: soft to medium-hard.

FOOD: Omnivorous, enjoys both plant and animal foods; for best year-round color, vary prepared diets with fresh algae, lettuce, or spinach and occasional feedings of live food.

SPECIAL NOTES: Because of its fondness for vegetable manner, may be rough on delicate, soft-leaved plants in the aquarium; landscape with sturdy species (such as larger *Echinodorus*).

## Barbus titteya:
# CHERRY BARB

This small, brightly colored barb is so shy that it spends most of its time hiding in tanks crowded with large, active fishes. When kept with small, quiet tankmates, however, it acclimates well and shows off its magnificent coloration. Note that some tank-raised strains of this species are not as colorful as wild-caught specimens.

SIZE: 2 inches.

TEMPERAMENT/COMPATIBILITY: Peaceful and rather shy; best in a community tank with other small or sedentary fishes.

Tiger Barb

TEMPERATURE:  75–85°; ideal temperature 78–82°.

WATER CONDITIONS:  pH: slightly acid; hardness: soft.

FOOD:  Omnivorous, but regular meals of live food help keep its colors at their peak.

SPECIAL NOTES:  This species shows off its colors best and feels most at home in a heavily planted tank with a dark gravel bottom. Because these fish are frequent jumpers, make certain that their tank is tightly covered at all times.

Green Tiger Barb

## Barbus schuberti: GOLDEN BARB

Although listed here as a separate species for purposes of identification, this fish is probably the result of selective breeding within or between true *Barbus* species. Its bright color, ease of keeping, and agreeable disposition make it a welcome addition to many community tanks.

SIZE:  2–2½ inches.

TEMPERAMENT/COMPATIBILITY: Peaceful, good for most community tanks.

TEMPERATURE:  75–85°; ideal temperature 78–82°.

WATER CONDITIONS:  pH: slightly acid; hardness: soft.

FOOD:  Omnivorous, but regular meals of live food help keep its colors at their peak.

Cherry Barb

Golden Barb

97

Harlequin Rasbora

## Rasbora heteromorpha:
## RASBORA

One of the first tropical fishes I ever kept, the rasbora is still a favorite. Look at the tiny, frightened, pale-colored specimens in most pet shops, and you might wonder about my taste. But when these fish are properly raised, which is not hard at all, they are handsome in an understated way. A school in a well-planted tank with a dark gravel bottom and water filtered through peat is a sight to behold.

SIZE:   1–2 inches.

TEMPERAMENT/COMPATIBILITY:
Very peaceful, and highly desirable in the community tank. Does best in schools of at least half a dozen.

TEMPERATURE:   70–85°.

WATER CONDITIONS:   pH: neutral to slightly acid; hardness: soft.

FOOD:   Omnivorous; accepts prepared foods readily, but vary diet for best color.

SPECIAL NOTES:   Make any temperature changes slowly.

## Rasbora kalochroma:
## CLOWN RASBORA

This active and handsome species is usually not displayed to best advantage in pet shops, because it is often treated harshly and is pickier about sudden changes in water conditions than other *Rasbora* species. It is very handsome when well-kept at home.

SIZE:   4 inches.

TEMPERAMENT/COMPATIBILITY:
This peaceful, active species is a good addition to any community tank that offers some open space in which to swim.

TEMPERATURE:   75–85°; ideal temperature 78°.

WATER CONDITIONS:   pH: neutral to slightly acid; hardness: soft.

FOOD:   Omnivorous, but regular meals of live food help keep its colors at their peak.

Clown Rasbora

# Labeo bicolor:

## RED-TAILED BLACK SHARK

This species is rarely appreciated by casual visitors to pet shops. Because red-tailed sharks seldom dress up in full colors under stressful, overcrowded conditions, it looks more like a "pink-tailed gray shark." But under suitable conditions in the home aquarium, it quickly colors up. Its jet-black, velvety body contrasts beautifully with a bright red tail, making this one of the most attractive bottom-dwelling species for home aquaria. At maturity, this fish is suitable only for large tanks, but it grows slowly, and smaller specimens are quite attractive in small tanks.

SIZE:   4–5 inches at maturity.

TEMPERAMENT/COMPATIBILITY: Peaceful toward other species (the most peaceful member of its genus), and a desirable member of almost any community tank. *Labeo* is, however, territorial and quarrelsome with its own kind; one to a tank is the rule.

TEMPERATURE:   70–85°; ideal temperature 75–78°.

WATER CONDITIONS:   pH: neutral to slightly acid; hardness: soft to medium-hard.

FOOD:   Omnivorous; accepts dried food, but colors up best when periodically fed fresh algae or other vegetable matter and live foods, especially *Tubifex* worms.

SPECIAL NOTES:   Provide plenty of shady hiding places.

Red-Tailed Black Shark

# TETRAS:
## Family Characidae

Most species in this family (at least, twelve hundred of them) come from the Amazon and other rivers that wind through the disappearing rain forests of Central and South America. There are, however, about two hundred species in Africa. The family is extraordinarily diverse; its members range in size from inch-long tetras to giant tambaqui that grow to lengths of more than three feet and weigh seventy pounds. Species personalities vary just as much, from meek little neons to feisty black tetras to fierce piranhas that snip chunks of flesh from the bodies of their prey.

As a group, characins eat just about anything available: small shrimplike creatures, fishes, insects, and algae, in addition to fruits, seeds, and insects. The smaller characins popular in aquariums subsist in nature mainly on small shrimp and a steady diet of ants, termites, small beetles, and other insects that fall into the water from overhanging forest trees. In captivity they adjust readily to prepared foods, but several species (particularly members of the genus *Hyphessobrycon*) show their best colors when treated to such delicacies as small ants and wingless fruit flies.

Many tetras create their shimmering blue-green colors by using reflection, refraction, and interference phenomena created when light bounces off their scales at certain angles. These colors are most vivid under front-lighting that reflects off their bodies, rather than in light that comes through them from behind or bounces up off the gravel. Many species have also evolved colors that are most visible in the tea-colored, peat-stained water of their blackwater streams.

For these reasons, tetras show to their best advantage in peat-filtered water with medium to dark-colored gravel (rather than white or pale beige) beneath them. If you follow my advice about multiple-bulb lighting fixtures for plants, place the frontmost bulb on a separate switch so you can use it alone to display these fishes.

The scientific classification of characins and their relatives is problematical, and is revised often enough that books published at different times often list the same species under different names. Several groups of fishes once placed in this family (such as hatchetfish and headstanders) have been given their own families, and are discussed at the end of this chapter with members of other small families.

## Paracheirodon axelrodi:
## CARDINAL TETRA

Nearly twenty-five years after buying my first cardinal tetras, they are still, in my eyes, among the most beautiful and desirable of fishes. Their brilliant (almost fluorescent) colors rival the most florid of tropical-reef species, but their gentle disposition and undemanding nature make them easy even for beginners. Few sights in a freshwater aquarium are more arresting than a school of mature cardinal tetras in a well-planted aquarium.

More handsome and larger than the closely related neon tetra *(Cheirodon innesi)*, cardinals can be distinguished by the fact that their red coloration extends from head to tail, while that of neons begins a little more than halfway back on the body.

SIZE:  2 inches when mature.

TEMPERAMENT/COMPATIBILITY:
Peaceful and highly desirable in community tanks, this species does best in schools. Be careful about larger tankmates when introducing newly purchased immature cardinals; the tetras' small size makes them easy prey for even generally peaceable fishes.

TEMPERATURE:  72–78°.

WATER CONDITIONS:  pH: neutral to slightly acid; hardness: soft to medium-hard.

FOOD:  Omnivorous, does well on nearly any diet, although it enjoys periodic feedings of live food.

Cardinal Tetra

## Paracheirodon innesi:
## NEON TETRA

Neon tetras, smaller, slightly less brilliantly colored, and significantly less expensive than cardinals, are equally good members of any community tank.

SIZE: 1–1½ inches.

TEMPERAMENT/COMPATIBILITY: Peaceful and highly desirable in community tanks, this species does best in schools. Be careful about larger tankmates when introducing newly purchased immature cardinals; the tetras' small size makes them easy prey for even generally peaceable fishes.

TEMPERATURE: 70–80°.

WATER CONDITIONS: pH: neutral to slightly acid; hardness: soft to medium-hard.

FOOD: Omnivorous, does well on nearly any diet, although it enjoys periodic feedings of live food.

## Gymnocorymbus ternetzi:
## BLACK TETRA

Black tetras, longtime favorites, are strikingly patterned and constantly active when well-conditioned and displayed in a small school. Though generally suitable for community tanks, their habit of nipping fins can make life miserable for angelfish. Also, given their penchant for live foods, I would not trust full-grown specimens with bite-sized tankmates.

SIZE: 2–3 inches.

TEMPERAMENT/COMPATIBILITY: This active and periodically aggressive species is suitable for community tanks containing active fishes their own size or larger. They do not generally "attack" tankmates, but will often nip the long, flowing fins of angelfish, bettas, and veiltailed guppies.

TEMPERATURE: 70–85°.

WATER CONDITIONS: pH: neutral to slightly acid; hardness: soft to medium-hard.

FOOD: Voracious feeders, these tetras will devour just about any food you offer them, though they particularly relish live and frozen foods.

Neon Tetra

## Hyphessobrycon Species:

## FLAME, SERPAE, AND BLEEDING-HEART TETRAS

Members of this very popular genus, although distinct to experienced eyes, are similar enough in appearance to confuse beginners. All are generally rosy in color with markings of black and white. The species most commonly offered for sale are *H. serpae* (the serpae tetra), *H. erythrostigma* (the bleeding-heart tetra), and *H. flammeus* (the flame tetra). These species rarely show up well in the confusion and less-than-ideal conditions found in dealers' tanks, but they are gems when properly cared for.

SIZE:   1–2 inches.

TEMPERAMENT/COMPATIBILITY: Extremely peaceful and desirable members of nearly any community tank, all these species do best in schools.

TEMPERATURE:   70–85°; ideal temperature 74–76°.

WATER CONDITIONS:   pH: slightly acid (6–6.7); hardness: soft.

FOOD:   Readily take all kinds of prepared foods, but color up best when periodically offered live and frozen foods.

SPECIAL NOTES:   Because these species tend to be shy, they feel most at home in well-planted tanks in which dense clumps of plants alternate with open spaces.

Black Tetra

Bleeding-Heart Tetra

## Nematobrycon palmeri:
## EMPEROR TETRA

Relatively new to the aquarium trade in this country, the emperor tetra and its close relatives are gaining in popularity. Because much of their striking coloration is produced by iridescence, photographs rarely give a sense of how beautiful they can be in a properly lit aquarium.

SIZE: 2–2½ inches.

TEMPERAMENT/COMPATIBILITY: Peaceful fishes, well-suited to life in a community tank. These, like other schooling tetras, do best when kept together in small groups.

TEMPERATURE: 70–85°; ideal temperature 74–76°.

WATER CONDITIONS: pH: neutral to slightly acid; hardness: soft to medium-hard.

FOOD: Omnivorous, does well on nearly any diet, although it enjoys periodic feedings of live food.

Emperor Tetra

## Astyanax mexicanus:
## BLIND CAVE FISH

This species, which has evolved in lightless caves in Mexico, has been a popular "novelty" fish for years. Totally lacking eyes, it navigates and finds food through its well-developed lateral-line system and chemical senses. This species is not particularly aggressive, but because it can't see its neighbors, it tends to nip at any that get in its way. This species is therefore not a good companion for very small fishes or those with long, trailing fins.

SIZE: 3–3½ inches.

TEMPERAMENT/COMPATIBILITY: Generally peaceful, but inclined to nip fins. Small individuals may work out well in small community tanks. Full-grown specimens are suitable for tanks with large, active species.

TEMPERATURE: 70–85°; ideal temperature 74–76°.

WATER CONDITIONS: pH: neutral to slightly acid; hardness: soft to medium-hard.

FOOD: Readily accept most prepared, frozen, and live foods.

Blind Cave Fish

# THE CATFISH FAMILIES

The popular term "catfish" is loosely applied to a group of predominantly (but not exclusively) bottom-dwelling fishes that is nearly as large as the characins. There are more than twenty-two hundred catfish species worldwide, and more than a dozen species new to science are described every year. There are fourteen families in South America alone, and other families live on every continent except Antarctica.

Unlike most other fish, catfish are heavier than water, are flattened on their undersides, and spend a good deal of their time on or near the bottom. For this reason, fishkeepers particularly interested in catfish use long-style aquariums rather than tall ones to provide more bottom area for equivalent volumes of water.

Favorites in the aquarium trade, members of the genus *Corydoras* are appreciated for their habit of cleaning algae, uneaten food, and debris off the bottom of the aquarium. Many catfish, however, feed in midwater or near the surface in nature, and seek out a wide variety of foods. Some eat fruits and insects, others are voracious carnivores, and some even live like vampire bats by sucking blood.

Though these specialized feeders are rarely kept in home aquaria, no catfish should be expected to fare well on scraps and leftovers. Their needs for shelter, water quality, and proper food should be attended to carefully. Those catfish reluctant to come to the surface for floating flake food should be fed with a pellet food that sinks. Because the undersides of even most armored catfish are soft and vulnerable, they should never be kept in aquaria containing sharp-edged, crushed-glass gravel.

Catfish have experienced a meteoric rise in popularity over the last several years. As an indicator of catfish popularity, *Aquarium Fish Magazine* has one regular column devoted entirely to catfish, and several entire books have recently been devoted to the study and care of these amusing, popular, and generally easy-to-keep fishes.

# FAMILY CALLICHTHYIDAE:

## The Genus Corydoras: COMMON AQUARIUM CATFISH

The upper bodies of these armored catfish are covered with V-shaped bony plates, hence the group's common name. There are dozens of species within this genus, most of which make attractive, endearing, and easy-to-keep additions to any community aquarium. All have the same familiar body shape, but vary in coloration from one another.

SIZE:  Most members of this genus reach about 3 inches when mature.

TEMPERAMENT/COMPATIBILITY: All commonly imported members of this genus are extremely peaceful and get along well, both with members of their own species and with other catfish species.

TEMPERATURE:  72–85°.

WATER CONDITIONS:  pH: not critical; prefers neutral to slightly acid; hardness: not critical; prefers soft to medium-hard.

FOOD:  Omnivorous; accepts wide variety of dried, frozen, and live foods, especially *Tubifex* worms, which they devour until they appear ready to burst. If relying on dried foods, use some pelletized food that falls to the bottom.

Flagtail Corydoras

Copper Nape Corydoras

Leopard Corydoras

Bronze Corydoras

# FAMILY LORICARIIDAE

The Loricariidae, the largest family of South American catfishes, is characterized by a heavy plating of armor and a well-developed sucker-like mouth. Many live in fast-flowing streams, where they cling to rocks. Although loricariids look fierce because of their armored heads, most are peaceful with other fishes and with members of different catfish families. As a group, loricariids are herbivorous; they use their rasping, suckerlike mouths for scraping algae off submerged rocks and pieces of wood. One or two will do a lot to keep your tank algae nearly algae free. Their tank should be well-planted and furnished with rocks and driftwood to which these animals can cling.

SIZE: Many members of this family grow quite large; some reach over two feet, even in captivity.

TEMPERAMENT/COMPATIBILITY: Peaceful and welcome additions to most community tanks (when small enough to fit!). Some of the larger types, such as species in the genus *Plecostomus,* will quarrel with members of their own kind and should be kept singly.

TEMPERATURE: 72–82°.

WATER CONDITIONS: pH: not critical; prefer neutral to slightly acid; hardness: soft to medium-hard.

Snowy Sucker-mouth Catfish

FOOD: Loricariids accept dried foods and both live and frozen *Tubifex* worms without hesitation. They do best if offered vegetable matter in the form of fresh algae or boiled lettuce, spinach, or zucchini slices. (Zucchini slices, boiled until they sink, will be eagerly eaten from the inside out.) Many species also like to gnaw on driftwood. Deny these fishes the vegetable matter they need, and they may damage soft-leaved plants.

SPECIAL NOTES: Although these fishes are not too fussy about pH and hardness, they are used to rapidly flowing, clear streams, and do best in water that is regularly refreshed by water changes.

Whiptail Loricaria

Blue-Eyed Panaque

107

# FAMILY MOCHOKIDAE

This African family contains many handsome and peaceful species that are quite easy to keep. Only one or two are well-known to most aquarists, however, and the group deserves far more attention. Many are handsomely marked in bands and spots of silver and brown or black, and several carry long, gracefully arched barbels.

The best-known member of this family is *Synodontis nigriventris,* the upside-down catfish. This species spends most of its time literally upside-down near the surface or beneath overhanging rocks or pieces of driftwood. Another species, *Synodontis nyassae,* is native to Lake Malawi, and is at home in the hard, alkaline water preferred by African Rift-Lake cichlids.

SIZE: Many species grow to a foot or more in the wild, but seem to level off at around 6 inches in captivity. Those bought when small and kept in small tanks will grow more slowly and probably stay somewhat smaller.

TEMPERAMENT/COMPATIBILITY: Peaceful and desirable members of community tanks, these catfish tend to be a bit shy, and a few species dislike intense light. Give them enough hiding places and a densely planted tank, however, and once they are acclimated, they will show themselves regularly.

TEMPERATURE: 72–85°.

WATER CONDITIONS: pH and hardness not critical, but maintain water quality.

FOOD: Most accept a wide variety of dried, frozen, and live foods; several species are particularly fond of *Tubifex* worms.

# FAMILY PIMELODIDAE

This family, with at least two hundred species in the Amazon River, has recently been discovered by American aquarists. Generally omnivorous, the pimelodids commonly offered for sale are not difficult to keep, and with their long, arching barbels make fascinating additions to community aquaria.

SIZE: Up to 6 inches in captivity.

TEMPERAMENT/COMPATIBILITY: Peaceful and desirable in community tanks.

TEMPERATURE: 72–80°.

WATER CONDITIONS: pH and hardness not critical; maintain water quality.

FOOD: Most members of this family accept a wide variety of dried, frozen, and live foods.

Royal "Pleco"

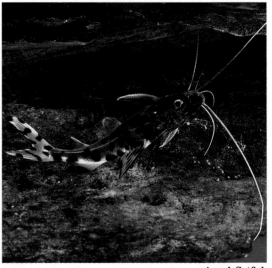

Angel Catfish

# FAMILY SILURIDAE

Although this is one of the most widespread catfish families, most members are too large, too predatory, or too homely for aquaria. The exception is *Kryptopterus bicirrhus,* the glass catfish of Thailand and Indonesia. Compressed from side to side and transparent except for its internal organs, this species behaves unusually for a catfish, spending most of its time hovering in midwater. Because its body lacks pigments, and reflects light in different ways depending upon the angle at which illumination strikes it, this fish can seem to shimmer in hues ranging from yellow through a dark purple-violet.

This shy, retiring species is more difficult to maintain than most other catfish; it is susceptible to shock from low water temperatures and requires ample live and frozen foods.

SIZE:   3–3½ inches.

TEMPERAMENT/COMPATIBILITY:
Shy and retiring, this species takes some time to acclimate to new surroundings. Good for a community tank with other slow-moving, peaceful species.

TEMPERATURE:   72–85°.

WATER CONDITIONS:   pH and hardness not critical; maintain water quality.

FOOD:   Ample live food in the form of *Tubifex,* daphnia, artemia, and mosquito larvae help keep this fish in good condition for long periods.

Glass Catfish

# CICHLIDS:

## Family Cichlidae

The large and widespread family Cichlidae is a favorite of hobbyists and scientists alike. (Popular cichlid species lacking common names have been the impetus behind many an aquarist's grudging acceptance of scientific terminology.) Ecologically diverse and often beautiful, cichlids display some of the most complex and fascinating behaviors of any aquarium fishes. They stake out and defend territories, battle with and court one another, and often care for their young diligently. Many species have been extensively bred and hybridized, so that gold, albino, and many other variously colored strains are now available.

Cichlids are wonderful fishes, and I recommend them highly to anyone who wants *pets,* rather than just decorative additions to their tank. But before you run out and buy just any cichlids, read the following entries carefully; this family is full of surprises for the uninitiated. Some cichlids remain under three inches in length and have exemplary dispositions, while others grow with extraordinary speed and rapidly take on personalities that make Rambo look like a pantywaist. Even long-term breeding pairs sometimes fight so violently that it is a good idea to have a spare tank to use as a recovery ward, just in case.

Some species are so difficult to keep that I recommend them exclusively to aquarists with years of experience. Others have such cast-iron dispositions that they would spawn if you tossed them into a garbage can half-filled with water. Several are excellent subjects for breeding; they spawn readily, produce relatively hardy fry, and care for their young rather than eating them. If a pair enters breeding condition, they will usually undo all your landscaping efforts to rearrange the tank as they see fit. You will be amazed at the way they move gravel, plants, and even rocks around to suit their needs.

Many books have been written on cichlids, and I can do little more than scratch the surface in describing them here. To make a few tentative generalizations possible, I will divide them into three groups, the first two of which are arbitrary and scientifically meaningless:

*Large cichlids,* including members of the genera *Cichlasoma, Astronotus* (oscars), *Hemichromis* (jewel cichlids), and *Pterophyllum* (angelfish), are long-lived (up to several years) and easy to care for. Acceptable members of community tanks when small, they get aggressive as they get larger, and a single pair may end up requiring a tank seventy gallons or larger. Because most will devour anything small enough to swallow, their list of possible companions shrinks as they grow. Full-grown specimens of several species are often vicious with other fishes (especially when in breeding condition) and prefer live guppies and goldfish as food, rather than as tankmates. As far as humans are concerned, however, these are "personality plus" fishes; they learn to recognize their owners, often like to be gently rubbed on their bodies or between their eyes, and—in part because they live so long—engender long-term relationships with humans.

*Dwarf cichlids,* including members of the genera *Apistogramma, Microgeophagus,* and *Pelviachromis,* are beautifully colored, even-tempered, and rarely exceed three inches in length when mature. A bit more demanding than their larger relatives, they are nonetheless relatively easy to care for. Because their behaviors are scaled down along with their body length, dwarf cichlids are more suitable for community aquaria, and can be bred in tanks under twenty gallons in size. Several species breed readily and exhibit fascinating brood-care behaviors.

*African rift-lake cichlids,* including members of the genera *Pseudotropheus, Melanochromis,* and *Lamprologus,* originate in Lake Malawi, Lake Tanganyika, and Lake Victoria. From an aquarist's point of view, they are brightly colored, active, and easy to care for. From a scientific perspective, they are the products of one of the most fascinating episodes in the evolution of living fishes. Isolated in landlocked lakes about forty thousand years ago (an instant by evolutionary reckoning) a few founding species have diversified in record time to produce hundreds of species found nowhere else in the world. Because these fishes prefer hard, alkaline water, and because they are active and rough on sedentary tankmates, they are best kept in their own aquaria.

A tank of Pseudotropheus Zebra Cichlids

## Cichlasoma meeki:
### FIREMOUTH CICHLID

The first of the larger cichlids I ever purchased, this species introduced me to both the joys and sorrows of its family. Handsomely colored, even when small, firemouths are active and engaging community tank species until they begin to grow. Then, while their colors intensify, their disposition sours, and they become not only territorial but downright nasty. Very easy to keep, but recommended only for "Rambo" tanks or for culture by themselves.

SIZE:  4–5 inches.

TEMPERAMENT/COMPATIBILITY:
Suitable in a community tank when no more than an inch long, it becomes aggressive and predaceous as it grows. Beyond 2 inches in length it is suitable only for communities of other large, pugnacious fishes.

TEMPERATURE:  70–85°.

WATER CONDITIONS:  pH: not critical; neutral to slightly acid hardness: not critical; medium-hard.

FOOD:  Eats just about anything it can swallow whole, including worms and small fishes; vary prepared diets with live foods for best color.

Firemouth Cichlid

## Cichlasoma festivum:
### FLAG CICHLID

Not as colorful as some other large cichlids, but not as aggressive either, flag cichlids are another good species for a hobbyist who wants to get started with cichlids. Once extremely popular, these and a few other species of reasonably attractive South American cichlids have been eclipsed by the more dynamic African rift-lake species described on page 117.

SIZE:  5–6 inches.

TEMPERAMENT/COMPATIBILITY:
Relatively peaceful (as members of its family go); most individuals will probably behave themselves in a large community tank of all but the smallest fishes. Provide plenty of hiding places until the fish become well-acclimated. Keep an eye on them nonetheless.

TEMPERATURE:  70–85°.

WATER CONDITIONS:  pH: not critical; neutral to slightly acid; hardness: not critical; medium-hard.

FOOD:  Readily accepts a variety of prepared, frozen, and live foods; for best growth and health, offer live foods regularly.

## Astronotus ocellatus:

## OSCAR

Although *not* candidates for any community tank, oscars come highly recommended as personality fishes. Adult oscars are as attentive as most dogs, and far more affectionate than most cats I have known. As long as they are given sufficient space, fed a varied diet, and kept in water of good quality, they are hardy and will live for several years.

The one- to two-inch juveniles usually offered for sale are strikingly beautiful, with bold markings in red, gold, and black, depending on their particular strain. But buyer *Beware*! Unlike many other fishes, oscars grow rapidly to their full size (over a foot), even in small tank. Once they pass about four inches in length, they will make short work of any tankmates and any aquascaping you attempt. A pair of adults require an absolute *minimum* of a fifty-five-gallon tank to themselves, and full-grown adults would be better off in seventy-gallon aquaria. Adults have voracious appetites; they can consume two to three small goldfish on a daily basis. Large oscars are common in public aquaria; they are usually supplied by aquarists who bought them as juveniles.

SIZE: Over 1 foot.

TEMPERAMENT/COMPATIBILITY:
Suitable for community tanks only when less than 2 inches in length; larger individuals are aggressive and predaceous and will attack even other large fishes.

TEMPERATURE: 70–85°.

WATER CONDITIONS: pH: not critical;

Flag Cichlid

neutral to slightly acid; hardness: not critical; medium-hard.

FOOD: Takes a variety of dried, frozen, and live foods when small; adults require large, pelleted food, whole freeze-dried krill, and—depending on size—live guppies or goldfish.

Oscar

## Pterophyllum scalare:

## ANGELFISH

Next to guppies and their kin, angelfish are probably the best-known and most popular of freshwater aquarium fishes. They are strikingly handsome and majestic fishes, and are hardy and easy to keep.

Selective breeding from several wild subspecies of *P. scalare* has produced strains that carry a variety of colors and fin patterns. Many strains are masterpieces of the fish breeder's art; though I usually prefer "wild type" fishes to artificially "gilded lilies," such angelfish strains as "black veils," "blushing angels," "marble veiltails" and "koi" are sights to behold.

Baby angelfish, do grow, however, and run into trouble in small tanks. Because many long-finned varieties are taller than they are long, they require large tanks with plenty of height and room to swim. Dense plantings of vertical plants such as *Vallisneria* offer security, and large-leaved species of *Echinodorus* offer a site upon which to deposit eggs when breeding.

SIZE:   6 inches in length; often taller than they are long.

TEMPERAMENT/COMPATIBILITY: Full-grown angels are not too aggressive, but will devour small guppies or tetras. Small and medium-sized angels are fine for community tanks that do not contain fishes small enough for them to swallow whole. Like many cichlids, mature angels may fight with one another; it is usually best to buy several young ones and allow them to grow up together. Angels' trailing fins are often nipped by such fishes as black tetras, tiger barbs, and blind cave fishes; to preserve those fins, provide only peaceful tankmates.

TEMPERATURE:   70–85°.

WATER CONDITIONS:   pH: neutral to slightly acid; hardness: soft to medium-hard.

FOOD:   Will readily accept a variety of prepared, frozen, and live foods; for best growth and health, offer live foods regularly.

Veil Angelfish

Leopard Veil Angelfish

# Pseudotropheus zebra:

## ZEBRAS

Arguably the most popular of the cichlids from Africa's great lakes, zebras are beautiful and captivating. The wild forms are stunning, with bright, iridescent blue strips alternating with jet black. Several artificial strains, although not necessarily any more attractive, are at least as good-looking. A fifty-five-gallon tank with a dozen or more small specimens fishes makes an energetic and attractive addition to any room.

These cichlids make short work of any except the most tough-leaved and deeply rooted plants; they will also move gravel around your tank constantly. Your best way to handle this behavior is to furnish the tank in imitation of the fishes' natural boulder habitat; cover the undergravel filter with small rocks, and build piles of medium-sized rocks throughout the tank.

SIZE:  5–7 inches.

TEMPERAMENT/COMPATIBILITY:
These fishes, like most other medium-sized rift-lake cichlids, are active, territorial, and aggressive species that form dominance hierarchies. Keeping several individuals together (rather than just two or three) seems to blunt the effects of aggression on fish lower in the hierarchy; for that reason, community tanks of zebras and related species are often stocked at higher densities.

TEMPERATURE:  72–80°.

WATER CONDITIONS:  pH: strongly alkaline (7.6–8.8); hardness: medium-hard to hard.

FOOD:  In nature, this species grazes on fuzzy algae that carpet the boulders around which it swims. In so doing, it eats both the algae and numerous small creatures that live in the algal mat. To match that diet in captivity, offer a variety of dried, frozen, and live plant and animal matter.

Mottled strain of Malawi Zebra Cichlid

"Albino" strain of Malawi Zebra Cichlid

# OTHER POPULAR RIFT-LAKE CICHLID SPECIES:

## MELANOCHROMIS AURATUS,

## LAMPROLOGUS BRICHARDI,

## JULIDOCHROMIS ORNATUS

These species, found only in Lakes Tanganyika, Malawi, and Victoria, are similar to *Pseudotropheus zebra* in size, disposition, and cultural requirements. They are but three of more than three hundred African lake cichlid species, many of which are becoming readily available in the aquarium trade.

Although most of these fishes are hardy and easy to care for, they do prefer the same hard, strongly alkaline (pH 7.6–8.8) conditions as *Pseudotropheus zebra*. Although this makes them incompatible with many other popular fishes, it does make them ideal pets for people in areas with hard, alkaline water.

Malawi Golden Cichlid

Lyretail Cichlid

Marlier's Julie

117

## Hemichromis bimaculatus:

# JEWEL CICHLID

Jewel cichlids are so easy to breed that I know hobbyists who have bought extra tanks to separate pairs that wouldn't *stop* breeding if kept together. Although fiercely aggressive toward other fishes in any but the largest tanks, jewels are exemplary parents; they care for their brood more conscientiously than some human parents I have known. Although very young specimens do not show their full colors, medium-sized juveniles and adults are strikingly patterned.

SIZE: 6 inches.

TEMPERAMENT/COMPATIBILITY: Aggressive and fiercely territorial; suitable only for a large Rambo tank with other fishes at least as large.

TEMPERATURE: 70–80°.

WATER CONDITIONS: Not critical.

FOOD: Greedily takes most foods offered; vary diet with live food for best growth and color.

## Pelviachromis pulcher:

# KRIBENSIS

A prince among dwarf cichlids, this species (formerly called *Pelmatochromis*) is handsome, easy to keep, and peaceful enough to get along in a community tank. Given proper conditions, a pair will enter breeding condition, excavate a small nest, and spawn, right in a community tank. You shouldn't expect the young to survive under those conditions, but the fascinating courtship and breeding behaviors of these fishes are a joy to watch.

**Jewel Cichlid with fry**

"Kribensis"

SIZE: 3–4 inches.

TEMPERAMENT/COMPATIBILITY:
Peaceful except when breeding; certain pairs may become aggressive toward other fishes during courtship and mating. Even this aggression is usually moderate, and may not be a problem if the tank is large enough and the other fishes savvy enough to stay away from the chosen nest site.

TEMPERATURE: 72–85°.

WATER CONDITIONS: pH: neutral to slightly acid; hardness: soft to medium-hard.

FOOD: Will take a wide variety of foods; for best color, and in order to encourage breeding, vary diet regularly with live foods. "Kribs" are particularly fond of *Tubifex* worms.

## Apistogramma agassizi:
### AGASSIZ'S DWARF CICHLID

The most common of several subtly colored yet handsome species within its genus, Agassiz's cichlid is a good addition to community tanks containing any but the smallest fishes.

SIZE: 2–3 inches.

TEMPERAMENT/COMPATIBILITY:
Peaceful and desirable in community tanks with other peaceful species; may become aggressive when breeding.

TEMPERATURE: 70–85°; ideal temperature 75°.

WATER CONDITIONS: pH: neutral to slightly acid; hardness: soft to medium-hard.

FOOD: Accepts a wide variety of dried and frozen foods, but colors up best when periodically offered live foods such as daphnia, *Tubifex*, and brine shrimp.

Agassiz's Dwarf Cichlid

## Microgeophagus ramirezi:
### RAMS

Rams, like most other dwarf cichlids, have particularly endearing personalities, intriguing behavior patterns, and attractive coloration. Several hybrid strains of this species including a "gold" strain are available; I still prefer the original color pattern, just as it evolved in the wild.

SIZE: 3 inches.

TEMPERAMENT/COMPATIBILITY:
Peaceful and desirable in community tanks with other peaceful species; may become aggressive when breeding.

TEMPERATURE: 70–85°; ideal temperature 75°.

WATER CONDITIONS: pH: neutral to slightly acid; hardness: soft to medium-hard.

FOOD: Accepts a wide variety of dried and frozen foods, but colors up best when periodically offered live foods such as daphnia, *Tubifex*, and brine shrimp.

"Ram"

## Symphysodon aequifasciata and S. discus:

## THE DISCUS FISH

Among the most beautiful and elegant of all tropical fishes, discus are also among the most difficult to keep, for they are very sensitive to water composition and quality. Native to slightly acid streams with flowing, soft water, these animals are used to water conditions not easily kept constant in small aquaria. They also do best at water temperatures significantly higher than those preferred by most other tropicals; pet dealers who really understand discus maintain them at a minimum of 82°.

Discus are usually kept by themselves. Slow to feed, they can easily be outcompeted by even peaceful tankmates. I recommend as companions only such small and peaceful species as rasboras, cardinal tetras, and *Corydoras* catfish. Besides, discus are such a treat to watch that you wouldn't want too many other fishes around as distractions.

Discus strains available today have been derived through selective breeding from several varieties of one or both wild species. New hybrids may be covered almost completely in brilliant turquoise or may be striped in bright red and cyan.

When buying discus, pay careful attention to their appearance; animals in less than perfect health are difficult to revive. Review the criteria listed in Chapter 2 and make certain they are feeding. In general, it is best to purchase several individuals at sizes ranging from a quarter up to a silver dollar; these are large enough to travel well, yet small enough to coexist with one another and become accustomed to new surroundings.

Discus

SIZE: 6–6½ inches in diameter.

TEMPERAMENT/COMPATIBILITY: Peaceful and generally shy, a slow and often picky eater, especially for a cichlid. Suitable tankmates should be small (such as tetras) and/or innocuous (such as *Corydoras* cats).

TEMPERATURE: 82–88°.

WATER CONDITIONS: Water filtered over peat; pH: slightly acid (pH 6.0–6.5); hardness: soft (from 3–5° DH); some strains are now being raised in harder water and will tolerate it.

FOOD: May take dried foods, usually accept a variety of frozen and live foods, including brine shrimp, bloodworms, and shredded beef heart, which is highly recommended. Although discus are fond of live *Tubifex*, they are susceptible to diseases and parasites those worms may carry, so use only carefully washed *Tubifex* that have been kept in cold, running water.

SPECIAL NOTES: Some breeders recommend 20 percent water changes as often as once a week. Because discus are so sensitive, the temperature, pH, and hardness of new water must be as close to those of tank water as possible.

# BETTAS AND GOURAMIES:

## Family Anabantidae

These lovely and engaging fishes range across most of Asia and Southeast Asia, where they evolved in periodically stagnant, oxygen-poor habitats. As an evolutionary response to the difficulty in breathing in such water, the members of this family have evolved a structure called a labyrinth organ. This complex of thin tissues and blood vessels near the gills allows them to extract oxygen from bubbles of air they swallow at the surface. Even in well-aerated aquaria, therefore, it is normal to see these fishes rising to the surface to "breathe," expelling old air and taking in new.

Many of these fishes are well-suited to aquarium life, and several are quite hardy. Most breed in an intriguing manner; males build nests out of floating aquatic plants and mucus-covered bubbles, and take care of eggs and young assiduously.

## Betta Splendens:

## BETTA, SIAMESE FIGHTING FISH

Aquatic equivalents of fighting cocks, strains of *Betta splendens* have been used in "sporting" contests in Thailand for several hundred years. They have been actively bred—both for battling behavior and for color and fin shape—for at least a century and a half. Dozens of varieties are available, ranging from albinos to solid reds and blues, and even bicolors. Males will fight fiercely with each other, and will even erect their fins and spread their gill covers in aggressive display at their reflections in a mirror. They can also get rough with females of their species, but are model citizens with other fishes.

I am fond of bettas, and object strongly to the way most of them are kept in this country. Because bettas—like other anabantids—breathe air and can tolerate water with little dissolved oxygen, they are usually kept in tiny

Siamese Fighting Fish

121

bowls no larger than an adult human fist. There they languish, unable to swim even a body length, their graceful fins hanging folded between trips to the surface for air.

But place these fishes in even a small tank and keep them warm enough (at least 75°), and they come to life, swimming around and waving their fins. Unfortunately, males' flowing fins seem irresistible to many other fishes, and any species that has the slightest tendency toward fin-nipping will cause problems with bettas. (Even guppies and platies may pick on them!) For that reason, bettas should be kept either singly (a five-gallon tank will do nicely) or together with gentle tetras and catfish.

SIZE:   2–3 inches.

TEMPERAMENT/COMPATIBILITY: Perpetually combative with members of their own species, bettas are peaceful with other fishes. They may be kept together with any very peaceful and sedentary fishes.

TEMPERATURE:   Survives from 68–90°; shows best vigor and activity at around 79°.

WATER CONDITIONS:   Not critical as long as extremes are avoided.

FOOD:   Will probably accept dried foods, but prefers frozen and live food of all types.

## Macropodus opercularis:
# PARADISE FISH

This attractive species is undemanding, active (in warm water) and easy to keep, but is too aggressive to be suitable for most community tanks.

SIZE:   3 inches.

TEMPERAMENT/COMPATIBILITY: Aggressive; can be kept in a community tank only with equally active species of its own size or larger.

TEMPERATURE:   Survives between 50 and 90°; does well at standard community tank temperatures in the middle 70s.

WATER CONDITIONS:   Not critical.

FOOD:   Accepts wide variety of food; vary diet with live foods for best color.

## Colisa lalia:
# DWARF GOURAMI

A charming and strikingly beautiful species, dwarf gouramies are ideal for peaceful community tanks because of their small size. These fish are often shy at first, and do best in a well-planted aquarium that includes some floating plants to give them a sense of security.

SIZE:   2–3 inches.

TEMPERAMENT/COMPATIBILITY: Very peaceful (shy, in fact) and should be kept in community tanks only with other peaceful fish.

TEMPERATURE:   70–85°.

WATER CONDITIONS:   Not critical.

FOOD:   Accepts many dried and frozen foods; vary diet with live foods such as mosquito larvae for best color and vigor.

Paradise Fish

Dwarf Gourami

Pearl Gourami

## Trichogaster leeri and T. trichopterus:

### PEARL GOURAMI and THREE-SPOT GOURAMI

These handsome gouramies grow quite large, and require ample room to swim. Although generally considered peaceful, individuals have been known to pick on slow-moving fishes smaller than themselves.

SIZE:  *T. leeri,* 5 inches; *T. trichopterus,* 6 inches.

TEMPERAMENT/COMPATIBILITY: Suitable with fishes their own size or larger, but may pick on smaller or more sedentary individuals.

TEMPERATURE:  70–90°.

WATER CONDITIONS:  pH: not critical; neutral to slightly acid; hardness: not critical; soft to medium-hard.

FOOD:  Accepts a wide variety of dried and frozen foods, offer live foods occasionally.

## Helostoma temmincki:

# KISSING GOURAMI

The most peaceful of the large gouramies, kissing gouramies are favorites in the aquarium trade because of their amusing use of their thick, protruding lips to scrape algae off aquarium glass and other surfaces. When the animals appear to "kiss" one another, however, the intent is not what it might seem; like many other fishes, these gouramies are known to lock lips in aggressive contests and threat displays.

SIZE:  8–12 inches.

TEMPERAMENT/COMPATIBILITY: Suitable with fishes its own size, but some individuals are unpredictable with smaller fishes.

TEMPERATURE:  70–85°.

WATER CONDITIONS:  Not critical.

FOOD:  Takes a wide variety of dried, frozen, and live foods; make certain to provide sufficient vegetable matter in the form of algae or boiled lettuce leaves.

Kissing Gourami

# LOACHES:

## Family Cobitidae

This family of primarily nocturnal fishes displays behaviors reminiscent of catfishes; living primarily along the bottom, they use their barbels to explore the gravel for food.

## Acanthopthalmus kuhli:

## KUHLI LOACH

The kuhli loach I bought for my first community tank turned out to be one of my favorite fishes, even though I rarely saw it during the daytime. Despite what some people might describe as a wormlike body shape, this species is both attractive in appearance and endearing in behavior.

Because it dislikes bright light, it should be given a sheltered hiding spot, preferably in the back of the tank. It will spend a great deal of time in those quarters; you will see more of it if you build a "cave" of sorts with one side open to a side of the aquarium that does not receive much light. It is also less timid when kept with several others of its own kind. Despite generally nocturnal habits, this species will usually come out at feeding time once it is well-acclimated. If all else fails, offer it live *Tubifex* and stand back!

SIZE:   Long and thin, up to 3 inches.

TEMPERAMENT/COMPATIBILITY: Very peaceful, suitable for a community tank.

TEMPERATURE:   70–78°; sensitive to high temperatures.

WATER CONDITIONS:   pH: not critical; neutral to slightly acid.

FOOD:   Takes a variety of dried and frozen foods; particularly relishes *Tubifex* worms.

SPECIAL NOTES:   Because this species is shy and dislikes bright light, it is most comfortable in a densely planted tank with ample hiding places.

Kuhli Loach

# Botia macracantha:

## CLOWN LOACH

This magnificently colored loach is less timid and less nocturnal than many other members of its family. Clown loaches are also very social creatures; to improve your luck with them, keep at least three together and watch them explore their surroundings together.

SIZE:   In nature, up to 12 inches; rarely larger than 5 inches in captivity.

TEMPERAMENT/COMPATIBILITY: Less timid and sensitive to light than the coolie loach, this species is welcome in a community tank with other peaceful fishes. Most comfortable when kept in a group of at least three of its own kind.

TEMPERATURE:   72–80°.

WATER CONDITIONS:   pH: not critical; neutral to slightly acid; hardness: not critical; soft to medium-hard.

FOOD:   Takes a variety of prepared and frozen foods; vary diet regularly with *Tubifex*, white worms, and other live foods. Enjoys dining on small snails, so is useful for snail control.

Clown Loach

# KILLIFISHES:

## Family Cyprinodontidae

This family, which nearly covers the globe, contains some of the most brilliantly colored of all fishes. As a group, they are not difficult to keep, but are not suitable for community tanks. Because they are rarely carried by large, commercial fish suppliers, they are seldom seen in pet shops.

Many of the most beautiful killifish are native to sub-Saharan Africa, where they live in seasonal streams and pools. Many of these bodies of water exist only during the rainy season, and dry down to mud soon when the rains stop. Although individual fishes in these habitats die each year, their species survive in the form of eggs that endure dryness and hatch when water returns. Adapted to these conditions, many killifish mature, spawn, and die within a year; some species live for no more than eight months. Experienced aquarists can keep their stock going by breeding them, but beginners end up replacing them regularly.

Although I am not a killifish fanatic, I have thoroughly enjoyed the killifishes I've kept. I recommend them to anyone with some experience and an extra-small tank or two. My killies did well and looked particularly good in a combination aquarium-terrarium that held about three inches of peat-stained water overhung with both aquatic and terrestrial plants.

## A KILLIFISH SAMPLER:

### Aphyosemion gardneri, A. gulare, Nothobranchius brieni

SIZE: 2–4 inches, depending upon species.

TEMPERAMENT/COMPATIBILITY: Best kept in small tanks in pairs by themselves.

TEMPERATURE: 70–85°, but life expectancy is significantly lower at the upper end of the temperature range.

WATER CONDITIONS: Most species appreciate water filtered over peat; pH: slightly acid; hardness: soft.

FOOD: Will usually accept a wide variety of dried and frozen foods; vary diet with live food for maximum color.

SPECIAL NOTES: The hardiest and most easily bred killifish occasionally show up in large, well-stocked pet shops. If you are interested in killies and cannot find any locally, look through aquarium magazines and contact the American Killifish Association (see page 228 for information). Many hobbyists sell eggs or young fishes through the mail.

Red Gularis

# WORTHY MEMBERS OF SMALL FAMILIES

## RAINBOWFISHES:

### Family Atherinidae

For many years, the only popular member of this enormous, primarily marine family was *Melanotaenia maccullochi,* the Australian rainbowfish. Though hardy and relatively attractive, the fish never really caught on in this country. In the last few years, however, a new round of exploration in the freshwater habitats of Australia and New Guinea has turned up a host of new *Melanotaenia* species and members of related genera that make good aquarium specimens. Some of these newly discovered fishes are extraordinarily beautiful, and—unlike many other new and exotic species—are both hardy and peaceful. Because they are now being imported for the first time, they are offered mostly by the larger, better-stocked pet shops, and are still relatively expensive. As soon as they are bred in large numbers, however, they will make ideal pets for the relatively new fishkeeper who wants something "new and different."

SIZE: 3–6 inches at maturity, depending on species.

TEMPERAMENT/COMPATIBILITY: Peaceful species, welcome in community tanks with other peaceful fishes.

TEMPERATURE: 72–80°.

WATER CONDITIONS: pH: slightly acid through neutral to slightly alkaline; hardness: medium-hard.

FOOD: Apparently omnivorous, most accept a wide variety of prepared foods. Vary diet often with such live foods as ants, wingless fruit flies, and daphnia.

SPECIAL NOTES: These fishes, like danios, are active swimmers that like to live in small

Celebes Rainbowfish

Boseman's Rainbowfish

schools; they therefore need reasonably sized tanks with ample open space. Rainbowfishes, like several tetras, are shown off to best advantage by light that reflects off their bodies from certain angles. Experiment with display lighting in your tank to achieve the best effects.

Cape York Rainbowfish

# HATCHETFISHES:
## Family Gasteropelecidae

Hatchetfish have always been popular with hobbyists, both because of their unusual shapes and because they spend most of their time at the surface of the water where few other fishes remain for long. Although not the easiest fishes to keep in good health (they are sensitive to sudden changes in their surroundings), hatchetfishes are not particularly difficult, either. The main problem is that these species are accustomed to leaping out of the water and landing several yards away. In their native haunts, this works well; in your home, it means trouble. Most hatchetfishes sold die not because they are mistreated but because they manage to jump out of their aquarium when no one is around. Keep a tight-fitting cover on your tank to keep these fishes inside.

## Gasteropelecus sternicla
## SILVER HATCHETFISH,

## Carnegiella strigata
## MARBLED HATCHETFISH

SIZE: Up to 3 inches, but usually closer to 1 inch.

TEMPERAMENT/COMPATIBILITY: Peaceful but timid; does best in peaceful community tanks. Floating plants beneath which hatchets can "hide" help make them feel more secure.

TEMPERATURE: 72–82°.

WATER CONDITIONS: pH: slightly acid; hardness: soft.

FOOD: Feeds only from the surface, where it will take many dried and frozen foods; vary diet with wingless fruit flies and other small insects.

Marbled Hatchetfish

Silver Hatchetfish

# HEADSTANDERS:

## Family Anostomidae

These unusual and attractive fishes have the peculiar habit of posing in at a 45° angle with their heads down; hence their common name. Interesting and generally suitable for community tanks when small, they require very large tanks at maturity, and should not be kept with very small fishes.

## Anostomus anostomus
## STRIPED ANOSTOMUS,
## Leporinus fasciatus
## STRIPED LEPORINUS

SIZE: *Anostomus anostomus*, 6–7 inches; *Leporinus fasciatus*, 8 inches.

TEMPERAMENT/COMPATIBILITY: Peaceful when kept with other fishes its own size or larger; needs a large tank when mature.

TEMPERATURE: 70–85°.

WATER CONDITIONS: pH: neutral to slightly acid; hardness; soft to medium-hard.

FOOD: Readily accept a wide variety of dried, frozen, and live food; be certain to provide ample plant material.

Spotted Headstander

Black-Banded Leporinus

# PENCILFISH:

## Family Hemiodontidae

Another popular and peculiar group of fishes, members of this family offer a counterpoint to headstanders by positioning themselves at angles ranging from 45° to vertical with their heads up, just beneath the surface of the water.

## Nannostomus unifasciatus
## ONE-LINED PENCILFISH,

## Nannostomus trifasciatus
## THREE-LINED PENCILFISH

SIZE:  2 inches.

TEMPERAMENT/COMPATIBILITY: Peaceful; amusing additions to community tanks.

TEMPERATURE:  70–80°.

WATER CONDITIONS:  pH: neutral to slightly acid; hardness: soft to medium-hard.

FOOD:  Accepts a wide variety of dried and frozen foods; for best results, vary diet with small live foods such as wingless fruit flies and ants.

Three-Lined Pencilfish

One-Lined Pencilfish

Black Ghost Knifefish

# THE BLACK GHOST KNIFEFISH:

## Family Apteronotidae

## Apteronotus Albifrons:

### BLACK GHOST KNIFEFISH

This strikingly patterned and unusually shaped fish is one of the few "electric fish" that can be safely kept in a community aquarium. Many other knifefishes—along with electric catfishes, so-called "elephant noses" and misnamed "baby whales" are either too shy or too aggressive and predaceous to get along with other fishes. Black ghost knives, on the other hand, are relatively hardy, and make fascinating additions to any tank large enough to offer them room to swim.

These fishes and their kin, while evolving in the dark waters of peat-stained rivers, evolved a unique way of navigating and communicating in situations where vision is nearly useless. These animals use specially adapted body tissues to generate weak electric fields around their bodies. (These should not be confused with electric eels or electric catfishes that generate enough power to stun prey and people.) These weakly electric fishes use specialized receptor cells in their skin to measure those fields. Any object—or other animal—entering that field deforms it slightly, in a manner that the fish can detect. Many electric fishes also use their fields to communicate with one another in a "private language" undetectable to most other animals.

SIZE: 10–20 inches.

TEMPERAMENT/COMPATIBILITY: One of the few peaceful yet robust electric fishes. Best kept one to a tank with peaceful nonelectric fishes.

TEMPERATURE: 72–80°.

WATER CONDITIONS: pH: neutral to slightly acid; hardness: soft to medium-hard.

FOOD: Once acclimated, will accept a variety of dried and frozen foods; offer *Tubifex* regularly.

SPECIAL NOTES: To be really at home in your aquarium, this species needs a densely planted tank where it can avoid bright light. As a highly sensitive electric fish, it appreciates an electrically "quiet" place shelter such as a piece of 1-inch diameter PVC tubing that will insulate it from external electric fields.

# CHAPTER 6

# SALTWATER AQUARIA:
# BALI HAI IN YOUR HOME

*If you take any activity, any art, any discipline, any skill, and push it as far as it will go, push it beyond where it has ever been before, push it to the wildest edge of edges, then you force it into the realm of magic.*

Tom Robbins

Imagine an underwater fantasyland—a magic kingdom where plants and animals put Disney's imagination to shame. Pastel-colored fairy-tale castles sport spires, turrets, battlements, and gargoyles. Schools of fishes sweep past, creating maelstroms of sparkling fins and scales. And lurking in nooks and crannies are creatures that look more like hallucinations than flesh and blood; sea lilies with feathery arms, worms with gills that look like feather dusters, and shrimp with bodies striped like candy canes.

Welcome to the coral reef, an ecological system of phenomenal beauty and staggering complexity that has perplexed, amazed, and challenged scientists for centuries. Reefs are home to more different kinds of plants and animals than any other aquatic habitat on Earth, for in addition to hundreds of fish species, there are thousands of invertebrates (animals without backbones) whose colors and shapes defy verbal description.

But appearances are only part of the story, for the behaviors of many reef denizens are as curious as their looks. Each species has its own distinctive rules of conduct governing relationships with other animals. And many reef fishes and invertebrates are bound together in relationships called symbioses—literally, "life together." Those symbioses, often vital to the survival of both partners, are symbolic of the complex web of life that is the reef as a whole.

## REEF BIOLOGY:
### An Aquarist's Primer

Given the beauty and otherworldliness of reef environments, it's no wonder that aquarists eagerly try to recreate pieces in their homes. Given the complexity of reef life, it shouldn't be surprising that those efforts require study, skill, and dedication. To put the challenge of marine fishkeeping in perspective, and to give you the best chance to surmount its difficulties, there are several things you must know about the reef environment and the ways corals and their neighbors interact with one another in nature.

It's difficult to describe coral reefs without superlatives. To begin with, several reefs are the largest creations of living creatures on Earth. The Great Barrier Reef, for example, is almost too large for us to consider it a single living system. Built by corals and coralline algae that have laid down a tiny fraction of an inch of carbonate rock each year for millennia, this reef extends more than two thousand kilometers (roughly twelve hundred miles) along Australia's coast, and consists of roughly twenty-one thousand cubic kilometers of limestone rock. Even the largest human metropolis is insignificant by comparison.

Then there is the structure of the reef itself. Because each coral colony grows independently, responding only to sunlight, currents, and its immediate neighbors, the reef has no master plan, no coherent pattern. Over the millennia, coral colonies grow around, over, and into each other, creating not a solid cliff but a labyrinth of tunnels, dead-end caves, and crevasses.

The reef's physical complexity goes even further, for each limestone boulder is itself a world in miniature. Living coral tissue covers only the reef surface; if colonies break during storms, are overgrown by their neighbors, or are attacked by predators, coral polyps die, leaving behind their rocky skeletons. But no sooner are those skeletons laid bare of living tissue than they are colonized by scores of plants and animals. Soon the once-solid rock is both covered by and riddled with algae, sponges, clams, worms, shrimp, crabs, and other invertebrates.

Even if a casual scuba diver notices all this during a midday dive, however, he or she sees only part of the living reef. For however many fishes and invertebrates are visible during the daytime, many more remain hidden inside its secret chambers. The coral labyrinth serves, in fact, like a residential hotel that works on two shifts, for it harbors both diurnal (day-active) and nocturnal (night-active) animals. At dawn, members of the day shift abandon nighttime refuges deep within the reef, and head out to make their living. On their way, they pass creatures of the night, returning to slumber by day in the shelter of the coral maze. In this way, the reef actually shelters nearly twice as many species as you can see at any single point in time!

Although a full and proper scientific explanation of reef diversity would take several books, part of the answer can be found in two words. Colloquially, those words are "different strokes"; scientifically, they are *ecological specialization*. In either case, they mean that reef animals— through the process of evolution over time— have divided up available food and space in ways that minimize competition between species.

To accomplish this, many species evolved mouth shapes, body forms, and behaviors that allow them to be remarkably efficient at utilizing one particular source of food, or one specific part of the reef habitat. Thus, you'll find certain species of fishes and invertebrates that feed only on the living polyps of certain types of coral, or that graze on just a few kinds of algae. Other species might nibble only on the tissues of a particular living sponge. Still others might feed on open-water shrimp, but only those shrimp that are active after dark. Thus, although many species seem to be feeding in the same place, each is actually utilizing a slightly different source of food.

## The Reef's Invisible Partnership: Coral Symbiosis

Another reason that reefs carry such density and diversity of life is that many of their algae, fishes, and invertebrates help rather than hinder each other by living together. Some reef symbioses are invisible to the naked eye, while others, no less important to the organisms involved, are easy for even the uninitiated to see.

The single most important symbiosis on the reef is also the least obvious to the casual observer. For this relationship—which makes the richness of life in the coral kingdom possible —occurs inside the living coral polyps themselves. There, nestled among the corals' own cells live countless single-celled guests—algae called zooxanthellae. Together, corals and zooxanthellae—animals and plants—form a sort of short-circuit ecosystem in which both members benefit.

Corals, like all animals, constantly take in oxygen. Coral polyps also absorb organic compounds from seawater and snag passing planktonic animals with stinging tentacles. As they digest this food and carry on their life processes, coral tissues release carbon dioxide and nitrogen-containing waste products.

That's where the zooxanthellae come in. For the coral wastes, though toxic to the corals themselves, are not only tolerated but needed by the algae. Zooxanthellae, like all green plants, take in carbon dioxide and require nitrogen-containing compounds as fertilizer. Thus, algae living inside coral tissues are in just the right place; they absorb carbon dioxide and nitrogen directly from coral tissues instead of working to concentrate these essentials of life from nutrient-poor seawater.

But what do the corals get in return? Experiments have shown that zooxanthellae bolster their hosts' health and well-being by manufacturing and providing several compounds essential to corals. We know this because corals without zooxanthellae (or corals kept in the dark where their zooxanthellae can't function) stop growing and slowly waste away. Corals with functioning zooxanthellae, on the other hand, thrive with a limited input of food from outside.

It turns out that a number of invertebrates other than corals also depend on algal symbionts in good health. Most shallow-water sea anemones, several shell-less sea snails, and even giant clams host zooxanthellae in their tissues.

Why should this symbiosis be of any concern to you as a potential marine hobbyist? Because all these "animals" depend on functioning algae within their tissues to do well in captivity, all of them must be treated as if they were both animal and vegetable! They will all eat if offered appropriate food (see below), but they also need the right kind and intensity of light for photosynthesis.

## Visible Partnerships

Although algal symbioses help the reef itself to thrive, many more partnerships on the reef are equally fascinating and more visible. The best-known of these is the classic case of strange bedfellows; clownfish that nestle contentedly amid the stinging tentacles of sea anemones, apparently as comfortable as children snuggling in a pile of down pillows.

Anemones—which are related to corals—normally feed by using tentacles to stun and subdue small fishes. Yet by themselves anemones are defenseless against several angelfish and butterfly fish that snack on tentacle tips.

Enter the clownfish. By covering themselves with a layer of body mucus, they mask the chemical stimuli that normally tell anemones' stinging cells "there's food here, fire away!" Gaining security from their own enemies by hiding in this armed nest, the feisty clownfish return the favor by chasing off anemone-eating fishes many times their own size. So endearing are the interactions between these fishes and anemones that many hobbyists have started keeping marine fish specifically to watch this relationship close at hand.

Other behavioral symbioses are just as intriguing; several brightly striped fish called cleaner wrasses, for example, remove troublesome parasites from the bodies, mouths, and gills of other fishes. Several species of coral shrimp behave in similar fashion, while other shrimp hitch rides on the backs of giant, shell-less sea snails.

## THE CAVEATS

As exciting as tropical marine animals are, the nature of their natural environment and the specifics of their biology create numerous practical and philosophical problems for home aquarists. Behind several of those problems is the fact that virtually no marine fish have been spawned commercially to date. As a result, all fish and invertebrates you see for sale (with the exception of some clownfish) were snatched from a reef somewhere within a few weeks of the time you see them. They are thus, in effect, wild animals that home aquarists must successfully tame and acclimate to captivity. This situation raises several points you should consider before launching your marine aquarium.

## Are You Ready for Overtime?

In the abstract, marine-aquarium maintenance is not all that different from its freshwater counterpart. Aside from the fact that seawater carries more salt than freshwater, success or failure in marine tanks hinges on precisely the same issues: water quality, lighting, proper diet, and selection of animals to create a congenial community. What is different, however, is the way marine animals respond to aquarium conditions that deviate from the ideal state.

Remember that most freshwater habitats—even tropical ones—expose their inhabitants to changing environmental conditions. Rainy seasons alternate with dry seasons, and hot, sunny days alternate with cool nights. Lakes and ponds experience major changes in water temperature, dissolved oxygen, and pH in spring and fall. To survive in these habitats, freshwater species (with exceptions such as discus) have evolved tolerance to changes in environmental conditions.

But the coral reef is one of the most benign, environmentally stable habitats on earth. Water temperature varies at most a few degrees over the course of the entire year. Salinity stays virtually constant. Clean, fresh seawater washes constantly over the reef, bringing food and carrying away waste products. Even day length and the strength of the sun vary little; reefs grow best close to the equator where sunlight is always intense, and where there are always between eleven and thirteen hours of daylight.

The upshot of all this is that reef fish, unused to fluctuating conditions in nature, are far less tolerant of them in captivity. To keep them healthy, therefore, you must do everything you do for freshwater tanks, but do it *better*. No overcrowding. The right food. Constant pH. Carefully designed filtration systems. Regular water changes to maintain water quality. Even small deviations from ideal conditions—slip-ups that would hardly be noticed in typical freshwater community tanks—can spell disaster for marine tanks.

## The Undersea Money Pit

Nearly all reef animals cost a lot more than most freshwater species. Marine aquarists don't bat an eye at forty-dollar fish, and regularly spend one hundred dollars or more on a single specimen. Much of the equipment currently in vogue for marine tanks can also be pretty pricey; the latest filter systems can run two hundred dollars or more for a fifty-five-gallon tank. So

don't be surprised if your dealer quotes you a price of two thousand dollars for a basic, fifty-five-gallon marine-aquarium setup—not including fish.

Even if you decide to start with a smaller tank (although I recommend a twenty-gallon long as the absolute minimum for a saltwater starter), you'll find that equipment costs per fish are high. Because seawater carries less oxygen than freshwater does, a given tank will support fewer marine species than freshwater ones. That is true both because of the limitations of tank-surface area and because of the limitations posed by the basic undergravel filters used to provide biological filtration.

Additionally, most reef fishes are used to more private space than their freshwater counterparts, and have no compunction about fighting for it. As part of the behaviors that help them divide up available food and space on the reef, many species have become fiercely territorial, and will viciously attack any other members of their own kind that infringe upon their turf. Even between-species relationships can be iffy in tanks; the spectacle of reefs swarming with fishes notwithstanding, very few individuals normally live in the tiny volume enclosed by even the largest home aquarium. Even though you may only intend to put two or three fishes in a twenty-gallon tank, you may still be crowding them psychologically.

Finally, remember that for most of us seawater suitable for aquarium use isn't as cheap as tapwater. Saltwater aquariums require water changes at least as frequently as freshwater tanks do. For reasons discussed below, even if you live near the sea, you're better off using artificial sea salts in your tank, and those cost several dollars for every five gallons. Because

of the sensitivity of reef animals to decreases in water quality, you cannot allow the cost of seawater to deter you from making those changes.

## Picky Eaters

There's another side effect of reef fishes' ecological specialization that makes keeping them difficult. As I mentioned earlier, many reef fishes are so specialized in their diets that they normally eat only certain types of live coral polyps or particular kinds of living sponge. Its important to remember that over the eons, much more than just the mouths and feeding behaviors of these animals have become specialized. In many cases, their stomachs and intestines have adjusted physically and chemically to digest their chosen foods.

The flip side of this efficiency is that the digestive systems of many reef animals can't handle any other kind of food. Even if these animals become hungry enough to eat things they normally would not touch, or even if you manage to force-feed them in captivity, they cannot extract the nutrients they need and slowly starve to death, despite full stomachs.

Unfortunately for fishes, fishkeepers, and pet shops, many marine fishes commonly shipped to this country will not survive for long because they are such picky eaters. Several beautiful and popular butterfly fish and angelfish fall into this category, yet they continually show up in retailers' tanks. Dealers who really care about these fishes have informed overseas suppliers that they do not want these species. But in a market where supply is often tight—and is steadily becoming tighter—dealers often feel forced to accept the chaff with the wheat.

As a conscientious (and fiscally wise) aquarist, you have two options in this situation. The simplest route—and the one I recommend for beginners—is to stick to those few fishes I suggest starting on page 83. Alternatively, you can invest in a comprehensive atlas of marine fishes that gives honest information about the dietary requirements of the hundreds of species carried in the trade. You must then carefully identify any fish you are interested in buying, and make certain you can provide for its needs before you bring it home.

## Typhoid Marys

Last but not least, disease is a much more serious problem in marine tanks than it is in freshwater aquaria for several reasons.

Because virtually all marine fish are wild-caught, most harbor parasites or infections. This is not to say that all imported fishes are "sick"; in nature most infections (with bacteria and fungi) and infestations (with larger parasites) either remain latent (without causing harm) or pass with no ill effects.

But two problems arise in captive situations:

First, as you'll see more specifically in Chapter 9, many fish parasites spend only part of their lives attached to fishes. At some point, they drop off, fall to the bottom, and reproduce like mad, producing tens, hundreds, or even thousands of progeny that swim around looking for new fishes to infect. In the great open spaces on the reef, few of those progeny actually encounter another host. In a small tank, however,

your fishes are sitting ducks, sure to be reinfected with more and more parasites on each go-round.

Second, even if fishes can normally fight off certain infections in nature, their immune systems are often seriously compromised by the stresses of capture, shipping, life in crowded dealer's tanks (where other parasites from past residents may still be lurking), and less than ideal conditions in your tank. Thus, infections that would stay latent in nature become active in home aquaria.

As if this weren't enough, most medications that kill fish parasites will also do a job on any invertebrates in your tank. Thus, if your clown-fish gets sick, you've got to have someplace else to put your sea anemone before you add medicine to the tank. This can be a real problem in the magnificent living-reef tanks discussed below, which are filled with invertebrates and where catching fish to remove them for treatment is often as difficult as it is on a real reef.

To avoid the problems discussed above, you *will* have a quarantine/treatment tank, and you *will* treat every newly acquired marine fish as a potential source of infection. Every new acquisition must be quarantined and treated as described in Chapter 9. Particularly if you intend to maintain fishes and invertebrates together in the same tank, you will always keep a second tank operating, ready to accept either fishes or invertebrates if medication proves necessary.

Furthermore, if, through a combination of science, art, and luck, you end up with a "happy" marine tank, you *will not* push your luck by periodically adding "just one more fish." Rigorous quarantine procedures can lessen the risk of disease introduction, but there's always

the chance that a single parasite passing through your medical net will wreak havoc in your tank.

## THE BREAK-IN PERIOD

Perhaps the most traumatic time for marine aquarists (and their fishes) is the first month or so immediately following the setup of a new marine tank. As is the case with freshwater systems, some time is required for beneficial bacteria to become established in the biological filter bed. But these bacteria grow more slowly in seawater than they do in freshwater, so levels of ammonia and nitrite often rise higher and stay higher longer in marine tanks than they do in freshwater systems. Because marine animals are more sensitive to ammonia and nitrites than their freshwater counterparts, those high levels of wastes pose greater threats to fish health.

Establishment and stabilization of the biological filter usually takes between three and five weeks in marine tanks, depending on particular circumstances. During all this time, only the hardiest animals should be kept. Part of the frustration newcomers to the hobby feel with this process is undoubtedly due to the fact that both ammonia and nitrite are invisible; eager aquarists can't *see* anything wrong in the tank except by using test kits. Thus, the process of breaking in a new marine tank requires a substantial amount of planning to make it run smoothly. For now, be forewarned that this planning is necessary; a specific list of procedures and rough timetable for the break-in period is provided in Chapter 8.

# EQUIPMENT FOR A MARINE AQUARIUM

## Understanding and Preparing Your Seawater

Seawater, I hardly need to inform you, carries a substantial quantity of dissolved mineral salts. As you may be aware, the mix of elements is fairly complicated; although there's plenty of "salt" in the form of sodium chloride, there are also calcium and magnesium salts and a variety of trace elements present in small amounts. This means you can't just add table salt or rock salt to your tapwater to create your miniature ocean.

Those of you who live along the shore might think it reasonable to collect natural seawater in containers. Once upon a time, that may have been a viable alternate, but there are few places I'd recommend it today, for two main reasons.

First, coastal waters near metropolitan areas often carry pollutants that make life tough for fishes. Water and sediments in Boston Harbor, for example, are sufficiently contaminated to give our harbor flounder outrageously high rates of skin cancer and liver tumors. (Do I eat lobster caught in our harbor? Not on your life!) Coastal waters near the mouths of rivers in agricultural areas, on the other hand, may be diluted with freshwater that carries either pesticides or fertilizer residues drained from cultivated fields. Because of such problems, of all major public aquaria located on or near the sea, only the Monterey Bay Aquarium in California can pump raw, natural seawater through its tanks on a daily basis. The others use artificial seawater made up from concentrated brine mixtures.

Second, on a less human-centered note, natural seawater often carries parasites. Of particular concern here is the question of putting tropical Pacific fishes into, say, seawater from the Gulf of Maine. The problem is that parasites and their hosts in any given area sooner or later "work things out"—in an evolutionary rather than conscious manner, of course—to their mutual advantage. Hosts acquire at least relative immunity to disease, and parasites evolve nonlethal strains. For though parasites, by definition, do harm their host, if they rapidly and invariably caused death, they would quickly be out of places to live! Thus, with certain notable exceptions, although local parasites might cause illness in local fishes, they don't invariably cause death.

Parasites and hosts from different parts of the world, on the other hand, have no such relationship. While working at an aquaculture laboratory in Woods Hole, for example, I kept dozens of tanks filled with local animals, and a single tank of tropical fishes on running seawater pumped out of Vineyard sound. The local fishes did fine. In fact, they broke several growth records. But the tropical species barely survived as they lurched from one plague to another. Even though their tank water was cleaned by microfine (one micron) filters, local parasites still slipped through. The same problem occurred in my home tanks as long as I insisted on using local seawater. Once I switched to artificial sea salts, however, the disease problems cleared up immediately.

The upshot of this is clear. If you live on the Florida Keys and are keeping Caribbean Reef fishes, or if you live in Baja California and in-tend to collect Sea of Cortez fishes, your local seawater is probably suitable. (I'd still store it in a dark closet or basement, in aerated carboys for three weeks before using it; that should give time for most fish-dependent parasites to die off without hosts.) In any other situation, it is best to use only artificial sea-salt mixtures in your marine tanks. Several brands are widely distributed today, all of which are more or less equivalent. (My personal favorite is the aptly named Instant Ocean.) In addition to being disease free, these salt mixes contain all the necessary trace elements, and include buffers to stabilize your tank's pH.

| 7.2 |
| 7.4 |
| 7.6 |
| 7.8 |
| 8.0 |
| 8.2 |
| 8.4 |
| 8.6 |
| 8.8 |

pH

**Measuring Salinity** Most aquarists don't measure salt content directly. Instead, we measure the water's *specific gravity,* an indicator of its density. Water that contains salt is denser than water that does not; the more salt it carries, the higher its density. Thus, as long as all the salts in your mix are present in the right proportions, you can adjust their concentration accurately by checking specific gravity with a device called a *hygrometer.*

Standard, scientific hygrometers are long, hollow glass tubes with weights in their sealed lower ends. These are floated, either directly in the tank or in a wide cylinder of water removed from the tank. The denser the water, the higher the hygrometer floats. Along their thin upper ends runs an easily read specific-gravity scale.

These devices are damnably fragile, however, and are awkward to use. I've honestly lost count of the number I've broken in my time, and I've been trained to be careful with scientific equipment! As an alternative, I recommend a more recently introduced style of hygrometer that measures specific gravity with a floating pointer inside a lucite container about the size of a deck of playing cards.

Water from the open sea, measured at a temperature of 70° F, usually has a specific gravity of about 1.024, but water collected elsewhere may vary. Water from coastal bays in high-rainfall areas often measures as low as 1.015, while readings of 1.026 or even higher are not uncommon in such landlocked, tropical areas as the Red Sea.

**Determining the Right Salinity** Most marine fishes in captivity can tolerate a fairly wide range of salinity, from around 1.016 to about 1.022. Invertebrates as a group, on the other hand, are less able to cope with salinity changes, and do best between 1.020 and 1.024.

Thus, to keep fishes and invertebrates together, maintain a salinity between 1.022 and 1.024. But if you are keeping fishes alone (as I recommend for beginners), it may be useful to maintain a pH closer to 1.016. Why? Many parasites of fishes are invertebrates, and some of those are as sensitive as their more benign relatives to low salinity. Thus, by keeping salinity near the low range for fishes you may be able to make life harder for potential troublemakers. (Note that if you receive your fish in water of specific gravity 1.024, you must acclimate them to a lower salinity slowly, over a period of several days.)

**Mixing Your First Batch of Seawater** Seawater mixes come in convenient sizes; rather than being packaged simply by weight, they are sold in quantites sufficient to create various volumes of seawater. Most brands are available at least in five-, ten-, twenty-five-, and fifty-gallon sizes.

When you actually prepare to fill your tank, don't just dump, say, a thirty-gallon seawater package into a thirty-gallon tank. The actual capacity of most tanks is a little less than the volume used to describe them, and gravel, coral, and decorations all take up space within the tank. Instead, fill the tank, add about two-thirds the amount of salt you think you'll need, and hook up the filtration and aeration systems. Then, wait overnight for the salt to dissolve completely and for the water to stabilize at around 70° F. At that point, measure the water's specific gravity and adjust it as needed by adding extra salt.

Over time, water will evaporate from your marine tank, just as it will from freshwater tanks. When that water evaporates, however, it leaves the tank as pure water; all its dissolved salts are left behind. Thus, to replace water lost by evaporation, you should add either distilled water or tapwater treated to remove chlorine and chloramine. Add more seawater only to replace water removed during water changes.

## Monitoring and Maintaining Water Quality

Because marine fishes are sensitive to both ammonia and nitrite, and because invertebrates are also sensitive to nitrate, you *must* maintain water quality in all marine tanks. Buy a good, complete test kit, and use it regularly to monitor pH, alkalinity, ammonia, nitrite, and nitrate. Because a reliable test kit is essential to your tank's health, don't skimp in buying one. Pick up a good master kit that consolidates all important tests in a single package. When buying your kit, check the expiration dates on the kit's reagents; all these chemicals have limited shelf lives, so you should buy a kit with the most current date possible.

**pH** The pH in your tank should never fall below 8.0, and should stay closer to 8.2. The hardier marine fishes can tolerate pH as low as 7.7, but invertebrates begin to suffer at 7.9.

Starting off with that pH is no problem, because all artificial sea-salt mixes contain pH-adjusting compounds, and most of the gravel types used in marine aquaria have some buffering capacity. Remember, however, that your biological filter continually releases hydrogen ions, and will slowly but steadily lower the tank's pH unless you take steps to counter its effects.

For that reason, as part of your regular tank maintenance schedule (see Chapter 8), you should test your system regularly for both pH and total alkalinity. You can't simply dump in lots of pH-raising compounds and ignore the problem, because your fishes can't live at pH 9. You can't depend entirely on alkaline gravel and coral rock to do that job, either, because their buffering ability declines with time. What you can do is utilize alkalinity-testing kits and such products as Aquarium System's Sea Buffer to build up the water's reserve alkalinity without changing its pH.

Filtration and Aeration  In theory, the filtration needs of marine aquaria are no different from those of freshwater systems; mechanical, chemical, and biological filtering must all be tended to, and water must be properly aerated. The principles behind these jobs and the types of equipment necessary to accomplish them were discussed in detail in Chapters 2 and 3. (If you don't remember the basics of water-quality maintenance and filtration, go back and review the relevant parts of those chapters now.)

In practice, experienced aquarists use more elaborate systems for marine tanks, primarily because of the lower tolerances of marine animals for organic wastes. But before I launch into a paean to advanced filter systems, let me say that if you're willing to exercise restraint in stocking your marine tank, you can get away with the filter system discussed for well-stocked freshwater systems in Chapter 3. A motor-powered, box-type outside filter loaded with filter floss and a layer of activated carbon can provide all the mechanical and chemical filtration you need, and a four-inch gravel bed will support the necessary biological filtration. The only real necessary difference between this system and its freshwater equivalent is that you should substitute dolomite or crushed coral gravel in your filter bed to help keep the tank's pH on the alkaline side.

The advantage of this is that it will allow you to convert an existing freshwater tank to saltwater use with a minimum of additional expense. Although not as sophisticated as the latest high-tech systems, this outside filter/undergravel combination allowed many of us to keep marine animals for years. Another way to use standard equipment in marine tanks—deploying a canister filter to power a reverse-flow undergravel filter—is shown on pages 50–51. Be certain if you choose this sort of system to provide sufficient aeration. Still another variation is the use of "power heads" to pull water through undergravel filter plates at high speed.

It is true, however, that water quality is of prime importance in marine systems, and dedicated marine hobbyists usually insist on the latest and most advanced equipment to maintain that water quality. The "latest thing" right now is the wet/dry or trickle filtration system described in Chapter 3. Such filters, coupled with protein skimmers (also described in Chapter 3) help provide the best water quality available in small, closed systems today. The addition of calcite to the biological filter bed in the trickle filter will provide extra buffering support to keep pH constant. In addition, the trickling itself helps to drive carbon dioxide out of the water, thereby helping maintain pH.

A more recent addition to some trickle filter systems is variously called a "nitrate remover" or "denitrifier," that is intended to address the normal buildup of nitrate. The most complex of these (which retail for between $200 and $300), use a precision pump to feed a sugar solution into a sealed box containing a foam-block culture of bacteria that grow in the absence of oxygen. Tank water is pumped very slowly through the block, where the bacteria are supposed to convert nitrates into a gas that leaves the system altogether.

In theory, this is an excellent idea. In practice, it is difficult to implement properly. If things go wrong—and if the commotion surrounding the device in the hobbyist community today is any indication, they seem to go wrong regularly—the denitrifier can backfire by churning out toxic nitrites or other compounds that could cause a disaster in your tank. Unless and until these problems are overcome, I'd steer clear of this accessory. It is possible, however, to establish a less sophisticated, less efficient, but more predictable denitrifier by simply placing a thick gravel bed in the sump area of the trickle filter. This gravel layer need be cleaned only when debris from filter material above cover its surface.

Permissible Levels of Organic Wastes  Once your tank is established, ammonia and nitrite should always remain scarce enough that your test kit can barely detect them. Ammonia should be less than 0.1 ppm, and nitrite should be below 0.5 ppm. Nitrate, which can go higher than 20 ppm without bothering most fishes, should be maintained below 10 ppm (some experts even say below 0.1 ppm) to keep invertebrates happy. To achieve these results, don't overload your tank (see Chapter 7), care for both your mechanical and biological filters carefully and regularly (see Chapter 8), and change at least 20 percent of your water at least once a month.

### The Importance of Water Changes

Water changes in marine tanks are even more critical than they are in freshwater tanks. The chemistry of seawater is complicated to begin with, and many marine organisms—particularly algae and invertebrates—both absorb elements from seawater and secrete various compounds of their own. On the reef, absorbed elements are replaced, and secreted compound washed away by waves and currents. In your tank, however, some trace elements in seawater may be depleted, and potentially toxic compounds will build up. To minimize these effects, regular water changes are absolutely essential.

## Foods and Feeding

At the risk of seeming redundant, I'll repeat (again) that it is absolutely essential to understand the dietary requirements of any reef fishes you intend to keep. Because some of those needs can be met only with difficulty, and others cannot be handled in captivity at all, you must familiarize yourself with your charges' needs *before* you purchase them. If you can't provide the proper diet, or don't want to go to the extra work or expense, don't buy the fish! Remember, even if your fish agrees to eat foods other than what it needs, it may not be able to digest them or may not obtain some critical nutrient from them, and will slowly pine away.

In general, the easiest reef fishes to keep are those that normally feed on other fishes, on shellfish, or on plankton, because simple substitutes for these natural foods are all readily available. Predatory species such as lionfish can be fed guppies or small goldfish. Shellfish and plankton eaters such as several triggerfishes can be fed on frozen and live brine shrimp, fresh shrimp from your neighborhood fish market, or on any commercially available freeze-dried plankton mix. Similarly, those species that normally graze on algae can be fed on lettuce and spinach leaves weighted to the bottom of the tank or on living algae that you grow either in the tank or elsewhere.

Tangs, for example, once acclimated in captivity, devour both flake foods and frozen brine shrimp with gusto. Despite constantly full stomachs, however, these beautiful animals tend to deteriorate slowly but steadily. First they begin to lose muscle tissue in the area between their dorsal fin and backbone. Then, the area immediately around the lateral line pores on their heads loses color, and the pores seem to enlarge. Although the fish may live for months, they look progressively less attractive, and ultimately die.

Why the poor prognosis? In nature, tangs subsist almost entirely on green algae. Although they readily eat other foods in captivity, they still develop nutritional deficiencies. Informed of the situation, however, you can keep your tangs happy by either cultivating a carpet of algae in your tank or by growing algae on rocks or small coral heads in another tank and periodically putting them into the tang tank for a treat. Lettuce and spinach leaves provided regularly are another option.

Specific information on the nutritional needs of several species is provided as part of the fish list at the end of this chapter.

## Light

For marine fishes alone, the nature and quantity of light in your aquarium is not all that important. As in freshwater aquaria, you want to provide enough light so that your fishes can see their surroundings, and so that you can see your fishes. If you want to maintain any sea anemones or corals, on the other hand, both the kind of light and its intensity become matters of real concern. Why? Recall that these soft-bodied animals host algal symbionts within their tissues; to keep anemones and corals in good health, you must provide enough light to keep their zooxanthellae healthy as well.

On this much, everyone who knows marine aquaria agrees. But toss out to half a dozen experienced aquarists an apparently innocent question about exactly what kind of lighting is best for zooxanthellae, and you will find yourself in the midst of an intense, even vituperative debate.

Some aquarists will tell you to use the same sort of fluorescent bulbs I recommended earlier for freshwater tanks (a mixture of wide-spectrum Grolux and Cool White). Most of these hobbyists agree that it's best to double the number of tubes; over a fifty-five-gallon tank, therefore, this recommendation would place a minimum of four 40-watt bulbs (although some folks prefer six).

Another group, while sticking up for a hood containing four fluorescent tubes, would recommend replacing one of the Grolux bulbs with intense blue actinic 03 bulbs. Still others would go along with the idea of actinics, but recommend swapping the Cool Whites for Vita-lites. Others would insist on tossing out fluorescents altogether in favor of metal-halide lamps, and still another group would recommend combining metal halide with actinics.

Arguments, claims, and counterclaims rage on among these groups, and there has been precious little in the way of controlled, scientific experiment to give an objective answer. It is probably safe to say that people have had success with all the above lighting configurations, depending on the location of their tank and the specific invertebrates being kept.

I would agree that four bulbs are probably indicated, and you might even want to locate the tank where it receives some supplemental natural light. (To those who insist that sunlight is necessarily bad for tanks, I'd counter that the Waikiki aquarium has excellent luck with live coral outdoors in full tropical sunshine.) But if you want to provide all the necessary light artificially, I'd recommend a total of roughly four watts per gallon of water as a guide. A mix of one actinic bulb, one wide spectrum Grolux, and two Vita-lites has worked well for many aquarists, although it is no guarantee of success. Those willing to invest the extra money in a metal-halide fixture are welcome to experiment with it, being careful to place it at least a few inches away from any animals. In general, keep all lights on for sixteen hours a day, although you can keep only a single bulb burning for display purposes on occasion.

## Problems in Paradise

You've probably noticed in the forgoing discussion that I've practiced uncharacteristic restraint in recommending the keeping of marine fish. You'll also notice in the following fish list that I've recommended relatively few animals for beginners to try. This controlled enthusiasm and selective listing have both been shaped by a simple fact mentioned earlier in the chapter: All marine fish are wild-caught. To those of us who consider ourselves ecologically minded—and particularly to those of us who set ourselves up as advocates for the hobby—that fact poses a profound philosophical conundrum: Can we really encourage the keeping of tropical marine animals with a clear conscience?

After a great deal of research, and an equivalent amount of soul-searching, I've decided that my personal answer to that question is a heavily qualified yes. What are those qualifications?

First, I recommend marine fishkeeping only to hobbyists who've acquired necessary expertise, who fully understand what they are getting into, and who are willing to shoulder both the additional work and the added costs of maintaining their pets properly. Although all of us need to learn from experience (and although all of us have been unintentionally responsible for the demise of numerous fishes), the situation with marine organisms is extreme. Right now, the majority of marine fishes and invertebrates sold here die far too soon, either because of hobbyist inexperience or because the animals are simply not suited for life in captivity.

To improve that situation, all of us must work to improve the hobby's record in keeping marine animals alive and healthy. To do that, hobbyists should agree to start with marine fishes only after having experience in freshwater systems. We should then make it our responsibility to purchase—and therefore subsidize the collection and importation of—only those animals that are, in fact, suited to life in captivity. If enough of us refuse to purchase highly specialized butterfly fish and invertebrates that will not live in tanks, the message will work its way back through dealers to wholesalers, importers, and collectors.

Second, I charge marine aquarists to take action, both to maintain a supply of animals to fill their tanks and to preserve the world's coral reefs for future generations. This action must face threats to reefs on two fronts:

First, the world's coral reefs are threatened just as surely as our tropical rain forests. Some reefs are being destroyed through uncontrolled development that covers them with asphalt; one tragic example is the Japanese decision to build an airport on top of the country's only surviving coral reef in a part of the Okinawa island chain called Ishigaki. (This despite the fact that there is already an airport on Okinawa.) Other reefs are threatened indirectly by marine dredging and filling operations or by nearby deforestation that smothers corals beneath a blanket of sediment. Still other reefs are literally blown to pieces by dynamite fishing—a technique that uses underwater explosions to stun fish and tear apart coral forests to "simplify" the collection of food fish. Many corals are also ripped off the reef and sold internationally as curios or as raw materials for the handicraft trade.

Second, we must police ourselves and the industry that supports our hobby, to make certain that we do not inadvertently subsidize activities that work to the detriment of our fishes and their native habitats.

What sort of activities do we want to discourage? Precisely because reefs are such good homes for fishes, they are particularly difficult places for fish collectors. The big nets used to round up freshwater fish by the thousands almost never work on reefs; they get tangled in coral thickets and tear while fishes vanish. Some fish—those that will come to bait—can be caught in traps. But in most cases, each fish must be individually caught in a hand net. And that (take it from one who's tried) is no easy feat; it requires skill, patience, and endurance on the part of the fish collector.

For this reason, it has unfortunately become widespread practice to catch coral fishes through the much simpler method of using "drugs" to knock them senseless. Unfortunately, most of the "drugs" used in commercial fish collection are actually poisons, rather than anesthetics. Sodium cyanide is the most popular, particularly in the Philippines. Fish *seem* to recover from cyanide—within a few hours they look well and eat well, and continue to appear healthy just long enough to end up in your tank. But cyanide-collected fish often sustain damage to their livers and other tissues, and mysteriously die some weeks later.

The best retailers and wholesalers are aware of this problem and are already doing their best to discourage this practice. We must all, however, be constantly on the lookout for quick-money types who think nothing of dealing in drugged fish to make an easy profit.

Is it really possible for aquarium hobbyists to help save the reefs? We should not underestimate the political power of thousands of aquarists across the world; if all of us raise our voices in support of national and international conservation measures, we will be heard. Additionally, we must remember that the collection and sale of tropical fishes is big business; even ten years ago, it generated $3 million in the Philippines alone.

Ideally, the industry—from individual hobbyists all the way back up the chain to major importers—should harness that economic clout to help set up research and training programs that encourage sustainable harvesting of fishes from reef areas. Although difficult to execute, this approach—similar to strategies being implemented to save tropical forests—can preserve nature in the most secure way possible, by linking the health of the natural habitat to the economic well-being of the local populace.

## TROPICAL MARINE ANIMALS FOR THE HOME TANK

If freshwater fishes enchant aquarists, marine fishes bewitch us. Their colors and shapes are brilliant and varied. Their personalities range from shy to nasty. Even their movements vary enormously; some dart, some glide, some slither, some crawl, and others seem to "hop" through their tanks. And there are *lots* of reef fishes; one major atlas of marine-aquarium species lists more than five hundred species, and still doesn't purport to be all-inclusive.

Many of these fish, however, are either quite rare, very expensive, or difficult to keep in small home aquaria. So, to provide the best possible service to the beginning marine hobbyists, I've exercised more restraint in this section than anywhere else in the book. I've forced myself to list only those species hardy enough to give beginning hobbyists a chance to succeed. Butterfly fishes, for example, are beautiful, peaceful, and ever so charming. As a group, they are also quite delicate and difficult to keep. That's why you won't find them on this list. To avoid frustration, I've also tried to list only those fishes common enough to be available in good pet shops.

Fortuitously, many of the hardiest species I've listed—such as damselfish—are among the least expensive, and several are quite attractive. Thus, although I've left out many personal favorites, there are still plenty of interesting choices. I have also left in just a sprinkling of moderately difficult species to tempt you as you grow into the hobby.

Although all these fishes like the same water conditions, you still have to be careful about the number of individuals and species that you place together in the same tank. Relatively few marine fishes are as peaceful as guppies or small tetras, many are as aggressive and territorial as large cichlids, and still others eat small fish on a regular basis. Importantly, even fish species that are congenial to other fishes regularly eat several kinds of invertebrates. Conversely, certain large crabs can make short work of slow-moving fishes. For your own sake and the sake of your fishes, pay close attention to the "temperament/compatibility" entries in the list, because finding a congenial mix of animals for a marine tank is tricky. Be careful not to use *your* tank as an inadvertent (and expensive) demonstration of marine food chains in action!

## Water Conditions for Tropical Marine Tanks

The hardier of these fishes are all compatible in terms of temperature and water-quality requirements. In captivity, reef fishes do well in temperatures between 72 and 82° F, at a pH between 7.8 and 8.2, and at a specific gravity between 1.016 and 1.022. Although hardy fishes (by definition) have higher tolerances for temporary exposure to high ammonia and nitrite levels than more delicate species, they all do best in water as free of organic wastes as possible.

## Do Fish and Invertebrates Mix?

It is true that marine aquarists who restrict themselves to fishes are missing half the fun of marine tanks. Even a quick glimpse at the colors and shapes of anemones and coral shrimps is enough to convince you of that. But mixing fishes and invertebrates is risky.

First, there's the "food chain" issue; you don't want tankmates—whose minimum price is usually at least twenty dollars—making meals out of one another.

Second, there's the fact mentioned earlier that most medications effective against diseases of marine fishes are toxic to invertebrates. That means medicating a mixed tank of fishes and invertebrates is usually not possible; either fishes must be treated elsewhere, or inverts must be moved out till the medication has done its job and has been removed.

The most practical setup for a serious marine aquarist who wants to minimize problems requires three separate tanks: one for fishes, one for invertebrates, and one for quarantine and "hospital" treatment. The more daring experienced hobbyists, however, aim for a different ideal; a "living reef" tank, the closest aquarists can get to duplicating a small piece of reef in their home. In this approach, the tank is decorated not with dried coral skeletons and limestone rocks but with living corals and "live rocks." Live rocks aren't alive themselves, of course, but they are rocks that have either been removed from living-reef areas or "seeded" by keeping them in living-reef tanks so that they support a host of invertebrates and algae.

Living-reef tanks are magnificent to behold, and they are within reach with current technology. Certain species, such as the psychedelically colored Mandarinfish (genus *Synchiropus*) are actually easier to keep healthy in a living-reef tank, because these normally picky eaters feed eagerly on the innumerable tiny organisms that populate the live rocks. Some professional aquarists also believe that—once established—living-reef tanks maintain themselves better than more sterile setups, and that fishes surrounded by a diversity of algae and small invertebrates to feed upon are healthier than those raised exclusively on prepared diets.

Living-reef tanks do, however, require substantial investments in equipment. Strong lighting is essential to maintain the growth of both desirable marine algae and the zooxanthellae within corals and anemones. A large trickle filter is strongly recommended to handle waste products, not only from fishes, but from the invertebrates—visible and invisible—that inhabit the artificial reef. Because the emphasis in living-reef tanks is on mixing fishes and invertebrates, all potential inhabitants must be carefully screened for compatibility problems. Finally, because fish diseases in such tanks would be disastrous, *all new arrivals must be rigorously quarantined to avoid introducing infections.*

*No exceptions!*

# DAMSELFISHES:
## Family Pomacentridae

Spunky, attractive, and hardy, damselfish are among the best possible choices for your first marine tank. Hardy enough that they are often used to "break in" tanks destined for other fishes, damsels lack only the size and mystique of some other families. Their main drawback is their aggressive personality; though several species gather in loose aggregations in nature, they often fight among themselves in small tanks.

Several species of damsels are often found "hanging around" sea anemones, but only one subgroup, the clownfish, has developed the relationship into a tight symbiosis. Several clownfish are easy to keep, and they are among the most peaceful members of the family. Clownfish also allow you an interesting opportunity to grow with your hobby. Keep these fishes until you're confident in your abilities to maintain water quality, and then, once you're ready, add a suitable anemone. If your fishes accept your choice of tankmates, the resulting behaviors will keep you fascinated for many hours.

SIZE:  6 inches when fully grown in nature; usually closer to 3 inches in captivity.

TEMPERAMENT/COMPATIBILITY:
As a rule, these fishes are aggressive toward others of their own kind. If acquired while small, introduced to the aquarium at the same time, and given sufficient room, several species of clownfish and members of the genus *Dascyllus* may behave well in groups of half a dozen or more. Generally compatible with good-sized invertebrates, they may nibble on any small worms and crustaceans that cross their paths.

FOOD:  Feeding on plankton and algae in nature, damsels take readily to a variety of prepared, fresh, and frozen foods in captivity. Vary diet with live foods when available.

SPECIAL NOTES:  In nature, clownfish are always found within a few body lengths of their symbiotic anemones. In captivity, however,

they can be picky about which anemones they will accept. (The anemone seems to have no say in the matter.) You have the best chances of success with Pacific species from the genera *Radianthus* and *Stoichactis*, but be aware that clownfish sometimes refuse to perform in captivity. Many aquarists end up offering two or three potential partners before making an acceptable match.

Blue Damsel

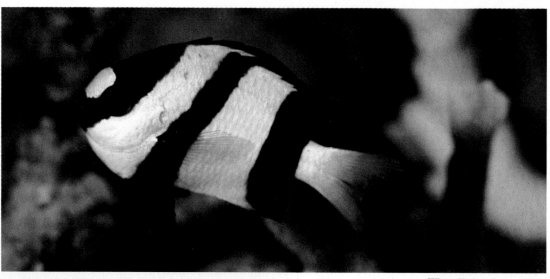

White-Tailed Damselfish,
also known as
Three-Striped Damselfish

Three-Spot Damselfish

Clark's Anemone Fish

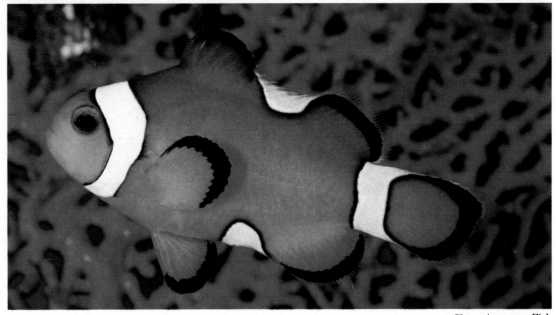

Clown Anemone Fish

# TRIGGERFISH:

## Family Balistidae

Judging by comments from other aquarists, I am nearly alone in my affection for these attractive and fascinating—but often aggressive—fishes. The family get its common name from a dorsal spine it uses to wedge itself into crevices when it sleeps at night. When the spine is fully erect, an adjacent spine can literally lock it in place, making it impossible for either predator or fish collector to pry the fish loose.

I used to spend hours watching my triggerfish, although sometimes I watched mainly to defend their tankmates. Triggers tend to act very much like schoolyard bullies; they chase other fishes around, snapping their beaklike jaws audibly at regular intervals, but run for cover the moment they feel threatened. Triggerfish, like many other reef species, feel most comfortable when they have a suitably sized cave or seashell to wedge themselves into at night. They are quite amusing as they jockey in and out of their shelter, keeping an eye on you constantly as they do so.

Several triggerfish are reasonably priced, although one of the most spectacular, the clown triggerfish *(Balistoides conspicillum)* runs close to one hundred dollars. In all cases, buy these animals as small as you can find them; they will grow quickly once acclimated to your tank.

SIZE: Many triggerfish species grow to 20 inches or more in nature, but rarely reach more than 8–10 inches in captivity.

TEMPERAMENT/COMPATIBILITY:
Some of the most beautifully colored triggerfish

—such as *Balistapus undulatus*—are too nasty to share a tank with any except the largest species. Others, such as members of the genera *Odonus, Rhinecanthus,* and *Balistoides* can usually be trusted with other fish their own size or larger. None of them can be trusted, however, with either very small or very sedentary fishes, and all triggers will make short work of most invertebrates.

FOOD: In nature, most triggerfish dine on plankton, shrimps, crabs, and any other invertebrates—such as sea urchins—that they can get their jaws around. When crowded into small tanks, they may make meals of tankmates. These fishes eagerly accept freeze-dried krill, but you should vary their diets with a variety of frozen and live foods.

SPECIAL NOTES: Don't underestimate the power in these fishes' beaks. Even small ones can deliver a painful nip, and large specimens can take a sizable chunk out of an aquarist's hand.

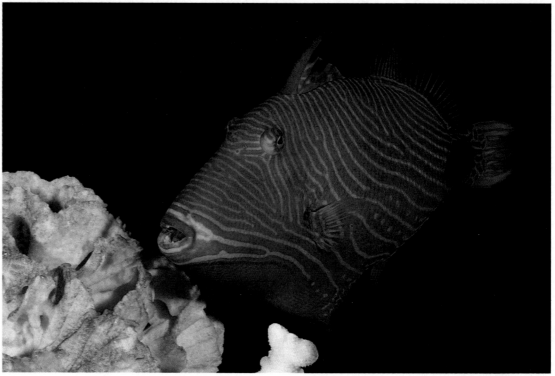

Undulate Triggerfish

Clown Triggerfish

Red-Tooth Triggerfish

Picasso Triggerfish

# GROUPERS:
## Family Serranidae

Commonly called sea basses, groupers are a large and diverse family better known as sport and table fish than as aquarium specimens. That's a pity, because many groupers are hardy, attractive, personable, and peaceful. In terms of their ability to recognize and bond to their owners, groupers are the closest of all marine fishes to cichlids. Their only drawbacks are a tendency to outgrow their tanks rapidly, and a habit of making meals out of tankmates that don't grow as quickly.

The brightly colored groupers are rarely seen in aquarium stores, perhaps because they are difficult to catch when small enough for home aquaria. One commonly seen species that I heartily recommend is the pantherfish or polka-dot grouper, *Cromileptes altivelis*. Unfortunately, these fishes grow rapidly, and if you succeed in keeping them healthy you will eventually have to trade them in, no matter how large your tank. Buy them as small as you can, therefore, to enjoy them for as long as possible.

SIZE:  Although some groupers grow to several feet and can weigh hundreds of pounds, those common in captivity rarely grow more than 2 feet, even in the largest tanks, and some will stay under 10 inches in small tanks.

TEMPERAMENT/COMPATIBILITY: Groupers are not particularly aggressive, toward other fishes their own size, but they are predators, and will devour anything—fish or invertebrate—that they can swallow whole.

FOOD:  Exclusively carnivorous, groupers do best on live foods; start them on baby guppies and watch them grow until they graduate to large goldfish.

Pantherfish

# LIONFISH:

## Family Scorpaenidae

Lionfish are hard to beat for drama; nothing in freshwater comes close to their long-spined, trailing fins and engaging expressions. In nature, many are active mainly during dawn and dusk twilight periods when they stalk their prey. They are fascinating to watch as they use their fanlike pectoral fins to herd their quarry into corners and devour them with a gulp so rapid that it cannot be seen with the naked eye.

SIZE:   Growing to between 4 and 10 inches in nature, most lionfish reach only half that size in captivity. A few dwarf species grow no larger than 3 inches.

TEMPERAMENT/COMPATIBILITY:
Although they are strictly predators, lionfish are peaceful with fishes their own size, and are easily intimidated in too frenetic an aquarium. Aggressive fishes such as damsels and triggerfish will often nip at lionfishes' fins, sometimes worrying them to death. I like to keep these fishes by themselves in a large tank where they can show off their fins to best advantage.

FOOD:   Exclusively carnivorous, lionfish do best on live foods such as guppies and small goldfish. With patience, you may be able to wean them onto frozen foods by dangling the food in front of them on a thread.

SPECIAL NOTES:   All members of this family have venomous spines. The sting of scorpionfish, the most deadly genera, can be lethal, so steer clear of these rarely imported fishes. Lionfish venom is far less toxic; depending on species, the severity of their sting can vary from a severe wasp sting to a mild snakebite. In any case, caution is necessary, and these fish should never be handled without caution and protective gloves. Not recommended for households with inquisitive children or cats.

Volitans Lionfish

# BLENNIES:

## Family Bleniidae

Although not the most brilliantly colored fishes, blennies are hardy, peaceful, and interesting to watch as they scuttle from place to place across the bottom of the tank.

SIZE: 3–4 inches.

TEMPERAMENT/COMPATIBILITY: Generally peaceful fishes, some blenny species defend territories against members of their own kind. They are compatible with most invertebrates, and several species are welcome additions to living-reef tanks.

FOOD: Offer a varied diet; if blennies are not kept in living-reef tanks, offer a variety of live and frozen foods.

# TANGS:

## Family Acanthuridae

Perpetually active, even skittish, tangs add animation to any marine tank. Several species— such as the powder-blue tang, *Acanthurus leucosternon*—have dispositions as delicate as their air-brushed color patterns, but others are quite hardy if fed properly.

SIZE: Although many tangs grow to nearly 2 feet in length on the reef, in captivity they rarely grow larger than 8–10 inches.

TEMPERAMENT/COMPATIBILITY: Tangs get along well with most other fishes. Because they are active and incessant swimmers, however, they need lots of room to swim; larger individuals of several species may become aggressive if cramped. Small specimens should be kept in of tanks at least 20 gallons; larger specimens in tanks not smaller than 55 gallons. Several species are armed with razor-sharp spines near their tails; these weapons are used only in defense, but can inflict nasty wounds, either on tankmates or on careless aquarists.

FOOD: Although tangs will gorge themselves on flake foods and frozen brine shrimp, they are naturally strict herbivores, and will starve to death despite their appetites. They must be offered an abundance of fresh plant material in the form of living algae or lettuce and spinach leaves weighted to stay on the bottom of the tank.

Redtail Blenny

Blue Tang *(yellow phase)*

SPECIAL NOTES: Tangs are particularly susceptible to the ailment known as "lateral-line disease" or "hole-in-the-head syndrome." Although some aquarists blame this on poor water conditions, and others suspect a bacterial infection, recent evidence supports the theory that a vitamin deficiency in captive diets is at the root of the problem. Offer plenty of plant foods from date of purchase; once the disease is present, it may never regress. Some species may go into shock on introduction; it is best to leave them in peace in dimly lit aquaria overnight before exposing them to full daytime illumination in their new home.

Hepatus Tang

Powder Blue Tang

# CARDINALFISH:

## Family Apogonidae

This attractive collection of species is easy to keep, and generally peaceful. Primarily nocturnal in nature, apogonids require shaded hiding places in brightly lit aquaria, and will be most active at dawn and dusk. The illustrated representative, *Apogon nematopterus,* has an odd appearance, almost as if it were composed of pieces of several different fishes.

SIZE:  Usually seen in aquaria at sizes between 2 and 3 inches.

TEMPERAMENT/COMPATIBILITY:
Peaceful, shy, and retiring by day, most active at night. Compatible with invertebrates other than very small crustaceans.

FOOD:  Accepts a wide variety of foods in captivity; vary diet with live and frozen foods.

# ANGELFISH:

## Family Pomacanthidae

I include angelfish on this list with some trepidation, for although they are beautiful and commonly offered for sale, they are not easy to keep alive for long periods of time, and tend to be expensive.

Aquarists often divide these fishes into two groups: regular and pygmy-sized. The full-sized angelfish are among the most beautiful of all reef fishes, but most of them are aggressive, territorial, and require large tanks (seventy gallons or more) when mature. Several species commonly offered for sale are nearly impossible to maintain because in nature they feed primarily on live sponges. Several pygmy angel species are also difficult, but a few will adapt to aquarium life.

Among those species that can be kept without too much difficulty are the pygmy angels *Centropyge bicolor* (bicolor pygmy angel), and *C. loriculus* (flame angel), and the larger *Pomacanthus semicircularis* (Koran angel).

SIZE:  Pygmy angels around 3 inches; larger species 8–10 inches in aquaria, up to a foot or more if captured as adults.

TEMPERAMENT/COMPATIBILITY:
Generally peaceful toward other species, many angelfish are fiercely territorial, and will not tolerate other members of their own kind. Some will also attack other angelfish species, although this tendency seems to vary among species and from individual to individual. Pygmy angels as a group are less aggressive than larger species. Most angels will graze on corals, macroalgae, and attached invertebrates, so they are not suitable for living-reef tanks.

Cardinalfish

Flame Angelfish

FOOD: In nature, angelfish often graze on a wide variety of encrusting algae and invertebrates. One key to long-term success with all angelfish species seems to be the provision of varied foods that come close to approximating this diet. Live and frozen foods should be offered in variety, along with plenty of fresh algae and vegetable matter.

SPECIAL NOTES: Angelfish do not tolerate changes in water conditions; they should be added only to aquaria in which the biological filter is already well-established. Some individuals of large angelfish species will adapt to aquarium life when small, but most species are extremely difficult to acclimate if captured as adults.

(Juvenile) Koran Angelfish

Queen Angelfish

(Adult) Koran Angelfish

(Juvenile) Lemon Peel Angelfish

(Adult) Lemon Peel Angelfish

# DRAGONETS (MANDARINFISH):

## Family Callionymiidae

These fish are colored so brilliantly that they hardly seem real. They are peaceful, slow-moving, and amusing to watch, and get along well with most species of invertebrates.

SIZE:  3–4 inches.

TEMPERAMENT/COMPATIBILITY: Peaceful and easily intimidated, they do best in very quiet community tanks where they need not compete for food with more active species.

FOOD:  Although they will sometimes take frozen brine shrimp, and do accept live foods, mandarinfish are difficult to feed properly in sterile aquaria. This species does particularly well in living-reef tanks; apparently they feed on the myriad unseen invertebrates that crawl in and out of the live rocks in such tanks.

Mandarinfish

Clown Dragonet, also known as "Psychedelic Fish"

## HAWKFISH:

### Family Cirrhitidae

Although not the most brilliantly colored of reef fishes, hawkfish are among the most endearing. Active and inquisitive, they alternately scuttle around the aquarium and pose on the ends of coral branches, "standing" on their pectoral and pelvic fins.

SIZE: Although several species grow to 5 inches or longer in nature, they are usually seen in aquaria between 3 and 4 inches.

TEMPERAMENT/COMPATIBILITY:
Peaceful with similarly sized fishes, hawkfish will prey on small fishes. Compatible with invertebrates other than small crustaceans, they make good additions to living-reef tanks. Some species are aggressive toward their own kind; keep one to a tank.

FOOD: Relatively easy to feed, hawkfish will eagerly track down live food such as baby guppies, but will also accept frozen foods appropriate to their carnivorous habits.

## ROUNDHEADS (MARINE BETTAS):

### Family Plesiopidae

These spectacularly beautiful fishes, nicknamed "marine bettas" after their graceful, flowing fins, are no relation to freshwater anabantids. They are easy to feed and relatively hardy, but are rarely seen in aquarium stores. They usually command high prices, and are therefore recommended only to aquarists with confidence in their ability to care for undemanding—but still not "foolproof"—species.

SIZE: Grows to greater than 6 inches in nature; usually seen in aquaria at between 4 and 5 inches.

TEMPERAMENT/COMPATIBILITY:
This is a very peaceful, even shy species that should be kept only with "polite" tankmates. Damsels, triggerfish, and others with pushy dispositions have a habit of nipping its fins and worrying it too much. Compatible with invertebrates except for very small crustaceans.

FOOD: Not difficult to feed, though particularly fond of live foods, including small guppies.

Falco Hawkfish

Marine Betta

# FAIRY BASSLETS:

## Family Grammidae

Imagine a ripe lemon peel dipped in violet mascara and highlighted with eyebrow pencil; that's a rather accurate description of the royal gramma *(Gramma loreto),* one of the most popular marine fishes in this country. Hardy, generally peaceful, and relatively easy to keep, royal grammas are also priced well within the range of most hobbyists. Easily the easiest to maintain of the truly showy fishes, this species is a favorite with beginners and advanced hobbyists alike.

These animals, like many other reef species, like to find a cave or burrow they can call "home"; given the opportunity, they will excavate a private retreat in the gravel beneath coral heads and shells.

SIZE:   Grows to about 3 inches.

TEMPERAMENT/COMPATIBILITY: Royal grammas are aggressive only toward members of their own kind, are compatible with invertebrates other than the smallest crustaceans, and should be kept (one to a tank) with other peaceful fishes.

FOOD:   Accepts a variety of prepared, frozen, and live foods; be certain to vary diet regularly.

SPECIAL NOTES:   This species, although among the easier marine species to keep, is often imported in large numbers and inadvertently mistreated by dealers. Grammas are highly aggressive toward other members of their species. When dozens are crammed into a single tank, fighting stops only at feeding time, and the resulting stress gets the fish off to a bad start. Buy only grammas that have been properly maintained, and examine them closely for battle scars and active, healthy behavior.

Royal Gramma

# INVERTEBRATES:

## A Magical World Apart

As colorful and unusual as reef fishes are, they meet their match in the forms and shades offered by the tropical seas' invertebrates. Ranging from familiar starfish, coral shrimp, and sea urchins to exotic nudibranches, corals, and anemones, invertebrates are an integral part of the reef community.

As discussed earlier, the keeping of invertebrates and fishes together is a touchy business, both because of compatibility issues and because of problems in treating diseased fishes in a tank containing inverts. A separate tank dedicated exclusively to invertebrates is fascinating for the connoisseur, but most beginning hobbyists will find themselves longing for the flash and action of fast-swimming fishes. I will repeat once again, however, that mixing fish and inverts is not a good idea for beginners.

The term "invertebrates" itself is so broadly applied as to be nearly useless taxonomically; it covers numerous phyla of animals, far more different from one another than humans are from hummingbirds. Some invertebrates have changed little since their appearance close to the dawn of life on Earth, while others have evolved many new species over the eons.

As a group, invertebrates are less tolerant of ammonia, nitrite, and nitrate than fishes are, and they are also less able to handle fluctuations in salinity. With some exceptions (such as certain hermit crabs), therefore, inverts are best reserved for those with some marine-aquarium experience, and I have listed only a few of the hardier and more popular varieties here.

WATER QUALITY WARNING: Invertebrates as a group are intolerant of even small amounts of copper in their water, so before investing in invertebrates, buy a test kit or have your tapwater professionally tested for dissolved copper. If your water contains significant amounts of copper, either find a way to get around the problem or avoid invertebrates. Remember that if water drawn from the tap first thing in the morning or evening has picked up copper from your pipes, you may be able to get around the problem by using water for bathing, washing dishes, watering houseplants, etc., before drawing water for your tanks.

# Phylum Crustacea:

## SHRIMPS, CRABS, AND LOBSTERS

Crustaceans are an extraordinarily varied group of animals, ranging in size and habit from nearly microscopic fish parasites, to free-swimming members of the plankton, to giant crabs more than six feet across. Those kept (intentionally) in aquaria are usually bottom-dwelling members of the group called *decapods* after their ten appendages or "legs."

Crustaceans can present some thorny compatibility problems, as they are predators on certain organisms and prey to others. All crustaceans must shed their external skeleton—a process called molting—in order to grow. Just after molting, they are soft and helpless, and must be offered secure hiding places or they will become expensive meals for tankmates.

Small crustaceans are favorite foods of nearly all marine organisms (including other crustaceans), and even large crustaceans fall prey to such sharp-beaked species as triggerfish.

# Shrimps

The most popular crustacean species in marine tanks are commonly called coral shrimps, cleaner shrimps, or "candy cane" shrimps. They are peaceful, relatively hardy, fascinating to watch, and live full lives in well-balanced aquaria. Several species live together in mated pairs and will even reproduce in living-reef tanks. The young rarely survive, but they do serve the most useful purpose of providing live food for corals nearby!

Hawaiian Deepwater Shrimp

Porcelain Anemone Crab

Anemone Shrimp

Candy Cane or Cleaner Shrimp

# Crabs

There is no such thing as a "typical" crab; those kept in aquaria vary from tiny species less than one inch long that live nestled in coral branches to hermit crabs that grow to six inches or more. Several of the commonly available medium-large-sized crabs are voracious feeders, and will try to grab any fishes that stray too close. For this reason, keep only the smallest, most peaceful species with fishes.

SIZE:   Most common aquarium shrimps are about 3 inches in length, not counting their long antennae. Select only crabs smaller than 2 inches for mixed aquaria.

FOOD:   Crustaceans as a group prefer frozen seafood of all types, including fish, shellfish, and fellow crustaceans. Offer small pieces one at a time on the end of a long stick.

Hermit Crab

Red Hermit Crab

Reef Lobster

Regal Slipper Lobster

# Phylum Echinodermata:

## STARFISH AND SEA URCHINS

This phylum, whose name means "spiny-skinned" contains numerous animals that can justifiably be called living fossils, because they have changed little in more than 250 million years. Those most commonly kept in aquaria include the plant-eating sea urchins and the omnivorous or carnivorous starfish.

SIZE: Various.

TEMPERAMENT/COMPATIBILITY: Urchins are welcome additions to living-reef tanks, where they help keep algal growth under control. Starfish can be kept only in tanks that contain no living clams or scallops. Some starfish may graze on encrusting invertebrates, but the real coral-eating kinds are rarely imported.

FOOD: Urchins are plant-eaters, and require large amounts of algae to do well. Starfish can be fed bits of clam or scallop by tucking the food under an arm until the animal grabs it. Both urchins and starfish do far better in living-reef tanks than they do in sterile tanks containing only fishes.

Bat Starfish

Tropical Starfish

Red-Spined Starfish

Rock-Boring Sea Urchin

Pencil Urchin

Purple Sea Urchin

# Phylum Cnidaria:

## SEA ANEMONES AND CORALS

Members of this phylum are the true "signature" animals for marine tanks. Corals are responsible both for the very existence of reefs and for much of their beauty, while anemones are spectacular visual grace notes, both in nature and in aquaria.

As discussed earlier, many members of this phylum are host to symbiotic algae that live within their tissues. Because the good health of these photosynthetic guests is vital to the survival of both anemones and corals, these plant/animal combinations *must* be given adequate lighting or they will survive only a short while, even if fed regularly.

Although anemones are hardier than corals, all cnidarians are quite sensitive to water quality, and should be added only to aquaria with established biological filters. Don't forget, also, that although they look like plants, these animals do release organic wastes into the water, and must be considered in figuring out the total load on your biological filtration system.

Identification of anemones and corals to species is often difficult, even for experts, although genera can usually be recognized fairly easily. In terms of care and handling, these animals can be broken roughly into three informal groups.

## Hard Corals

These spectacular reef-building animals are—for better and for worse—very difficult to keep alive for more than a few months in home aquaria. They are extremely sensitive to both water and light conditions, and only one or two species survive even at the hands of experienced aquarists. I wouldn't mind a ban on importing these animals to protect their home reefs from crowbar attacks. Because these animals grow very slowly, even a coral the size of a baseball is apt to be ten or twenty years old.

## Soft Corals

"Soft coral" is a catchall term applied to a wide variety of organisms with differing requirements. Several species usually referred to by this common name, however, are more amenable to aquarium life than the reef-building corals. Those species that live in caves, on overhanging ledges, or in deeper water require less intense light and appear to be somewhat more tolerant of changes in water conditions. Most of them do, however, prefer strong water currents, both in nature and in the aquarium.

## Anemones

Although "sedentary" by nature, anemones can "walk" slowly on their fleshy bases. You can "plant" them where you want them, but chances are the animals will relocate to a spot they "like" better. Be careful if you try to move them yourself; their bases attach firmly to rocks, coral, and glass, and you can cause severe damage by tearing them loose. This warning also applies when removing animals from dealers' tanks; accept no anemone with a gash in its base or any other obvious damage.

**TEMPERAMENT/COMPATIBILITY:** Despite their much-touted stinging tentacles, most cnidarians pose little threat to healthy tankmates. Anemones and corals are, on the other hand, favored foods of several butterfly fish and angelfish, and should not be kept with those animals.

**FOOD:** Cnidarians really must be treated as both plant and animal. Along with sufficient light, they should be offered suitable food regularly. Anemones, when "hungry," will ingest small pieces of fresh fish or shellfish; offer pieces no larger than a dime at a time, for overfeeding can cause serious gastric distress. Corals, which expand their polyps to feed primarily at night, benefit from regular feedings with prepared invertebrate foods available commercially.

**Pink Anemone**

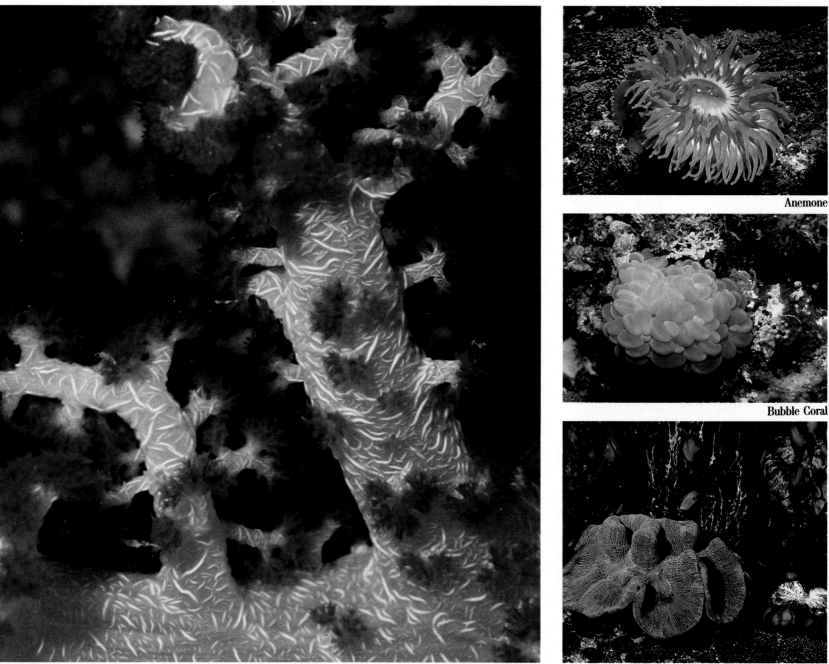

Anemone

Bubble Coral

Soft Coral

Corals and macroalgae require intense light.

Moon Coral

Orange Tube Coral

Soft Coral

## "LIVE ROCKS"

As living-reef tanks gain in popularity, more and more well-stocked aquarium stores are beginning to stock what are called "live rocks." The rocks, of course, are not alive themselves; the name refers to the fact that they are covered with—and often filled with—a variety of invertebrates and algae. Live rocks are much like marine "surprise packages," for if conditions in your tank are good enough, almost anything can grow out of them. Typical passengers on live rocks include feather-duster worms, macroalgae, colonial sea anemones, soft corals, myriads of tiny shrimp, and the like.

The more savvy dealers now offer live rocks in two categories: "fresh collected" and "seeded." Fresh-collected rocks are just that; they have recently been removed from a reef area and are teeming with attached and burrowing reef critters. Seeded rocks—offered at more reasonable prices—are previously dried pieces of coral rock that have been kept in established reef tanks in the company of live rocks. Their once-sterile surfaces have thus been "seeded" by bacteria, algae, and those invertebrates that reproduce in such systems.

Live rocks form the backbone of living-reef tanks, but are, as a rule, not a good idea for beginners. Their handling and role in aquaria will be discussed in Chapter 8.

Tubeworms on live rocks

## MACROALGAE

Very few flowering plants grow in the sea, and those that do are used to conditions it is nearly impossible to reproduce in home aquaria. Saltwater hobbyists can, however, cultivate a few species of marine macroalgae, so-called to differentiate them from the smaller, single-celled, and filamentous algae that often blanket our tanks whether we want them to or not.

The macroalgae best suited to marine tanks are several species of the genus *Caulerpa*. These are just now becoming available in this country commercially; if your local pet shop doesn't stock them, you can order them through the mail. While growing, *Caulerpa* species are welcome additions, both to living-reef tanks and to fish-only tanks.

*Caulerpa* require the same sort of intense, broad-spectrum illumination recommended for zooxanthellae. Even under the best conditions, however, these algae tend to be temporary residents, for they periodically enter a reproductive stage, release invisibly small reproductive cells, and then die off.

Caulerpa

171

# TEN TANKS THAT WORK

Aquarists experienced enough to write books about fishkeeping often forget the difficulty beginners have in assembling fishes into harmonious groupings. Sure, species descriptions in our books all carry notes on compatibility, but with so many fishes to choose from, and with so many variables involved, there are just as many chances for trouble as there are chances for success.

It struck me that species descriptions for fish in books such as this one are a lot like labels on the jars of herbs and spices used for cooking; they are accurate and often evocative, but can't tell you how to combine the individual elements together in groupings that work well. It's not enough to know that oregano is especially good with tomatoes and eggplant, or that rosemary is superb with lamb. An experienced chef must know how to blend various spices and foods in combinations that create interesting yet harmonious meals. That's why people read cookbooks; labels on jars just don't provide the right information.

This chapter is designed for you to use much the way you might employ a cookbook on an unfamiliar cuisine. It contains stocking sug-gestions for six freshwater and four saltwater tanks of various sizes and dispositions, and degrees of difficulty ranging from beginner to expert. Like the recipes of a master chef, these suggestions have been assembled from experience with the help of some friends, and they're meant to serve as guides, rather than as absolute proscriptions. If you do decide to experiment, though, keep the following rules in mind:

**Match Fishes with Similar Requirements.** Don't mix fishes that prefer soft, acid water with those that like hard, alkaline conditions. Although hardy species of both types will survive in medium-soft water and a pH close to neutral, neither will be in tip-top shape.

**Match Fishes with Similar Temperaments.** Don't mix boisterous, aggressive fishes with shy retiring ones; even if the roustabouts don't physically injure the wallflowers, they can intimidate them at feeding time and bully them into poor health.

**Keep Track of Your Fishes' Adult Size.** Don't buy oscars or pantherfish to keep in a twenty-gallon tank unless you are planning either to trade in your fish or to buy a larger tank within a year. Remember, too, that while baby oscars, firemouth cichlids, and triggerfish are cute and not too aggressive, they will show their true colors as they grow.

**Observe Interactions Carefully.** Even the most carefully planned tanks can be upset by particularly pugnacious fishes. Some individuals are rougher than others, and even previously peaceful pairs can treat their tankmates roughly during courtship and spawning.

**Don't Overstock.** For all the reasons discussed in earlier chapters, don't overcrowd your tank. Overcrowding can turn minor errors in judgment into catastrophes, and is probably the single most common cause of failure among beginning aquarists.

**Be Realistic About Your Skills, Time, and Energy.** Hobbies are most fun when challenges are learning experiences, and when reasonable inputs of time and energy lead to success. To ensure that you enjoy fish-keeping, don't buy more tanks and fishes than you can take care of without impinging on other important parts of your life. Buy one tank at a time, live with it for a few months, and judge how much time you need to keep it running smoothly. Add new tanks slowly as time and interest permit.

## SIX TYPES OF FRESHWATER TANKS:
### From Beginner to Expert

If you're just starting out, follow these recipes closely, because they teach by example how various groups of fishes work with one another. Once you gain some experience, though, feel free to spice things up on your own. Just as an experienced chef can guess whether a new recipe could use a bit more pepper or a little more ginger, you'll soon be comfortable deciding whether your tank can take another catfish or dwarf cichlid. Every now and then, your "ingredients" might clash, or one might overpower another, but sooner or later you'll get the hang of it.

# 1

## GAGGLES OF GOLDFISH:
### Simple and Low-Maintenance

Goldfish and small koi, among the simplest of all fishes to keep in the home, are available in a host of odd, unusual, and beautiful shapes and colors. Many are inexpensive, all are hardy, and they don't require an aquarium heater in most homes.

**The Fishes**  As an admitted nonconnoisseur of goldfish, I have no personal favorites among available breeds. With the exception of celestial-eyed varieties (as discussed in Chapter 5), most are compatible with one another and with small koi. Shop around to check on which breeds are common in your area, and choose a mix of black, gold, pearl-scaled, and oddly shaped breeds that suits your fancy.

For koi, on the other hand, I have unrestrained enthusiasm. Many are living works of art. Although the finest show specimens in Japan run into the thousand-dollar range, breeders' culls are beautiful enough for most of us nonexperts. I admit to poorly concealed envy for those with sufficient space and resources to build koi ponds outdoors or in sunrooms attached to their homes. For these magnificent fishes outgrow small tanks quickly when they are well-cared-for, and must be considered temporary residents in small aquaria. Stock koi sparsely, unless you are willing to buy additional tanks or are prepared to give away fishes as they grow.

**IN A 10-GALLON TANK:**

10 small (1.5–2″) goldfish,
or 4 medium-sized (2–4″) goldfish
(Larger fishes should not be kept in a tank this small.)

**IN A 20-GALLON (LONG) TANK:**

20 small (1.5–2-inch) goldfish,
or 6 medium-sized (2–4-inch) goldfish,
or 2 or 3 medium-sized (4–5-inch) show goldfish or koi could fit in a tank this size, but it gives them little room to swim; if you really want fish this large, use a bigger tank.

**IN A 55-GALLON TANK:**

24 small (2-inch) goldfish
or 11 medium-sized (3–4-inch) goldfish
or 5 medium-sized (4–5-inch) show goldfish or medium-sized koi

**The Plants**  Most "bunch plants" offered for sale in pet shops do quite well in brightly lit goldfish tanks. Many of these plants—often collected from or grown in temperate-zone lakes and ponds—prefer cool water, and grow denser and stockier in goldfish tanks than they do in tropical tanks.

Two of the most common bunch plants, *Elodea* and *Cabomba,* are particularly good choices for goldfish tanks. Plant these in groups across the back and sides of the aquarium, leaving the central region open for the fish to swim through. For a low-growing foreground plant, try *Acorus gramineus,* a small green or green-and-white plant available from mail-order suppliers and some pet shops.

**Potential Problems**  As these fishes can live in outdoor pools as long as the water doesn't freeze, they certainly don't require heaters in most homes. But if your house (like mine) has rooms whose temperatures dip into the lower 50s in January and February, take care not to overfeed animals in unheated tanks. Fishes, as "cold-blooded" creatures, have body processes that speed up and slow down with warmer and cooler temperatures, respectively. Under cool temperatures indoors, they need very little food. In cold weather outdoors, fish in ponds should not be fed at all until water warms up to 50° in spring.

Because these temperate fishes are accustomed to cool water, summer heat can cause problems for crowded aquaria in un-airconditioned rooms. If your tank is heavily stocked, watch it carefully during hot spells. If fishes collect near the surface and gasp for air, increase aeration, lower water temperatures, or decrease stocking density to alleviate the stress. Make certain to protect the tank from direct sunlight, and—as an emergency measure—float small plastic bags of ice cubes in the tank to bring temperature down.

# 2

## A COMMUNITY OF LIVE-BEARERS

This selection can offer many hours of pleasure to beginners and their families, while minimizing the angst involved in maintaining a first tank. Fancy guppies, platies and swordtails are available today in so many different color varieties that you could easily keep a dozen pairs of any species without having two that look alike.

All these fishes will present you with offspring sooner or later, so keep a breeding trap and/or baby net handy. You'll probably also want to leave a little extra room in the tank so you can keep the kids together with their parents once the little tykes have grown large enough to fend for themselves.

### The Fishes

| | |
|---|---|
| Fancy guppies | *Poecilia reticulata* hybrids |
| Platies | *Xiphophorus maculatus* hybrids |
| Swordtails | *Xiphophorus helleri* hybrids |
| Mollies | *Poecilia latipinna* hybrids |
| Syno cat | *Synodontis* sp |
| Cory cats | *Corydoras* sp |

### IN A 10-GALLON TANK:

2 pairs of fancy guppies (full grown)
2 pairs of platies
1 pair of swordtails
3 cory cats

### IN A 20-GALLON (LONG) TANK:

2 pairs of fancy guppies (full grown)
1 trio of swordtails (1 male, 2 females full grown)
2 pairs of platies (full grown)
1 pair of black mollies (full grown)
1 syno cat
3 cory cats
or
2 pairs of swordtails (full grown)
2 pairs of platies (full grown)
1 pair of sailfin mollies (full grown)
2 syno cats
3 cory cats

### IN A 55-GALLON TANK:

3 pairs of fancy guppies (full grown)
2 pairs of swordtails (full grown)
3 pairs of platies (full grown)
1 pair of black mollies (full grown)
1 pair of sailfin mollies (full grown)
3 cory cats
1 "pleco" cat

Any variation on the above will work. You can temporarily increase the number of fishes in each size tank if you buy smaller platies, swordtails, and mollies. Remember, however, that sailfins raised in your tank will not grow the large dorsal fin.

**The Plants** Among rooted plants, "Corkscrew val" *(Vallisneria)* and *Sagittaria* are most at home in the medium-hard, alkaline water preferred by live-bearers. Plant these species individually and carefully, either in gravel or in the planting mix recommended in Chapter 4. Be certain that the crown of each plant (where new leaves emerge) is even with the top level of gravel in the tank; planting it higher will leave roots exposed, and planting it lower will cause rot. Provide plenty of light for this tank, and these plants will create an attractive screen wherever you place them.

You can create a handsomely diversified aquascape in a well-lighted live-bearer tank by assembling groups of different sizes of variously colored and textured bunch plants including *Lobelia, Rotala, Ludwigia,* and *Alternanthera.*

As a treat for your fishes, you add duckweed or any of several lacy floating plants; your larger fishes will enjoy (and benefit from) these fresh greens in their diet.

**Potential Problems** The poeciliids listed are hardy enough to tolerate the high levels of ammonia and nitrite they will encounter during the tank's break-in period (Chapter 8). Several *Corydoras* species, on the other hand, are quite sensitive to nitrite, and should not be added until after the tank's biological filter has equilibrated.

Remember that the natural processes of biological filtration and the accumulation of organic wastes in the water will make your tank more acid over time. Check pH to make certain that your regular water changes and replacement of GAC counteract this tendency. If they do not, use the appropriate pH adjusting and buffering compounds (Chapters 2, 3, and 8).

**Variations** Because poeciliids are such hardy and adaptable fishes, they do not absolutely require the hard, alkaline conditions recommended for them. With the possible exception of black and sailfin mollies, they generally do well in neutral, medium-hard water. For that reason, you can mix them with a variety of egg-laying species—from angelfish to tetras—that tolerate neutral water. You could also mix in one or two pairs of rainbowfish, or a pair of the smaller African cichlids, such as *Julidochromis.*

Alternatively, you can take the water preferences of your poeciliids in the other direction; raise the salt content and pH and mix them with truly brackish-water species such as monos or scats *(Monodactlyus argenteus* and *Scatophagus argus).*

# 3

# A STUDY IN BLACK AND WHITE

The idea here is to produce a striking combination of black and white fish that—displayed in a black-trimmed tank on a modern piece of black-lacquered furniture, would fit into the most contemporary decorating scheme. The fishes are chosen for hardiness, striking markings in black, white, or black and white, and for their distinctly different body shapes and styles of movement.

To carry this theme to its extreme, forgo plants and driftwood, and decorate the tank exclusively with black, white, or black-and-white rocks and gravel.

## The Fishes

| | |
|---|---|
| Kissing gourami | *Helostoma temmincki* |
| Black veil angel | *Pterophyllum scalare* |
| Blushing angel | *Pterophyllum scalare* |
| Black neon tetra | *Hyphessobrycon herbertaxelrodi* |
| Black ghost knifefish | *Apteronotus albifrons* |
| | *Panaque suttoni* |
| Albino cory | *Corydoras aeneus* "albino" |

## IN A 10-GALLON TANK:

1 pair small (2–3-inch) kissing gouramies
1 pair small black veil angels
2 albino corys

## IN A 20-GALLON (LONG) TANK:

1 pair kissing gouramies (medium)
1 pair black veil angels (small)
1 pair blushing angels (small)
1 *Panaque suttoni*

## IN A 55-GALLON TANK:

1 pair kissing gouramies (large)
1 pair black veil angels (medium-large)
1 pair blushing angels (medium-large)
1 black ghost knifefish (5–6 inches)
6–8 black neon tetras
1 *Panaque suttoni*
3 albino corys

**The Plants**  See suggestions under A Blackwater Spectacle, page 179, or omit altogether.

**Potential Problems**  When selecting your decorations, avoid crushed-glass gravel and small, sharp rocks; catfish and black ghosts can injure themselves on those sharp edges.

If you want to go all-out on this theme, use predominantly black (rather than white) rocks and gravel. Even if you don't light your tank brightly, you'll get some algal growth sooner or later. Algae looks shabby on white objects, and regular maintenance will be necessary to keep light-colored accents looking clean and white. A few white "boulders" here and there—or some black marble veined in white—won't be too much trouble, but white gravel will quickly try your patience. Additionally, most fishes look better displayed against a dark bottom.

**Variations**  I chose a black-and-white scheme for this tank because achromatic decorating schemes (in black, white, and gray) are modern urban classics. I also restricted the fish list to those species that are exclusively black and/or white. If you're willing to stretch the boundaries a bit (as do many Italian designers), you can add such fishes as red-tailed black sharks, marbled hatchetfish, or pencilfish, which extend the color range to red and silver.

For reasons I don't totally understand, breeders are constantly working to produce "albino" or "gold" strains of tropical fish. With few exceptions, I prefer the original species—with all their natural colors—to these varieties. I don't see the point, for example, in creating an albino version of a black shark—other than to prove it can be done. One reason for including this tank type was to provide a use for such varieties! Keep your eyes open for any that appeal to you; more are appearing all the time.

Finally, by leafing through fish atlases, and by shopping around in pet shops for various kinds of quartz rocks and colored gravel, you can come up with other color schemes. Among freshwater fishes, pink, red, orange, and cyan are colors that are easy to come by. In marine species, you'll easily find blue, violet, and yellow, in addition to black and white.

# 4

# THE AFRICAN EXPERIENCE

If you're after an action-packed aquarium filled with fishes that are relatively easy to care for, unusual, colorful, and interesting, consider a tank of African cichlids. Be forewarned, however, that this tank is not for the weak of heart. These fishes never sit still, and rarely drift around calmly; they are always dashing around, often chasing each other, and sometimes fighting. But their flashing colors, their ability to change color as you watch, and their constant activity make them irresistible pets.

**The Fishes**  Most African cichlids have no useful common names. Varieties derived by selective breeding from wild animals are often given such names as "electric blue" or "peacock," but are still referred to by their Latin monikers.

|  |  |
|---|---|
|  | *Haplochromis* "electric blue" |
|  | *Pseudotropheus zebra* |
|  | or |
|  | *P. elongatus* |
|  | *Melanochromis auratus* |
|  | *Labeotropheus fuelleborni* |
|  | *Tropheus moorii* |
|  | *Lamprologus brichardi* |
| Malawi syno cat | *Synodontis nyassae* |
| Plecostomus | *Plecostomus* spp |

## IN A 10-GALLON TANK:

Place no more than one trio of small adult Africans (such as *Julidochromis*), or a group of appropriately sized juvenile individuals of the larger species in a tank this small. Provide plenty of hiding places in a rockpile near the back of the tank.

## IN A 20-GALLON (LONG) TANK:

Try ten assorted three-inch Africans and one each of the suggested catfish; see Potential Problems.

## IN A 55-GALLON TANK:

You can mix and match up to twenty 3-inch Africans, or fifteen 5-inch specimens along with one or two of the suggested catfish in a fifty-five gallon tank; see Potential Problems.

**The Plants**  Only firmly rooted, thick-leaved plants that enjoy hard, alkaline water will survive in this tank. This is one place where I would recommend including some nonaquatic plants with tough leaves and stems that you can buy with established roots.

| Corkscrew val | *Vallisneria* |
|---|---|
|  | *Sagittaria* |
| Prayer plants | *Maranta* sp |
|  | *Calathea* sp |
| Chinese evergreens | *Aglaonema* sp |

**Potential Problems**  Recommended stocking densities for these fishes are higher than for other cichlids, because Africans tend to get along better in groups. If just a few of these aggressive fishes are kept together, one unfortunate individual often ends up at the bottom of the pecking order, is perpetually attacked, and soon succumbs to stress-related disease. High-density stocking tends to dilute the aggression meted out by the leader of the pack by providing more targets and constant distraction.

Sometimes, though, this strategy doesn't work; if the personality and size mix isn't quite right, one fish may end up looking like it's been through a meat grinder. This can either happen within a day or so of stocking the tank or it can happen days or weeks later. (Usually while you're away for a weekend.) Naturally, given Murphy's First Law of Fish Behavior, it is invariably the most attractive and expensive fish that gets picked on. So inspect each individual regularly and be on the lookout for such signs of fighting as frayed fins, missing scales, and unusually shy or reclusive behavior. If the situation doesn't improve, that fish should be moved to a different tank or it will eventually weaken and die.

Note that the *Synodontis* species listed above is native to Lake Malawi (which was called Lake Nyasa when Malawi was known as Nyasaland), and is therefore at home in hard, alkaline water. Select a large individual, and watch carefully that it doesn't end up becoming cichlid chow. The armored *Plecostomus* species, though used to different water conditions, usually adapt well; get one large enough to hold its own against the aggressive cichlids.

Because many popular African cichlid species scrape algae off rock surfaces in nature, they will shred delicate plants. These fishes are also self-trained (and strong-willed) decorators who constantly rearrange any gravel you place in their tanks. My solution is to decorate African cichlid tanks with a layer of silver-dollar-sized rocks over the undergravel filter, and piles of fist-sized and larger rocks on top of that.

# 5

## A BLACKWATER SPECTACLE

This type of tank, when well-designed and well-managed, is the epitome of the freshwater community aquarium. By carefully selecting fishes, you can create a constantly shifting kaleidoscope of shapes and colors that fills the entire tank. Surface-dwelling species skitter about the top of the tank, midwater species cruise the central area, and bottom-dwellers meander over gravel and among the bases of plants.

### The Fishes

### FOR THE TOP OF THE TANK:

| | |
|---|---|
| Marbled hatchetfish | *Carnegiella strigata* |
| or | |
| Silver hatchetfish | *Gasteropelecus sternicla* |
| or | |
| Pearl danio | *Brachydanio albolineatus* |
| or | |
| Zebra danio | *Brachydanio rerio* |

### FOR MIDWATER:

| | |
|---|---|
| Cardinal tetra | *Cheirodon axelrodi* (a school of at least 6) |
| Rasboras | *Rasbora heteromorpha* (a school of at least 6) |
| Rosy or bleeding-heart tetras | *Hyphessobrycon* sp (a school of at least 6) |
| Angelfish (small) | *Pterophyllum scalare* |

| | |
|---|---|
| Kribensis | *Pelviachromis pulcher* |
| or | |
| Rams | *Microgeophagus ramirezi* (preferably as a trio; one male and two females) |

### FOR THE BOTTOM:

| | |
|---|---|
| "Pleco" | *Plecostomus* sp |
| Cory cat | *Corydoras* sp |
| Clown loach | *Botia macracantha* (at least 3) |
| Kuhli loach | *Acanthopthalmus kuhli* |

### IN A 10-GALLON TANK:

1 trio, your choice of surface-dwelling species above
6 cardinal tetras
6 rasboras
1 pair small rams or kribensis
1 small pleco
3 cory cats

### IN A 20-GALLON (LONG) TANK:

1 trio, your choice of hatchetfish
1 trio, your choice of *Brachydanio* species
6 cardinal tetras
6 rosy or bleeding-heart tetras
1 trio (small) angelfish
1 trio rams or kribensis
3 cory cats
1 pleco

### IN A 55-GALLON TANK:

6 individuals, your choice of hatchetfish
6 individuals, your choice of *Brachydanio* species
1 dozen cardinal tetras (large)
1 dozen rasboras (large)
6 rosy or bleeding-heart tetras
2 pairs of small angelfish of different varieties, or 4 individuals of the same type
1 trio rams
1 trio kribensis
4 small clown loaches
3 cory cats
3 kuhli loaches
2 plecos

**The Plants** In addition to a diverse selection of fishes, tanks with relatively soft, slightly acid water and good light allow you to assemble a magnificent aquascape. Most of the rooted plants listed below (with the exception of certain Amazon swordplants) are not carried by most pet shops and are best ordered by mail. The bunch plants are common.

Leave yourself time to landscape and plant this tank before buying fishes. Provide as much three-dimensional variety in the setting as you can, and be sure to work in clumps of dense vegetation, small "caves," and a variety of nooks and crannies for fishes to swim through and hide in.

| | |
|---|---|
| Java moss | *Vesicularia dubyana* |
| Underwater ferns | *Ceratopteris* |
| Java fern | *Microsorium (Polypodium) pteropus* |
| | *Cryptocoryne* |
| "Amazon sword-plants" | *Echinodorus* species: |
| Broadleaf sword | *E. bleheri* |

| | |
|---|---|
| Micro sword | *E. tenellus* |
| | *E. maior* |
| | *E. osiris* |
| Assorted bunch plants | *Cabomba* |
| | *Lobelia* |
| | *Rotala* |
| | *Ludwigia* |
| | *Alternanthera* |

**Potential Problems**   Note that the suggested mix specifies *large* cardinals and *small* angelfish. If the angels are too large and the tetras too small, I take no responsibility for the consequences. Some pet shops stock only tiny (read: bite-sized) cardinals; when large ones are available, they are often pricey. If you can't get (or prefer not to spend the money on)

larger cardinals, buy the tetras early on and don't add angels until the cardinals have grown larger. Then buy the smallest angels you can find, and watch them carefully as they grow.

**Variations**   This mix of fishes and plants offers what I consider to be the best of both South American and Asian species. If you find yourself becoming a geographical purist, consider assembling a tank stocked entirely with fishes and plants from either the Amazon river system or the Far East. Both faunas, separately and together, offer enough species to make dozens of attractive variations on this theme.

If you exercise extreme artistic restraint, you'll find few displays more peaceful, elegant,

and striking than a well-planted fifty-five-gallon tank stocked with just five dozen full-grown cardinal tetras and a trio of *Corydoras*.

Once you've become adept at maintaining water quality, you might want to gamble on the magnificent discus *Symphysodon aequifasciatus*. Discus are notoriously difficult to care for, both because they are fussy about water quality and because they are shy enough to be bullied or injured, even by peaceful fishes. Some species of otherwise peaceful *Plecostomus*, for example, seem to be attracted to the heavy mucous coat of discus, and sometimes attach themselves to discus, damaging the cichlids' delicate body coverings. I'd advise mixing discus only with cardinals or other small, inoffensive tetras, and a few *Corydoras*.

# 6

## THE RAMBO TANK

For some hobbyists, peaceful tanks are pretty, but ultimately boring. Some of these folks also like pit bulls and Dobermans. Others, I suppose, can't stomach wimpy pets. Luckily, there are several attractive and hardy large cichlids that —if they had arms that could hold assault rifles—could easily take over the world. That they haven't taken over the rivers and lakes they inhabit is a tribute to the efficiency of predators and other natural population controls.

These fishes are *tough*! While personable, even affectionate, with their owners, they are perpetually ready to reduce tankmates—including others of their kind—to fishburgers. They are equally vicious with plants, and are never happy with any aquascaping you attempt. Yet they come closer to aquatic "dogs" or "cats" than any other fishes, and their complex spawning behaviors are fascinating to watch.

### The Fishes

| | |
|---|---|
| Jewel cichlid | *Hemichromis bimaculatus* |
| Oscars | *Astronotus ocellatus* |
| Firemouth cichlid | *Cichlasoma meeki* |

### IN A 10-GALLON TANK:

In this small tank, you can keep two or three small individuals of any of these fishes, along with two cory catfish.

### IN A 20-GALLON (LONG) TANK:

This size tank will hold 6–8 young individuals and a couple of catfish; watch out for psychological and physical crowding as they grow.

### IN A 55-GALLON TANK:

This size tank can hold either

> 1 dozen medium-sized cichlids, along with 3 or 4 small armored catfish

or

> a single mated pair of full-grown cichlids in breeding condition.

**The Plants**  Use the same plants as for the African Experience tank. Don't expect the plants to last once these fishes grow beyond four or five inches however, as these fishes have their own ideas about tank decorating. Some have been known to shred even plastic plants.

**Potential Problems**  Cichlids can change overnight from model citizens to vicious gangsters, using any means necessary to intimidate their tankmates. This can happen either among young individuals growing up together, or between long-established breeding pairs. Sometimes, combat rituals that are part of normal cichlid behavior are hard to tell from real violence. I recall an hour one afternoon spent with two colleagues trying to decide whether two adult cichlids were engaging in a normal mating ritual or trying to kill each other. (As it turned out, this particular pair was "courting.") Keep an eye on these fishes for signs of madness and mayhem.

Unlike many live-bearers, whose growth can be permanently stunted in small tanks, large cichlids just keep growing. For that reason, you must keep up with water changes and monitor water quality regularly, to make certain your pets do not exceed the tank's carrying capacity.

Because large cichlids can live for several years, it is particularly important to provide them with a balanced diet and good water conditions. One of the most common problems from improper diet is lateral-line disease. This syndrome, described in more detail in Chapter 9, begins as a subtle enlargement of lateral-line pores in the head region. As it progresses, the pores enlarge and deepen, and the skin around them loses color and begins to look ugly. The exact cause of the problem is not clear, but it has been linked both to poor water quality and to a diet lacking in vitamins. In cichlids, at least, it can be avoided by proper diet and attention to water quality.

## FOUR SALTWATER TANKS:
### Spectacle and Cachet

Assuming that you are new to the keeping of marine fishes, I have avoided recommendations for saltwater tanks smaller than twenty gallons. Although such tanks are not impossible for experts, their size makes them difficult to manage well. You will have better success as a beginner with twenty-gallon or larger tanks.

With few exceptions, buy saltwater fish as small as you can find them in good condition. When young, these fishes are less feisty and less likely to devour one another. Additionally, several species, including blue tangs, adjust better to captivity when small than as adults. And, of course, the smaller your fishes are, the more of them you can keep in a single tank. The only real exceptions to this rule are some of the larger Pacific angelfish prized by experienced hobbyists. These animals do not reliably change from juvenile to adult coloration in small home aquaria, so those who want adult fishes usually buy them as mature specimens. (It remains true, however, that smaller specimens adapt better to aquarium life.)

# 7

## A COMMUNITY OF COLOR AND NOVELTY FOR BEGINNERS

Ideally, this tank should be as close as possible to the community tanks described for freshwater: a mixed group of interesting and colorful fishes that get along with one another.

Unfortunately, marine "community" tanks are rarely as peaceful as their freshwater counterparts. Why? There aren't many reef fishes that are small enough, colorful enough, and hardy enough to keep in home aquaria that are also as mild-mannered as guppies and tetras. As a rule, even the most peaceful fishes listed will either attack other members of their own species or band together and attack other fishes. Most—including the diminutive damselfish—are as feisty and bad-mannered as large cichlids. For that reason, mix them with caution, and keep on the lookout for serious fighting.

This tank contains no invertebrates for two reasons. First, treatment of fish diseases is simpler in a tank that contains only fishes (Chapters 6 and 9). Second, eliminating anemones and their kin helps keep costs under control by allowing the use of a single-bulb reflector instead of the four-bulb fluorescent or metal-halide fixture needed to maintain symbiotic algae in these animals.

### The Fishes

| | |
|---|---|
| Blue devil | *Glyphidodontops cyaneus* |
| Three-striped damsel | *Dascyllus aruanus* |
| Three-spot damsel | *Dascyllus trimaculatus* |
| Common clownfish | *Amphiprion ocellaris* |
| Royal gramma | *Gramma loreto* |
| Bicolor pygmy angel | *Centropyge bicolor* |
| Flame angel | *C. loriculus* |
| Koran angel | *Pomacanthus semicircularis* |

### IN A 20-GALLON (LONG) TANK:

If you're starting out with this as your first saltwater tank, stick with the hardy, active, and colorful damselfish (including clownfish) listed above. In a tank this size, you can keep five small clownfish, or roughly the same number of assorted damsels.

Once you've gained some experience, you can substitute one of the *Centropyge* angels and a blenny or two for a couple of damsels in this formula.

Alternatively, you can mix three or four clownfish with a single royal gramma.

See Variations for additional options.

### IN A 55-GALLON TANK:

Most aquarists willing to set up a fifty-five gallon tank (myself included) want to fill it with large, exotic specimens, rather than with smaller, more common fishes such as those listed above. All I can say (and I say this from experience) is that if you're not sure you are ready for a major investment of time and energy, give an "easy" tank a try; stock your first fifty-five with one of each of the fishes listed above. The selection may not be as exotic as you might ultimately want, but if you design and set up this aquarium properly, you may be able to get it going without losing a single fish.

Because damselfish are both aggressive and territorial, provide enough three-dimensional coral and rock structures for each fish to stake out its own individual turf. Two or three isolated coral heads scattered through the tank won't do that, and your fishes will battle each other constantly. To minimize lopsided territorial disputes, it's also a good idea either to introduce all your damsels at the same time, or to completely rearrange the tank when adding new individuals.

**Variations**  Once you've had enough experience with marine fishes to feel comfortable in treating diseases, and if you are willing to invest in a hospital/quarantine tank, add an anemone to keep your clownfish company. You could keep a single medium-sized anemone with a pair of small clownfish and a couple of small damsels in a twenty-gallon tank. You can also substitute an anemone for a medium-sized fish in a larger tank. Remember, though, that anemones require intense light for their symbiotic algae, and will be killed by most fish medications.

For larger tanks (fifty-five gallons and up), and after you've had some experience, you can consider mixing and matching the above individuals with some of the following:

Pantherfish: *Cromileptes altivelis,* or other grouper
Red-tailed blenny: *Ecsenius frontalis,* or similar species
Marine betta: *Calloplesiops altivelus*
Lionfish: *Pterois volitans* or similar species

Note that the latter two species are slow-moving and can be slow to feed in captivity. If you mix these animals with more active tankmates, therefore, make certain that they receive ample food. Note that lionfish are hard to mix successfully with damselfish; some damsels will nip the lionfish's long, trailing fins, and large lionfish may make a meal of small damsels.

You can also try adding either a Hepatus tang: *Paracanthurus hepatus,* or blue tang: *Acanthurus coeruleus,* as long as you provide plenty of fresh algae or romaine lettuce for these herbivores to eat.

Additionally, if most of your fishes are large (over three inches), or fast and agile (like tangs), you might try adding a *small* individual of one of the less aggressive triggerfish, such as one of the *Rhinecanthus* species. Watch carefully, however, as the little devils grow.

**Potential Problems**  Remember that no matter how "empty" your tank may seem to you, your fishes are still obliged to live in much closer proximity to one another than they would ever choose on the reef. Many reef fishes are territorial, and even though their territories may be closely spaced on the reef, there are plenty of caves to duck into and coral heads to hide behind if squabbling gets too intense. The degree that you can crowd marine fishes successfully in your tank depends both on the size of the fishes and on the number of hiding places you provide for them. As a rule, the more complex the rock-and-coral structure of your tank, the more likely your pets are to coexist successfully.

Remember, too, that pantherfish and lionfish are predators that will hunt down and swallow nearly any fishes they can get into their deceptively large mouths. You must therefore pay close attention to the relative sizes of individuals in your tank, lest a community tank turn into a expensive demonstration of a food chain. Pantherfish and lionfish (other than the dwarf species) grow rapidly when well-kept; if they get large enough to start eyeing their tankmates, you must move either potential predators or prey to another tank.

# 8

# THE "RAMBO" TANK, SALTWATER VERSION

The inhabitants of this marine Rambo tank co-exist in the same sort of uneasy truce as the African cichlids described previously. All these species are aggressive, but all are relatively easy to maintain. Once these animals are large, they will make short work of feeder goldfish.

## The Fishes

| | |
|---|---|
| Picasso triggerfish | *Rhinecanthus aculeatus* |
| Black triggerfish | *Odonus niger* |
| Undulated triggerfish | *Balistapus undulatus* |
| Moray eel | *Echidna* or *Lycodontis* |

## IN A 10-GALLON TANK:

You can try keeping a single, small two- to three-inch specimen of any of the above triggerfish species in a ten-gallon tank, but don't add any more. Even if the tank could hold them physically, they'd probably tear each other apart as soon as they're acclimated.

## IN A 20-GALLON (LONG) TANK:

In this tank, you can experiment with a single, small moray and a small triggerfish; just be certain that the trigger is too large for the moray to swallow. Although the trigger's locking spine mechanism would probably make it about as easy to swallow as a half-open umbrella, any attempt by the eel to do so would probably damage both fishes.

## IN A 55-GALLON TANK:

In a fifty-five-gallon tank you can play more, and might succeed with two large triggers or a trigger and a good-sized moray eel. (In either case, don't plan on putting your hand in the tank!) Unfortunately, triggers don't pair off in captivity the way large cichlids do, so two young adults might or might not get along with one another. Still, a tank with a single six-inch trigger or a large, brightly spotted moray should provide enough dazzle and excitement for anyone's taste.

**Potential Problems** The only difference between these fishes and large, aggressive cichlids is that while cichlid teeth are relatively innocuous, these guys can take serious chunks of flesh out of one another (and your hand, if you're not careful). On the reef, many of these fishes spend most of their time hunting down and devouring shrimp, crabs, worms, and other invertebrates, so do not put invertebrates into this tank unless you intend them to serve as food.

**Variations** There are several other triggerfish that make good pets; several species in the genus *Rhinecanthus* are quite attractive, and share the Picasso trigger's relatively mild disposition. If you choose triggers of this milder variety, if they are small enough, and if your tank is sufficiently large, you could try adding a medium-sized tang or two, as long as you're willing to provide the necessary vegetable food.

# 9

## THE STAR TANK

This "star" tank houses just one or two magnificent specimens, whose size, disposition, or feeding habits exclude it from polite company. Because the tank is conceived without small fishes and with bare, rather than live, rocks it can hold one or two larger animals more successfully than either community or living-reef tanks.

### The Fishes

Lionfish          *Pterois volitans*
Clown triggerfish *Balistoides conspicillum*
Pantherfish       *Cromileptes altivelis,* or
                  other grouper

### IN A 20-GALLON (LONG) TANK:

In a tank this size, you might try three small lionfish (or dwarf lionfish), or a small clown trigger and small pantherfish or other grouper. In the latter case, leave extra space (and plan to trade up in tank size or trade in your fish eventually) because groupers grow with surprising speed.

### IN A 55-GALLON TANK:

In this, a more impressive configuration, you could display either a single six-to-eight-inch specimen (such as a clown trigger) or two or three good-sized lionfish. If you've never seen a six-inch clown trigger, believe me that it is a sight to behold. The same is true of one, two, or three lionfish drifting slowly and gracefully through a tank of fifty-five gallons or more.

**Potential Problems** All these fish grow rapidly if cared for properly after they are acclimated. Monitor ammonia, nitrite, and nitrate levels in your tank to make certain that the growing animals don't outstrip the capacity of your biological filter. One six-inch triggerfish, for example, contains a lot more body tissue—and puts out a lot more waste—than six 1-inch specimens of the same species.

# 10

## THE LIVING-REEF TANK
### A Piece of the Pacific or Caribbean

The living-reef tank is the sine qua non of marine fishkeeping; the goal to which most marine hobbyists aspire. When living reefs work, they are a source of endless fascination; live rocks crawl with invertebrates and sprout new and unexpected forms of algae. Tiny coral shrimp crawl in and out of crevices, and fishes inspect the reef surface, nibbling here and there as they do in nature.

Full-fledged living reefs contain not only fishes but scores of invertebrates, large and small. That's a lot of living tissue. For that reason, living-reef tanks require a great deal of oxygen to supply their needs and extensive biological-filter activity to process their wastes. I therefore don't recommend well-stocked living reefs for tanks smaller than thirty gallons. Even in fifty-five gallon tanks, undergravel filters alone are not sufficient; good-sized, external wet/dry filters are necessary for best water-quality control.

**The Fishes** Because invertebrates are co-stars in living reef tanks, care must be taken in selecting fishes that will live with (rather than dine on) shrimps, small crabs, and corals. The following species provide a good working list of compatible animals. Stock your tank according to your preference among these species, but only load the tank with half as many fish-inches as you would in a fish-only aquarium.

| | |
|---|---|
| Pantherfish | *Cromileptes altivelis* |
| Lionfish | *Pterois volitans* |
| Red-tailed blenny | *Ecsenius frontalis* |
| Hepatus tang | *Paracanthurus hepatus* |
| Blue tang | *Acanthurus coeruleus* |
| Powder-blue tang | *Acanthurus leucosternon* |
| Mandarinfish | *Synchiropus splendidus* |
| Marine betta | *Calloplesiops altivelus* |

**The Invertebrates** Invertebrates selected for living-reef tanks include solitary and colonial sea anemones of several types, a handful of soft corals, and a variety of coral shrimp and crabs. In addition to these organisms, your living reef will also be populated by several types of "feather duster" worms and other odd creatures that spend their lives burrowing through the limestone rock that forms the backbone of the reef.

The following short list includes several of the best invertebrates for home culture. I'd advise you to avoid any animals not specifically listed here—at least at first. Many visually attractive invertebrates are not really good candidates for reef tanks because they die fairly quickly in captivity. And if something like a sponge decides to call it quits while you're away for a long weekend, you can kiss the rest of your reef good-bye on your return.

Remember that corals and sea anemones require intense light for their symbiotic algae, so follow the lighting recommendations in Chapters 3 and 6. The absolute minimum lighting requirement for a successful reef tank is four fluorescent tubes. (Many hobbyists use six tubes in a custom, fan-cooled fixture.)

small gorgonian (horny, not stony) corals
pipe-organ corals (*Tubastrea* spp)
"sunflower corals"
"Bubble corals" (*Plerogyra* spp)
Mushroom corals (*Fungia* spp)
assorted solitary and colonial sea anemones
feather-duster worms (purchased as inhabitants of live rocks)
coral shrimps
small coral crabs (not large crabs, including hermit crabs)

**Stocking the Tank** Stocking a reef tank is a matter of more than a little controversy; few marine aquarists agree on a single "correct" procedure, and everyone has had success with at least one technique that has spelled disaster for others. The only thing for certain is that if you load up a new tank with fishes and invertebrates, most of them are likely to die. My humble recommendations for stocking are as follows:

Into a tank furnished with a reasonable number of "seeded live rocks" (see Chapter 6), place several hardy fishes such as mollies adapted to full-strength seawater, damselfish, or the like. These fish will not be permanent inhabitants of the reef, but are used to establish the biological filter. In the meantime, purchase the hardiest fishes you will want for your tank, and begin their quarantine and prophylactic treatment in a separate tank (Chapter 9).

Once the biological filter in the reef tank has cycled and is carrying its load smoothly (Chapter 8) remove the "break-in" fish, and finish aquascaping with "inhabited" live rocks. Monitor water conditions carefully for ten days to two weeks. If there is no sign of either excess ammonia or nitrite, add the fish from the quarantine tank and monitor water conditions again.

Once things have settled down, both ammonia and nitrites should be below measurable levels. If they do not fall to near zero, the tank is probably overstocked; remove some fishes or invertebrates and watch water conditions again for a week to ten days, to make certain that the situation has been remedied. At this point, you can add anemones and soft corals, and hope for the best.

**Potential Problems** The delicate constitutions of many desirable invertebrates require top-notch water-quality control. Con-stant water testing, regular partial water changes, and careful changing of the mechanical filter medium are absolutely essential. A foam fractionator (aka "protein skimmer") is also strongly recommended, as many invertebrates secrete large amounts of mucus that can foul the water if not removed by such a device.

A minimum three-week quarantine period is absolutely essential, both for fishes and for new invertebrates, because if you introduce fish diseases into a reef tank, you're in for serious trouble. You must either remove all fishes to a treatment tank (which is no easy feat, with all the hiding places they'll have among the live rocks and invertebrates) or remove all invertebrates to a drug-free holding tank (essentially destroying your reef system).

I therefore *strongly* recommend treating all new fishes as though they were infected, and proceeding with a prophylactic course of medication against the most common parasites (See Chapter 9). I also recommend quarantining invertebrates if they have been freshly imported or held in dealer's tanks along with fishes. Under such circumstances, they might conceivably harbor free-swimming forms of fish parasites.

# CHAPTER 8

# GETTING YOUR HANDS WET

By now, you've learned almost as much about fishkeeping as you can without getting wet, so it's time to start assembling your tank. You'll discover that as you gather materials and choose animals, you gain experience every time you lift a finger. Like a child who has watched parents walk but only now prepares to stand on two legs, every step is new, and every step is an opportunity to learn. And there is still much to learn—from pricing equipment, to evaluating fishes in dealer's tanks, to helping your pets settle into their new home.

To ease your transition from gathering information to making specific decisions, this chapter provides step-by-step information on assembling a tank that works. If I make a point repeatedly, it's not because I enjoy being either pedantic or self-righteous, but because I'm trying to protect you from mistakes *I've* made —often many times. If I seem insistent about quarantine procedures for marine tanks, for example, or about overcrowding, or about mixing incompatible animals, it's because if I had only listened to advice offered to me when I was starting out, I could've spared myself a lot of trouble, expense, and dead fishes.

## BECOME AN EDUCATED CONSUMER

Marketing strategists for some aquarium-equipment firms are as clever (and occasionally as unscrupulous) as those who advertise children's toys. It is true that a lot of research has gone into today's aquarium products, many of which are far more efficient and reliable than those of even a decade ago. It is also true that the marketing hype used to sell aquarium supplies has increased exponentially, and often pressures novices into investing in sophisticated (but frivolous) paraphernalia at the expense of more mundane (but more useful) equipment.

Dedicated aquarists approach their hobby logically and scientifically, searching through new products for technological advances that really make a difference in keeping fishes alive and well. Unfortunately, this worthwhile intention makes some hobbyists susceptible to impressive-sounding, but meaningless, technobabble, which comes in both high-tech and low-tech forms.

One of my favorite examples of low-tech technobabble was part of the marketing strategy for one aquatic-plant fertilizer a few years ago. In addition to providing essential nutrients, the package proclaimed, this product added "vital electrolytes" (written in italicized, "electric" letters) to your tank water. Well, anyone who remembers just a little high school chemistry may recall that an electrolyte is simply any substance that carries electricity when dissolved in water. Common table salt is an electrolyte. So are most of the nitrogen, phosphorus, and potassium salts that provide nutrients in fertilizer. So this particular claim—while it was by no means false—was spurious; every soluble fertilizer in the world must contain electrolytes, or it wouldn't dissolve!

Similarly, emphasizing the undisputed fact that "plants require carbon dioxide to survive" does *not* mean that to grow healthy aquatic plants you must invest several hundred dollars in devices that pump extra $CO_2$ into the water. Such devices have applications in specific cases, but most planted aquaria—freshwater and marine—do fine without them.

High-tech technobabble can be sufficiently

misleading that it may border on fraud in some cases. Claiming that products are "genetically engineered" in these days of biotechnology leads people to believe that those products are the result of the latest gene-splicing or transfer techniques. So far, however, the term usually just means that the organisms have been selectively bred to enhance certain qualities.

## Mainstream Products in the Aquarium

Whenever you're in the market for a device to do something around your aquarium, broaden your search from pet shops to hardware and building-supply stores. Products designed and marketed for aquaria invariably cost more (sometimes a *lot* more) than similar items sold for general use.

Now, some specially designed aquarium products are, in fact, the best for use in tanks because they incorporate functionally important design features. But others are indistinguishable from less-expensive equivalents, and cost more just because of the way they are packaged and marketed.

Many aquarium chemicals, for example, are unconscionably overpriced. The last time I picked up a container of sodium bicarbonate in a pet store, it was *four times* the supermarket price of common baking soda, which is exactly the same stuff. Sphagnum peat moss packaged for aquarium use can be more then ten times as expensive as the moss you buy by the cubic foot at garden centers.

Aquarium light fixtures are another case in point. Top-of-the-line light fixtures manufac-tured specifically for aquarium use water-resistant bulb fittings, encase metal parts in plastic to avoid electric shocks, and are designed to complement tanks aesthetically. The extra cost of these amenities is worthwhile in many circumstances. If you have small children running around, for example, any electrical aquarium appliance that grounds and water-proofs its parts will earn its keep by preventing wear and tear on itself and on your kids. If, on the other hand, you plan to make a sleek and modern aquarium the centerpiece of your Eurostyle living room, you may opt for the top-quality fixture for aesthetic reasons.

Getting down to dollars and cents on this particular item, though, may surprise you. The four-foot, four-bulb fluorescent fixture that I recommend for freshwater plants, corals, and sea anemones is not yet a standard item in the aquarium industry, and is therefore priced as a special-order item. Aquarium fixtures of this size were listed recently at prices ranging from $179 (the least expensive) to as much as $279 (plus shipping and handling) for what appears to be the top of the line.

But at typical building suppliers, grounded, plastic-bodied, two-bulb, four-foot "shop light" fixtures sell for $11.99 each. You can place two of these side by side above your tanks to achieve the same light intensity for less than *one tenth* the price of the luxury aquarium fixture! Some building-supply houses also stock four-bulb, four-foot fixtures with protective translucent covers for $87.50—less than half the price of even the least expensive aquarium product. Because both these fixtures are designed to hang, rather than to sit atop tanks, they require a little ingenuity for use over your aquarium, but either could suit your needs.

I recently shared the surprise and dismay of one aquarium-magazine columnist who discovered that a national group of pet-shop owners had voted a glitzy gizmo called the Bubble Gum Machine Aquarium as the "Best Aquarium Product of 1988." Not an improved filtration system that keeps animals healthier longer. Not a better lighting system that keeps plants healthy. Not even new aquarium medications that actually cure sick fishes. But an ersatz gumball vending machine that confines hapless fishes in a plastic globe holding no more than a gallon or two of water.

That retailers' vote—grounded in the reality of relative sales of gumball aquaria and more practical equipment—goes a long way to explain why so many people try to keep fishes, fail, and give up.

Is the gumball aquarium whimsical? Yes. Does it provide a practical environment for keeping fishes? No! It can house—though less than adequately—a single betta or goldfish, or a couple of guppies, but it is about as far away from a real aquarium as one can get.

So please, in the interests of your fishes and in your own interest as a potential aquarist, think of life from your fishes' point of view as you buy aquarium equipment.

## Networking for Fish

There are more ways to learn about fishkeeping today than ever before. Even if you're not interested in attending local aquarium-society meetings, you can still keep up on the latest in new products and fishes.

First, there are many specialty books that

cover particular aspects of fishkeeping or specific groups of fishes in far more detail than I could in a general introductory volume such as this. There are many books dedicated entirely to cichlids, for example, and an increasing number that deal exclusively with catfish. There are also several aquarium-fish atlases that parade hundreds of full-color photos past your eyes, though usually with a bit less cultural information per species than novices might want. These books are available at well-stocked pet stores and by mail order.

Second, there are three full-fledged aquarium magazines, several aquarist newsletters, and dozens of special fish-society publications. I recommend the best of these to both novices and advanced aquarists; they feature regular beginners' columns, advice on finicky fishes for the experts, and information about (and sources for) the latest in aquarium products.

To my eyes, the newest journal, *Aquarium Fish Magazine,* is the best in terms of writing style and factual content. But pick up a copy each of *Tropical Fish Hobbyist* and *Freshwater and Marine Aquarium,* and see which appeals to your own taste. (I subscribe to all three.) (If you can't find any of these at your local pet shops (they are not carried in general magazine stores, for some reason) addresses and subscription information, along with the names and addresses of several major national aquarium societies with newsletters, can be found in the appendix.)

Third—and most exciting—is the dedicated group of aquarists who make up a lively special interest group called FISHNET on the CompuServe Information Service. CompuServe is a nationwide computer telecommunications network open to anyone with a computer and a modem. You can "converse" with other members online, participate in conferences and classes, leave and respond to messages left on bulletin boards, and browse through an extensive library on every aspect of fishkeeping.

The FISHNET experts—many of whom write for *Aquarium Fish Magazine* and other publications—are knowledgeable and dedicated aquarists. They spend an extraordinary amount of time debating fine points of aquarium management with one another and dispensing sage advice to novices. The only compensation they receive is the sense of conviviality and the satisfaction of making life easier for fishes and fishkeepers across the nation. Several FISHNET regulars work for major public aquaria, some have operated retail aquarium stores for decades, and others are aquarium-industry professionals. Together, they offer an unparalleled and invaluable mix of humor, consolation, and helpful hints. (Several parts of this book, in fact, have been shaped by discussions with FISHNET members.) I recommend FISHNET to anyone with access to a computer; subscription information is listed in the appendix.

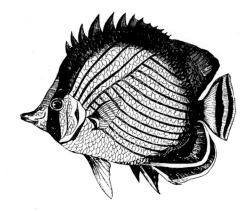

## CHOOSING YOUR FISH SHOP

Your road to fishkeeping success will be a lot smoother and more enjoyable if you can find a local pet shop with the right combination of information, service, and reasonable prices. The good news is that while many fish stores don't meet this ideal description, many others do.

How do you find the right store for you? Spend some time visiting and evaluating pet shops in your area before you buy anything. Look over their tanks. Pay close attention to both the selection of animals and their general health. Examine their supply racks for a variety of equipment and foods from several manufacturers. Find out whether or not they stock live and frozen foods. Walk around with a notepad, marking down prices on items you will be buying often, such as activated carbon and other filter materials, fish foods, air stones, and so on. (Pet shops within a few miles of each other here in the Boston area have prices on equipment and supplies that vary as much as 50 percent!)

Finally, watch the sales help as they deal with other customers. Are they friendly or curt? Do they make people feel stupid or uncomfortable for asking questions, or do they offer polite and intelligent answers? Do they act like they care about their fishes and customers? Do you feel like you can trust them, or do they act like stereotypical used-car salesmen? This last set of observations is the most vital, for in the end the only product pet stores have to offer that you can't get elsewhere is knowledgeable, helpful, and friendly advice.

## RETAILERS VERSUS MAIL-ORDER HOUSES:
### Pros, Cons, and Con Games

If you have another hobby, such as photography, home computers, or stereo equipment, you know that there are two sorts of places you can buy the things you need. You can patronize shops whose personnel offer goods at full retail price but who also provide advice based on training and personal experience. Alternatively, you can order cameras and CD players from high-volume mail-order firms that offer rock-bottom prices and limited—though often courteous—product information, but no repair service or emergency help.

Precisely the same situation exists in the aquarium trade. Aquarium magazines are filled with advertisements from mail-order houses that offer their goods at prices close to whole-sale. That means you can mail-order certain items at anywhere between 20 and 50 percent less than their price in pet shops.

What do you do in this situation? To my way of thinking, pet shops that satisfy the criteria I gave earlier deserve our support; without them, beginners and those seeking to grow in the aquarium hobby would be in rough shape. As a group, we can benefit greatly from their personal brand of service and advice—advice that is not offered by mail-order firms.

Many conscientious shops, for example, don't stock everything on the market, but decide what to offer based on either positive or negative experience with the reliability and service records of different manufacturers. That informed, long-term judgment is hard to come by. Additionally, most of us prefer buying fishes we can pick out, pick up, and carry home ourselves, rather than ordering blind through the mail. For that kind of service, we should allow our retailers reasonable markups to cover overhead.

Some shops, however, don't offer the services they should. Certain large chains, for example, hire managers and salespeople who barely know how to net fish without hurting them, and who are unreliable sources of information. Some stores are only interested in selling you as much equipment, as many different kinds of food, and as many fishes as possible, with no concern for either the well-being of your pets or your success as an aquarist. And some stores charge intolerable markups on hard goods. Not surprisingly, these establishments often fear and resent the large discount houses, and refuse to stock aquarium magazines that carry mail-order ads. I refuse to patronize stores of this type; my VISA card works fine over the phone, thank you very much.

Choose a local pet dealer carefully, and patronize him or her regularly to build a good working relationship. That doesn't mean you can't order occasionally from the mail-order houses—we all do, now and then—but it does strike a balance between getting everything at the lowest price and making a connection with a knowledgeable professional who has a great deal to offer.

## STARTING RIGHT:
### The Shopping List

Often, a beginning hobbyist will walk into a pet store for the first time and buy a starter kit containing a ten-gallon or twenty-gallon aquarium with "everything you need" all packaged together and slightly discounted. Trundling home, he or she soon discovers a variety of additional items—some large, some small—that are also really necessary. A net, perhaps. Or a siphon tube. Several trips to the pet store later, they're finally set—until the first problem with their fishes, at which point they find themselves running back and forth for salt, medication, and heaven knows what else. To avoid this problem, here's a basic shopping list of what you'll need.

### First Trip to the Fish Store

**Tank** Buy only all-glass or acrylic tanks. Glass tanks are available with acrylic top and bottom bands in either black or imitation wood-grain finishes. Acrylic tanks may be all clear acrylic. Tank sizes and shapes are discussed on page 42.

**Tank Stand** For tanks larger than twenty gallons, either buy an aquarium stand in a pet store or be certain that the furniture you have in mind for a stand will, in fact, support the several hundred pounds of equipment, water, rocks, and gravel. Options for support furniture are discussed on page 65.

**Tank Cover** Tightly fitting tank covers are essential for all tanks, both to retard evaporation and to keep fishes from jumping out. Covers are available in two models for most tank sizes:

*A piece of Plexiglas that covers the entire tank, with cutouts at the corners for heater wires, air tubes, and the like.* These are great for fish rooms and other places where tank lights are hung above the tank. They are sturdy and durable, but have two drawbacks. First, cutting additional holes for filters must be done carefully with an appropriate drill and/or fine-toothed saw to avoid cracking the cover. Second, these covers make it difficult to get your hands (or nets) into the tank; you must remove light fixtures and lift off the entire cover.

*A multipiece cover that uses long strips of glass held in acrylic channels.* The cover is designed so that glass covers most of the tank, while the back two inches is covered by a flexible plastic strip. This strip is easily cut with a kitchen shears to admit any filters or tubes necessary. The sliding-glass parts of the cover allow easy access to either the front or the rear of the tank for feeding and tank maintenance.

**Light Fixture** Avoid incandescent fixtures. Two- or four-bulb, rapid-start fluorescent fixtures recommended for planted tanks; four bulbs minimum for marine tanks with corals or sea anemones; metal halide to be considered as an expensive alternative for living-reef tanks. Many styles and types available; see detailed discussions on lighting in Chapters 3 and 6.

**Heater** Many styles available; calculate the size you need from information in Chapter 3. Look for newer heaters that are completely submersible and calibrated in degrees. For large tanks (fifty-five gallons and over) in cool rooms, consider making up necessary wattage with two half-sized heaters instead of one.

**Mechanical/Chemical Filter** Many styles available; see detailed discussions of filtration in Chapters 2 and 3. Simple, air-driven internal-box filters are adequate for ten- to fifteen-gallon tanks. For tanks of twenty gallons and larger, choose an appropriate outside power filter of either hanging box or canister type. For maximum filtration efficiency and long-term cost-effectiveness, avoid filters that require expensive (and inefficient) prepackaged bags or cartridges of filter medium.

**Mechanical Filter Media** Spun polyester "filter floss" or "filter wool" is as efficient as any other mechanical medium, and more reasonably priced than most. Because you want to change this medium regularly as dirt accumulates, and because it is most reasonably priced in bulk, buy the largest bags you can find.

**Chemical Filter Media** "Research grade" granular activated carbon (GAC) is the most cost-effective. Buy in large sizes for substantial savings. Miscellaneous resins often sold mixed with GAC are expensive and of questionable value.

**Biological Filter** For freshwater tanks, buy an undergravel filter powered by airlift tubes at the corners. These come properly sized for virtually all standard tank configurations.

For lightly loaded marine tanks carrying only fishes, buy a standard undergravel filter plate, but drive it more vigorously, either with a pair of "power heads," or with a canister filter hooked up in reverse-flow configuration (Chapter 3).

For heavily loaded marine tanks or living reefs consider an external wet/dry filter system (Chapters 3 and 8).

**Biological Filter Substrate** For freshwater tanks, use sufficient gravel to make a minimum depth of three to four inches. For soft/acid fishes, select standard, washed number-3 gravel, or any suitably colored "decorator" gravel, other than crushed glass. For African cichlids, select dolomite and/or crushed coral gravel for their buffering ability.

For marine tanks without wet/dry filtration, use sufficient gravel to achieve a minimum depth of four to five inches.

For marine tanks with wet/dry filtration, use dolomite or crushed coral for the undergravel filter, and either crushed coral or one of the synthetic filter media in the trickle filter (see Chapters 3 and 6).

**Starter Culture for Biological Filter** Your tank's break-in period will be shorter and less traumatic if you inoculate your biological filter with a living culture of beneficial bacteria. If you have access to an established, disease-free tank, a handful of biological filter media from that tank will "seed" your tank nicely. Otherwise, buy any of several brands of "freeze-dried bacteria" prepared for either freshwater or saltwater. Use these as described in the Setting Up section on page 197.

## Chlorine/Chloramine Remover

If your local water supply even occasionally uses chloramine, don't risk your fishes' lives; use Kordon's AmQuel both to set up your tank and for all water changes thereafter. A little of this stuff goes a long way, but it is much cheaper in bulk. If you're setting up a sizable tank, buy it by the quart or gallon.

## Test Kit

All test-kit reagents degrade with time, so check the dates on kits you buy. Do not buy undated kits. For freshwater tanks, a pH kit is absolutely necessary, and will suffice if you intend to keep only the hardiest of fishes. Better yet, buy a master kit that includes hardness, ammonia, and nitrite tests. For marine tanks, you must start out with a complete test kit that includes a high-range pH test along with ammonia, nitrite, and nitrate kits.

## Nets

Buy two nets of slightly different sizes, large enough to hold your largest fish but small enough to be maneuverable in your tank. (You'll find that catching fish with two nets is much easier than chasing them around with one.)

## Air Pump

Many brands and styles available. After selecting your filtration system, consult with your salesperson about the appropriate pump for your needs.

## Air Tubing

Standard. Buy sufficient tubing, not only to connect your air pump with filters and air stones, but to set up an antisiphon loop as described in the setup procedures.

## Gang Valves

Several brands and styles available. These multiple valves, used to distribute air from pump to appliances, are now made of plastic suitable for either marine or freshwater tanks. Buy a valve with one more outlet than you need; this will be used to prevent excess pressure buildup in the line that can harm your pump.

## Assorted Rocks and Driftwood

(see Chapter 4).

## Siphon Tubing

To help you get water out of your aquarium with minimal fuss, get a six-foot length of clear, flexible plastic (tygon) one-half inch to three-quarters of an inch in diameter to use as a siphon.

## Salt

For freshwater tanks, if you plan on keeping either live-bearers or African cichlids, pick up a small package (five-gallon size) of artificial sea-salt mix. You will use this salt at much lower doses than package directions to adjust salinity, pH, and hardness. Kosher salt (noniodized) is not quite as good, but is acceptable in a pinch.

For marine tanks, you will be needing salt, both for setup and regular water changes. If you are certain you can store opened bags in a *dry* place, the salts are less expensive in large bags. If you live in a humid area, you're better off to buy one large bag appropriately sized to set up your tank, and several smaller bags (five-gallon size or so) for later water changes.

## Compounds to Adjust pH

If you know your water's pH (and you should by now), include in your first pickup any materials you'll need to adjust it up or down to suit your fishes. (See Chapters 2 and 3.) If you plan to keep either marine animals or African cichlids, try Aquarium System's Sea Buffer, a mixture of buffering compounds that helps prevent pH from dropping below 8.0.

## Second Trip to the Fish Store

### Live Aquatic Plants

See Chapter 4; pick up your plants after making certain your tank is ready to go, but before you buy your fishes. This will allow you to landscape your tank in a leisurely fashion. Use mail-order suppliers if your local store doesn't carry healthy plants.

## Third Trip to the Fish Store

### THE FISHES!

### Fish Foods

Purchase at least two varieties of dried foods and two or more kinds of frozen foods. Buy small packets to start off with; once you've determined which foods your fishes like best, buy enough to last about a month at a time. Dried foods are one item you should *not* buy in bulk (unless you've got a lot of fishes) because certain vitamins and other important trace nutrients are lost in long-term storage.

## Household Supplies for Your Tank

Several items you'll need around your aquarium don't fall under the strict definition of aquarium supplies (although they should). Some of these are items you undoubtedly have around the house, but beware! *Because all soaps, detergents, floor waxes, and cleansers are highly toxic to fishes, never carry water to your tank in your everyday kitchen buckets or use kitchen sponges or brushes to clean either the tank or aquarium accessories!* It is very difficult to remove *all* soap film from rubber and plastics, and even a little in your tank can spell disaster. I am certain that a substantial proportion of unexplained fish deaths follow the unwitting introduction of toxic household compounds into tank water. Any items on the list below that you or someone else in your household might be tempted to use for other purposes should be labeled in Day-Glo tape or marker FOR AQUARIUM USE ONLY!

**Buckets**   Two three- to five-gallon, heavy-duty, nonmetallic buckets should be reserved strictly for aquarium use. These are invaluable for rinsing gravel and GAC, for holding water to be added to your tank, and for receiving water siphoned out of your tank.

**Sponges**   Always have handy two or three sponges of assorted sizes, again reserved strictly for aquarium use. These should never be contaminated with any soap or cleansers.

**Carboy or Garbage Can**   For salt-water tanks, you will need at least one 5-gallon carboy in which to mix and store artificial water for water changes. The containers used to deliver spring water to office water coolers are about the right size, but their openings are too narrow to be convenient for pouring salt in and water out. In a pinch, a sturdy, nonmetallic garbage can will do.

**Timer**   To relieve you of the task of turning your aquarium lights on and off, use any standard, twenty-four-hour appliance timer, available at most hardware stores. Buy one that is grounded and that accepts a three-prong plug.

**Multisocket Power Strip**   You will need a minimum of four plugs for your aquarium to handle lights, heater, air pump, and filter. To avoid messy and dangerous "octopus" extension cords, invest in a grounded, multiple-outlet power strip. I don't like the flimsy ones I usually see in pet stores; just a few dollars more in a hardware store will buy a heavy-duty, fuse-protected model with its own "on-off" switch that can handle as much current as you want to push through it.

**Ground-Fault Interrupt Protector**   Place GFI protection on your aquarium circuit, especially if there are kids around or if the aquarium is located near a radiator or sink. You can either install one to replace your existing wall outlet or buy a plug-in model. One socket will allow you to plug your power strip and protect all your appliances at once.

**Single-Edged Razor Blades**   Single-edged razor blades are invaluable around the aquarium for cutting tubing, trimming plastic accessories, pruning aquarium plants, and (in glass aquaria only) for scraping algae off the glass. Keep a few handy at all times.

**Paper Towels**   If your aquarium isn't located within panic distance of your kitchen, keep a roll of paper towels nearby for those inevitable and unforeseeable little spills and accidents.

**Notebook and Pen**   To keep the log I recommend, use a plastic-covered, spiral-bound notebook with good, thick pages and a good-quality waterproof pen or a dark pencil. To keep both together so you can log without hunting around, attach the pen or pencil to the notebook with a string or elastic cord.

**Peat Moss**   If you'll be keeping fishes that prefer soft, acid water, you may want to filter your tank water through peat moss (Chapters 2 and 3). If you don't have a bale of moss around for garden use, you can usually find a small bag at a supermarket or garden center. (The peat moss packaged for aquarium use and sold in pet shops is much more expensive.)

**Miscellaneous Materials for Plants**   If you plan to follow my advice for handling rooted aquarium plants (Chapter 4), pick up the peat pots and sterilized organic potting-soil mix (without either perlite or vermiculite) at any good garden center.

## Nonessentials Worth Considering

Pet stores are filled with "laborsaving" gadgets. Some of these are useful, others are fun to use, and still others are strictly toys.

**Algae Scrapers** Sooner or later, all aquarists have to deal with unwanted algae. Although I oppose the use of algicides in the aquarium, I agree that staring at a wall of green hairy stuff is no pleasure. The solution is to clean algae off the front and sides of the aquarium regularly. You can do this by rolling up your sleeves and scraping away with a single-edged razor blade. Or you can buy either a razor-edged scraping tool or an algae-scraping sponge attached to the end of a stick. In acrylic tanks, stick with the latter; in glass aquaria use either.

**Breeding Traps** These devices, which separate newborn live-bearers from cannibalistic parents, are good to have on hand if you keep guppies, platies, or any of their relatives. Most breeding traps are clear plastic and either float in your community tank or attach to its rim with metal clips. Be certain that the kind you buy has plenty of slots and holes in it to allow water circulation; some of the least expensive varieties can suffocate the fry after saving them from being eaten! One brand is set up to accept an airline from your pump that moves water through the trap.

**Gravel Vacuums** Yep, you guessed it: vacuum cleaners for the aquarium. The simplest (and most useful) styles attach to a siphon tube (or come equipped with one), and help separate gravel from debris as you siphon water from the tank. Because this type encourages partial water changes, it gets my strongest vote. The powered varieties are fun to use, but if they encourage you to skip water changes, don't buy one.

**Automatic Water Changers** These two-in-one devices (Chapter 3) are a clever idea, but only if (a) you have a sink near your tank and (b) water straight from your tap is safe for fishes. My tanks fail on both counts, so I do without these.

**Automatic Feeders** These devices, which dispense food automatically at present intervals, are a mixed blessing. If you travel regularly and must leave your tanks unattended for weeks at a time, they can be useful. But if you just wander off on long weekends and an occasional ten-day trip, your fish would be better off if you ignored them on weekends and hired a fish-sitter for the longer trip. Don't buy a feeder for daily use while you're home; the few minutes you spend feeding your pets is an important time to check aquarium conditions.

**Aquacomp** It was bound to happen: the computer-controlled aquarium. Aquacomp, designed to monitor tank temperature, turn your lights on and off, and generally take care of things for you, is a cute toy, but worthless as far as I'm concerned. It requires several inches of space behind your tank, but is neither innocuous nor highly visible in a useful way when installed. And instead of "remembering" all your settings in case of a power failure, it returns to default values and resets its clock to midnight when power returns. For its price, it should do a lot better. Or rather, you'd do better spending the same money on a larger tank or on improving your filtration or lighting systems.

## KEEPING A LOG

It's a good idea to keep a detailed log of everything that happens in the aquarium from the day you set up your tank. Because the log doesn't seem to do anything to keep the aquarium running well, it may seem like a childish or even obsessive task. But keeping a complete record of everything that is done to a tank can be invaluable—even life-saving for fishes—if two or more people share fishkeeping duties. Many mistakes in fishkeeping are caused by lack of communication among busy family members: "I didn't know you fed them this morning!" "Oh, didn't you change the water this week?" "You mean you already adjusted the pH once today?" Keeping a log near the tank can provide just the three or four words necessary to keep things running smoothly.

A good log is also important if anything begins to go wrong with your setup. Believe me, nothing is as frustrating to a pet-store person, an experienced fishkeeping friend, or a FISH-NET adviser than a desperate message that "my angelfish is swimming funny and the catfish is floating belly-up!"

Just think of what happens when you visit a doctor; as soon as you finish explaining what ails you, the physician asks about your medical history, what you've eaten recently, and any unusual things that might have happened to you of late.

The same is true for fish doctors. To offer sound advice, they need your tank's equivalent of a complete medical history, starting from "birth": accurate information on tank temperature, filtration techniques, water-changing history, pH, and water chemistry. Without those data, the people you turn to for advice can do little more than guess at what's wrong. That, in turn, can cost you money for unnecessary medications, and can also obscure the real problems until it's too late to save your fishes. If you keep a log, when problems arise (invariably when you are preoccupied with something else), you'll have all the information you need at your fingertips.

## How to Log

Logging doesn't take much time. On the first page of the log for each tank, list all the important pieces of tank equipment: lights, mechanical filter, biological filter, air pump, heater, and so on, as shown in the sample page at the end of the chapter. Keep that page as a reference, and record the dates of any changes made later on, such as filter replacement, changes of light bulbs, and so on.

On the second page, begin a record of tank-water chemistry. Photocopy the chart at the end of the chapter, paste it into your notebook, and fill it in as you go along. For the first two weeks or so after setting up the tank, check the water chemistry every two days or so. Once these chores become routine—and as long as you are making the recommended water changes—once-a-week water-chemistry checks are sufficient.

On subsequent pages, make brief notes of anything you do with the tank: feeding, gravel cleaning, filter changing, chemicals or medication added, etc. Keep the entries short; they aren't meant to be literary masterpieces, or even diary notes. For example, "4/18: Changed 5 gallons" is fine. If you are the only person caring for the aquarium, don't bother to list each feeding, but if your family is sharing the task, enter and date feedings to help prevent inadvertent overfeeding.

If your fishes start performing upside-down water ballet or show other signs of discomfort, turn to the first page of your log, check the most recent water tests you've performed, and review any significant changes you've made in the tank since setup. Add to that the additional information listed at the end of the chapter, and you're ready to ask for help in an intelligent manner. You'll be surprised at the quality of the answers you receive if you provide the right information.

## SETTING UP:
### A Beginner's Aquarium Calendar

By offering the following schedule, I am assuming that you are willing to do things a step at a time in a leisurely fashion, rather than trying to set up and stock a new tank in a single afternoon. Not only is this approach easier on you, it's a lot better for your fishes.

If your children want to know, "Why can't we go get the fishes *now*, Daddy?," take the opportunity to make tank setup both a family project and a learning experience. Explain to them—on a level appropriate for their ages— exactly why you need to set things up in a certain way. In the process, you'll convince yourself that you're doing the right thing!

One simple but essential precautionary note: Although today's aquariums are sturdily built and should last for years, they are *not* meant to be carried with water inside. Never try to move an aquarium that is even half-full; you may stress the seams enough to cause a leak. Siphon out as much water as you can, leaving no more than an inch or two inside.

## Equipment

Wipe your empty tank inside and out with a clean sponge, and rinse a few gallons of water through it several times. Do not use soap or detergent of any kind. If you need some a mild abrasive to remove dirt from a used tank, try a soap*less* plastic scrubbing pad or sprinkle some rock salt or table salt on a moist (not dripping-wet) sponge.

Move the stand or support furniture into place, and position your tank where you want it.

Assemble and position the underwater filter plate and tubes.

Following manufacturer's directions, assemble and position the undergravel filter plate and lift tubes.

Using your aquarium-only buckets, rinse your gravel clean of dust and dirt. Taking care to keep the undergravel filter plates flat on the aquarium bottom, spread an even layer of gravel two to three inches deep on top of them.

Following manufacturer's instructions, install the power filter, airline tubing, and heater(s). Do not plug in or turn on any of these appliances yet.

## Dry Aquascaping

Arrange rocks and driftwood into a composition that pleases you and suits your fishes' needs for swimming space and/or shelter. (See general information in Chapter 4, and cultural notes on specific fish species from Chapter 5.) Have fun with this process and don't rush it. It's a

lot easier to change things around now than it will be when the tank is stocked with fishes!

If you need to glue rocks or pieces of wood to achieve the effect you want, do so now, using only specially designed aquarium sealant. This stuff takes twenty-four hours to dry, and does not reach its full strength for forty-eight hours, so plan accordingly.

Make any rearrangements of filter tubes, heaters, and the like necessitated by your aquascape. Once you are certain that all equipment is in its final location, check the fit of your aquarium cover and cut any necessary holes.

## Water Leveling Check

Pour in enough water to make a layer an inch or so deeper than the gravel, using a rock or small plate to diffuse the force of the water stream as you pout. Using this water level as a guide, check to make certain that the aquarium

is completely level from side to side and from front to back. If it isn't, shift the stand or support furniture as needed. It's a lot easier to do this with just an inch or so of water in the tank than it is when the tank is almost full!

## Planting

Buy your plants. Having completed your dry aquascaping, you should have a good idea of where you want large specimen plants, where you want low-growing ground covers, and so on. That way, you'll have a good idea of what sorts and sizes of plants to buy. If you are lucky enough to live near a fish shop that carries good aquatic plants, buy them there. (If not, order from the mail-order plant suppliers listed in the appendix.) In either case, be certain to have all the necessary materials (Chapter 4) ready when your plants arrive; delaying them for several days will set them back unnecessarily.

Spread an even, two- to three-inch layer of gravel on the filter plate.

After adding an inch of water above the gravel, make certain the aquarium is level.

It is easier to reposition a tank that has a small amount of water in it.

A day or two before you expect to have your plants in hand, fill the tank half to two-thirds full. This will give the water a chance to reach room temperature before planting.

Arrange plants carefully and slowly, taking care not to damage leaves, roots, or crowns in the process. Refer back to the detailed instructions in Chapter 4.

When your arrangement is complete, add enough warm (not hot) tapwater to bring the water level within about 3 inches of the tank rim. Place the light in position, switch it on, and stand back for a critical inspection. Although the water will be a bit cloudy, you should be able to see how the plants stand up. Use your imagination to envision the way the scene will mature as your plants grow. Make final adjustments before you fill the tank all the way. If you are satisfied with your work, add a final layer of washed gravel to cover any exposed bits of peat pot or other planting materials.

Use a net to scoop up leaves or bits of planting medium that float to the surface. Double-check to make certain that the tank is level before filling it the rest of the way.

## Equilibration

You are now ready to prepare the tank to receive your fishes. Plug in and start filters and air pumps, making certain that they are operating properly. If you have purchased a heater with a calibrated temperature scale (Chapter 3), set your temperature and plug it in. If you will be keeping either live-bearers or African cichlids, add the recommended doses of artificial sea salt (usually one tablespoon per five gallons) now.

If there is any question at all about the chemicals used to treat your tapwater supply, add the appropriate quantity of AmQuel. Assemble

and position the tank cover and light, and relax. Wait twenty-four hours for the system to equilibrate.

The next morning, use your test kit to check the pH. If it is where you want it to be, pat yourself on the back and proceed to the next step. If it isn't right, make any adjustments necessary.

Check the thermometer to make certain that the heater is set properly. If it is, you're ready to add fishes. If it isn't, make the adjustments indicated and wait another twelve hours to be certain that water temperature has stabilized.

Remember to note all these procedures in the tank log.

## FINALLY THE FISH!

The night before you buy your fishes, add a dose of freeze-dried bacteria to the tank follow-

Connect the filter and air pump. Check to see they are working properly.

Place rock, seashells, or driftwood securely in the tank.

Add water to fill the tank approximately two-thirds full.

ing the manufacturer's instructions. This will allow the resting bacteria time to rehydrate and get primed for action.

## Purchase and Transport

Select fish carefully, according to the directions in Chapter 6. Start off with the hardiest species you've chosen; postpone the acquisition of touchier varieties until the tank's biological filter is fully operational. Remember that although *Corydoras* catfish are hardy and easy to keep, they are sensitive to high levels of ammonia and nitrites, and so should not be among the first fishes you buy.

Once your fishes are bagged, treat them carefully, and get them home as quickly as possible. Do not jostle them unnecessarily, and *don't* leave them in your car while you do more shopping; chills can cause disease, and overheating can lead to suffocation. In extreme weather, preheat or pre-cool your car as much as possible, and transport the fishes in an insulated picnic cooler.

## Adding Fish to the Tank

Traditional wisdom has it that you must float fish bags in your tank for thirty minutes, mix bag water with tank water, and then tip the bag over and allow the fishes to swim out on their own. I prefer, however, a radical departure from this technique that has been successfully championed by FISHNET member and aquacultural chemist John Kuhns. John's "dose and dump technique," which aims to get the fish out of the bag and into the tank as soon as possible, seems preferable any time there are not dramatic temperature differences between bag and tank water. The method is simple: Add a little squirt of NovAqua water conditioner to the bag, add the appropriate dose to the tank, remove the fishes from the bag, and dump them into the tank.

This advice will disturb many old hands at the hobby, but there is sound reasoning behind it, and it has worked well for John and numerous retailers and hobbyists who have followed his advice. Why? While in their shipping bags in small volumes of water, fish are constantly excreting both ammonia (which can build up to harmful levels) and carbon dioxide (which lowers the pH). As soon as you open the bag at home, the $CO_2$ begins to leave the water, and the pH rises, initiating a chain reaction that makes any ammonia in the bag more toxic. So as long as conditions in your tank are suitable, the faster the fish get out of the bag and into the water, the better.

Once the fish are in the tank, add another dose of the bacterial starter culture.

Repot plants in three-inch peat pots with sphagnum moss and potting soil.

The crown of the plant should be even with the layer of gravel in the pot.

Arranging plants in a partially filled tank shows how they will float without spilling water.

## The Critical Break-in Period

Your aquarium has now entered the most critical stage of its life, and the period during which both fishes and fishkeepers are exposed to the highest levels of stress. During this time, the beneficial bacteria discussed in Chapter 2 become sufficiently well-established to carry out their work in the nitrogen cycle. Tanks undergoing this process often suffer from what is called "new tank syndrome," during which sensitive fishes become distressed and die for no apparent reason. But the events during tank establishment are far from mysterious, and they can be handled intelligently as long as you understand what's going on.

### The Timing of Nitrogen Cycling

A newly filled tank is free of nitrogen wastes and contains few of the bacteria that participate in the nitrogen cycle. There are always a few of those bacteria drifting around in soil and even in clean water, but their populations don't amount to much. When you "seed" your tank with bacteria—whether you do so by adding gravel from an established tank or by adding freeze-dried bacteria cultures—you add only a small fraction of the bacteria necessary to process the fish wastes.

During the first few weeks of tank life, your fishes begin adding ammonia to the tank water. This ammonia is used as "food" by the first group of beneficial bacteria, which slowly begin to grow, to multiply, and to convert the ammonia to nitrite. At first, the fishes add ammonia much faster than the small number of bacteria can remove it. For this reason, the ammonia concentration in the tank rises steadily. Then, sometime between one and two weeks after tank setup, bacterial growth "catches up" with waste production, and the ammonia concentration in the tank drops quite rapidly.

That ammonia doesn't disappear, of course; it gets converted to nitrite. This waste product, in turn, accumulates faster than the second group of bacteria can take it up, so nitrite concentrations rise rapidly as ammonia levels fall. Then, between ten days and a month after tank setup, the second bacterial population gets established, and nitrite concentrations plummet.

Once the system is fully established, both ammonia and nitrite concentrations should drop nearly to zero. Over time, concentrations of the much less toxic nitrate rise steadily. Some of this nitrate will be taken up by live plants and algae in the aquarium, and excess is controlled by regular water changes.

Note that the specific timing of the events in this cycle depends on several factors, including water temperature, salinity, the number of fishes in the tank, the amount you feed your fishes, the size of your biological filter bed, and the size and viability of the culture you use to inoculate your tank. Exactly the same process occurs in both marine and freshwater aquaria, although the bacteria take longer to become established in saltwater.

### What to Do During the Break-in Period
You can follow the establishment of the nitrification process—and consult the nitrogen cycle on page 30—by testing your water daily with ammonia and nitrite test kits. Do *not* add any more fishes—particularly delicate ones—until the nitrite levels fall. If, at any time during this process, your fishes show such signs of distress as rapid breathing or gasping for air at the surface, change between 20 and 40 percent of the tank water twice at twenty-four-hour intervals. After that, sit back, keep watching, and keep testing the water.

You can expect the tank water to become a bit cloudy at some point. This is a normal result of various bacterial blooms in the tank as things get settled, so unless your fishes are obviously distressed, don't worry. As long as you are not overfeeding your fishes, the cloudiness should clear up in a week or so and not return.

### Equilibration
Once ammonia and nitrite levels have fallen, you and your fishes can both relax. Now, you can add some of the more sensitive species—such as *Corydoras* catfish—safely.

Note, however, that your biological filter has equilibrated to the amount of organic wastes the tank's current residents are producing. Each time you add new fishes, you will see "bumps" in ammonia and nitrite levels, the size of which will be proportional to the extra wastes the new fishes release. As long as you add new fishes a few at a time, and as long as you don't exceed the total capacity of the biological filter, these bumps will soon flatten out as the filter readjusts.

### Ammonia and Nitrite Tests: Signs of Balance or Trouble
If, at any time after equilibration, ammonia or nitrite levels rise and stay high, your tank is in

trouble. (This is why you should perform water tests regularly.) There are two possible causes for this problem:

If you've been steadily adding fishes (or if your tank was originally stocked with small fishes that have grown rapidly) you have probably exceeded what is called the *carrying capacity* of the biological filter. You must either increase the size of the biological filter bed or remove some of the fishes.

If you have added antibiotics or certain other medications to the tank recently, those chemicals may have either killed the beneficial bacterial or inhibited their growth (Chapter 9). Remove any traces of such compounds by adding fresh GAC to your mechanical filter, and make several water changes over the course of several days. Reseed the tank with bacterial culture, begin daily water testing, and hope for the best.

## Daily Maintenance

☐ Feed morning and evening with an appropriate mix of prepared and frozen food.

☐ Periodically, offer live food supplement.

☐ Check temperature.

☐ Look the tank over for signs of disease or fighting.

☐ Be certain that undergravel and outside filters are working properly.

☐ Top off with new water as necessary.

## Weekly Maintenance

☐ Check pH, ammonia, nitrite, and nitrate levels (check specific gravity for marine tanks).

☐ Adjust pH if necessary; retest in twenty-four hours.

☐ If levels of ammonia, nitrite, or nitrate are too high, take remedial action as described above.

☐ Change 20 percent of the tank water, using the opportunity to siphon debris from the bottom of the tank.

☐ Check mechanical filter; if filled with "gunk," change the filter medium, even if it isn't clogged.

☐ Using a sponge, single-edged razor blade, or aquarium scraper, remove algae from front and sides of tank. If algae begin to grow on plant leaves, try rubbing leaves gently between your fingers. If algae grow on (shudder) plastic plants, remove them and scrub with a stiff toothbrush.

## Twice Monthly

☐ Change GAC in filter when changing mechanical filter medium.

## Monthly

☐ Prune bunch plants as needed. If parent plants have lost their lower leaves, discard them and replace with top cuttings.

## BEYOND COMMUNITY TANKS:
### Breeding Egg-Layers

Sooner or later, nearly every aquarist who sticks with the hobby gets interested in breeding egg-laying fishes. It is not that any of us feel the need to increase the populations of our tanks, but surmounting a challenge is always fun. At the same time, some of the most intriguing behaviors, as well as the most brilliant body colors, are seen only during courtship, spawning, and fry-rearing behaviors. Fish courtship often involves an intricate series of "conversations" between male and female—conversations that are carried out through movement, color, and occasionally even sound. The males of many fish species—particularly though not exclusively among cichlids—often don dazzling breeding colors that put their daily garb to shame.

Although spawning habits are diverse enough to make any generalization difficult, most egg-laying fishes fit into one of four broad and arbitrary but descriptive categories:

**Egg Scatterers** These spawn with abandon, shedding eggs and sperm into the water and leaving those eggs strewn over the bottom, buried in groups in a loose substrate such as peat, or attached more or less randomly to aquatic plants or driftwood. As a group, these species provide little or no care for their offspring, and are, in fact, inclined to eat them. Many tetras and killifish fall into this category.

**Bubble-nest builders** Includes many anabantids such as bettas and gouramies, which build floating nests of bubbles made from a sticky mucous secretion, usually also incorporating floating plants into the design. Following an intricate courtship ritual, males use their mouths to retrieve eggs released by the female. Carrying them gently to the surface, they place them in the bubble nest, which they constantly guard and repair. When the eggs first hatch, the male often "herds" them into a group near the nest for a while, but soon loses interest.

**Substrate Nest Builders** Many cichlids excavate nests in sand and gravel, dig caves beneath rocks, or clean off and prepare parts of aquatic plants upon which they deposit their eggs. Such species often provide extended care for their young, protecting and watching over them even after they hatch.

**Mouth Brooders** Mostly African cichlids, they may excavate what looks like nests, but use them only for courtship and spawning. Females pick up their eggs almost as soon as they release them, and incubate them in their mouths. Even after the eggs first hatch, the females continue to provide shelter for the tiny fry, which dive into her open mouth whenever danger threatens.

# IS BREEDING DIFFICULT?

How difficult is it for you to see these behaviors in your tanks? Naturally, breeding is easier to accomplish with some species than others. Some species in fact *spawn* easily, but their young are difficult to raise. Many species have very specific requirements that must be met for breeding to succeed. To obtain that information, I recommend any of the books dedicated to particular families of fishes. There are, however, certain general requirements for all species, and those we can cover here.

## Preparing the Breeding Tank

With almost no exceptions, successful breeding requires a separate tank for the parents. Some fishes—particularly dwarf cichlids—will court and spawn in community tanks, but their young invariably fail to survive in those circumstances. Others, such as discus, killifish, and catfish, will not even attempt to breed unless given their own tanks, and even then may be tough to induce to spawn.

Although the ideal breeding tank varies with species, the most important requirements are simple. The tank should be large enough to allow the parents plenty of room to swim. Water conditions should be matched perfectly to the species' needs, and temperature should be at the species optimum. Parents should be fed diets as close to perfection for the species as possible; herbivores should get plenty of plants, algae, or romaine lettuce, while carnivores should get lots of live and frozen foods.

Aggressive species—such as many cichlids and some anabantids—require breeding tanks with ample hiding places in which females can take refuge if males get too overbearing. Some species need gravel substrates in which to dig nests, while others—such as certain killifish—prefer a bottom of soft peat into which they can burrow.

## Selecting Pairs

In many species of egg-layers, external sex differences are readily apparent; males are often larger or more colorful than females, and often carry longer, more impressive finnage. In such species, obtaining a pair is simple.

In other species, males and females are externally identical; they can tell one another apart quite easily, but we can't. In such cases, the practice is generally to buy half a dozen or so as juveniles. Raise them together in a large tank, and they will pair off as they mature.

## Spawning

As spawning time approaches, minimize disturbances around the breeding tank. Continue conditioning carefully, attend to tank water quality, and watch your fishes at various times of day. (Some fishes spawn at dawn, while many seem to prefer dusk.) Depending on species, it may be appropriate either to remove parents as soon as spawning is completed, or to leave parents to care for eggs and fry.

## Incubating and Hatching

Incubation time varies from species to species

## WATER QUALITY RECORD

| Test Date (month & date) | | | | | | | | | | | | | | | | | | | | | | | | | | | | | | |
|---|---|---|---|---|---|---|---|---|---|---|---|---|---|---|---|---|---|---|---|---|---|---|---|---|---|---|---|---|---|---|
| Tank Size | | | | | | | | | | | | | | | | | | | | | | | | | | | | | | |
| Temperature | | | | | | | | | | | | | | | | | | | | | | | | | | | | | | |
| pH | | | | | | | | | | | | | | | | | | | | | | | | | | | | | | |
| ammonia (ppm) | | | | | | | | | | | | | | | | | | | | | | | | | | | | | | |
| nitrite (ppm) | | | | | | | | | | | | | | | | | | | | | | | | | | | | | | |
| nitrate (ppm) | | | | | | | | | | | | | | | | | | | | | | | | | | | | | | |
| color/ cloudiness | | | | | | | | | | | | | | | | | | | | | | | | | | | | | | |
| water changed | | | | | | | | | | | | | | | | | | | | | | | | | | | | | | |
| specific gravity (marine only) | | | | | | | | | | | | | | | | | | | | | | | | | | | | | | |

## WATER QUALITY RECORD

| Test Date (month & date) | | | | | | | | | | | | | | | | | | | | | | | | | | | | | | |
|---|---|---|---|---|---|---|---|---|---|---|---|---|---|---|---|---|---|---|---|---|---|---|---|---|---|---|---|---|---|---|
| Tank Size | | | | | | | | | | | | | | | | | | | | | | | | | | | | | | |
| Temperature | | | | | | | | | | | | | | | | | | | | | | | | | | | | | | |
| pH | | | | | | | | | | | | | | | | | | | | | | | | | | | | | | |
| ammonia (ppm) | | | | | | | | | | | | | | | | | | | | | | | | | | | | | | |
| nitrite (ppm) | | | | | | | | | | | | | | | | | | | | | | | | | | | | | | |
| nitrate (ppm) | | | | | | | | | | | | | | | | | | | | | | | | | | | | | | |
| color/ cloudiness | | | | | | | | | | | | | | | | | | | | | | | | | | | | | | |
| water changed | | | | | | | | | | | | | | | | | | | | | | | | | | | | | | |
| specific gravity (marine only) | | | | | | | | | | | | | | | | | | | | | | | | | | | | | | |

## WATER QUALITY RECORD

| Test Date (month & date) | | | | | | | | | | | | | | | | | | | | | | | | | | | | | | | |
|---|---|---|---|---|---|---|---|---|---|---|---|---|---|---|---|---|---|---|---|---|---|---|---|---|---|---|---|---|---|---|---|
| Tank Size | | | | | | | | | | | | | | | | | | | | | | | | | | | | | | | |
| Temperature | | | | | | | | | | | | | | | | | | | | | | | | | | | | | | | |
| pH | | | | | | | | | | | | | | | | | | | | | | | | | | | | | | | |
| ammonia (ppm) | | | | | | | | | | | | | | | | | | | | | | | | | | | | | | | |
| nitrite (ppm) | | | | | | | | | | | | | | | | | | | | | | | | | | | | | | | |
| nitrate (ppm) | | | | | | | | | | | | | | | | | | | | | | | | | | | | | | | |
| color/ cloudiness | | | | | | | | | | | | | | | | | | | | | | | | | | | | | | | |
| water changed | | | | | | | | | | | | | | | | | | | | | | | | | | | | | | | |
| specific gravity (marine only) | | | | | | | | | | | | | | | | | | | | | | | | | | | | | | | |

## WATER QUALITY RECORD

| Test Date (month & date) | | | | | | | | | | | | | | | | | | | | | | | | | | | | | | | |
|---|---|---|---|---|---|---|---|---|---|---|---|---|---|---|---|---|---|---|---|---|---|---|---|---|---|---|---|---|---|---|---|
| Tank Size | | | | | | | | | | | | | | | | | | | | | | | | | | | | | | | |
| Temperature | | | | | | | | | | | | | | | | | | | | | | | | | | | | | | | |
| pH | | | | | | | | | | | | | | | | | | | | | | | | | | | | | | | |
| ammonia (ppm) | | | | | | | | | | | | | | | | | | | | | | | | | | | | | | | |
| nitrite (ppm) | | | | | | | | | | | | | | | | | | | | | | | | | | | | | | | |
| nitrate (ppm) | | | | | | | | | | | | | | | | | | | | | | | | | | | | | | | |
| color/ cloudiness | | | | | | | | | | | | | | | | | | | | | | | | | | | | | | | |
| water changed | | | | | | | | | | | | | | | | | | | | | | | | | | | | | | | |
| specific gravity (marine only) | | | | | | | | | | | | | | | | | | | | | | | | | | | | | | | |

and with water temperature. Until eggs begin to hatch, there is little for you to do, other than to be certain appropriate foods are on hand when needed. Be careful, as hatching time approaches, that mechanical filters are not liable to scoop up relatively helpless fry. For many species, it is advisable to discontinue mechanical filtration altogether; instead, feed parents carefully and rely on either sponge filters or undergravel filters to maintain water quality.

## Rearing the Young

The trickiest part of the entire procedure is providing suitable food for the young. Although newborn live-bearers are usually large enough to accept freshly hatched brine shrimp, many fishes that emerge from eggs are too small. These infants require much smaller foods in the form of microscopic single-celled animals called protists or protozoans by scientists and infusoria by aquarists.

The best way to grow infusoria is to obtain starter cultures called "infusoria pills" from pet shops. Place these pills along with some lettuce leaves in a jar of water in bright light but not direct sunlight. Infusoria will emerge from dormant stages and begin to grow within about two days; you can see them only because the water will get cloudy. Depending on the size and density of the culture, it will last anywhere from one to two weeks before dying off. Feed your fry with this mixture by transferring generous portions to the breeding tank with an implement such as a turkey baster. (After making certain that the baster contains no soapy residue.)

As the fry grow, they will take finely powdered flake foods, any of several prepared "fish baby foods" available in tubes, and, eventually, newly hatched brine shrimp. You must watch carefully to judge when your babies are ready for these various foods, and for the transition to adult diets. This is the most difficult stage in the process, but one that is enormously rewarding if you master it.

If you succeed and the fry thrive, be certain to give them plenty of room in which to grow. Even live-bearers such as mollies can be permanently stunted by small tanks.

## AQUARIUM MAINTENANCE LOG

General System Information:

_____ Water type (fresh or salt)
_____ Tank volume
_____ Tank location
_____ Lighting (type and number of bulbs)
_____ Date of tank setup
_____ Date on which nitrogen cycle completed

Filtration System:

*Mechanical/chemical filtration:*
Equipment type and model (inside, outside, canister): _____

Filter media used (floss, GAC, etc.):
_____

*Biological filtration system:*
Equipment type and model (undergravel, wet/dry): _____
Power source (airlift tubes, powerheads): _____

Substrate used (gravel type, dolomite, bio balls, etc.):
_____
_____

*Aeration:*
Pump type and model: _____
Number of air stones in tank (including UG filter): _____

## WATER QUALITY

Type of test kit used: _____

Temperature: _____ pH: _____ Total hardness: _____

Ammonia (ppm): _____ Nitrite (ppm): _____ Nitrate (ppm): _____

Specific gravity (marine): _____

Color/cloudiness (describe): _____

Water changes (percent of tank volume and frequency): _____

_____

Additives used (water conditioners, etc.): _____

_____

Additional information: _____

_____

_____

Most recent addition of fish/plants/invertebrates: _____

_____

_____

_____

Quarantine procedure: _____

_____

_____

## DISEASE REPORT FORM

The following form, adapted from the form currently in use on the FISHNET forum,
summarizes in convenient form most of the information necessary to get useful advice on disease problems.

### TANK INFORMATION

Volume: _____ Freshwater or marine: _____
Length of time in operation: _____

### FISH INFORMATION

Fish type: _____ size: _____ # animals: _____
Fish type: _____ size: _____ # animals: _____

### SYMPTOMS OF TROUBLE

Affected fish: _____ symptoms: _____
Affected fish: _____ symptoms: _____

### FOODS AND FEEDING

Types of food offered: _____ frequency of feeding: _____
Types of food offered: _____ frequency of feeding: _____

### FILTRATION SYSTEM

Mechanical filtration (filter type and model): _____
    Filtering materials used (floss, carbon, etc.): _____
    Frequency of filter changes: _____
Biological filtration: _____
    Filter type and model (undergravel, trickle filter, etc.): _____

    If undergravel, number and type of air stones or power heads: _____

    Gravel-cleaning procedure: _____

### AERATION

Number and type of additional air stones: _____

## ADDITIONAL INFORMATION FOR AQUARIUM PROBLEM REPORT

To ask for help in the most effective way possible, combine the contents of page one of your log,
your most recent water test results, and the following additional information:

TANK STOCKING INFORMATION:

Type of fish                                          Size (head to tail)                                          # in tank

_____

_____

_____

_____

_____

_____

_____

_____

DIETARY INFORMATION:

Food type                                             Feeding frequency

_____

_____

_____

MAINTENANCE INFORMATION:

Water changes (percent of tank volume and frequency):

_____

_____

Type of gravel cleaning performed: _____

        method: _____

        how often: _____

APPEARANCE OF AFFECTED FISHES:

(For details on what to look for and report, see Chapter 9)

_____

_____

_____

# TO YOUR FISHES' HEALTH

I was in tears. Again. It was scarcely a week since I'd discovered my prized albino swordtail mummified on the carpet behind the television. And Angie, my black angelfish, didn't look well at all. Her fins (I assumed, rather than knew, that "she" was a female) were not only ragged, they were shrinking. She'd stopped eating. Now, she was lying on her side. I gathered up every penny of my allowance, ran to the pet shop, bought every medicine I could afford, and dumped them all into the tank.

They didn't work; Angie died anyway. What's more, several other fishes in the tank started looking poorly, too. Luckily, the next day was my monthly housecleaning day. I siphoned lots of water out of the tank while cleaning the gravel, and replaced it with fresh, dechlorinated tapwater. Within hours the situation had improved! Encouraged, I cleaned even more, changing nearly half the water in the tank in the process. Within three days, the tank looked healthy again.

All of us who've ever kept fishes have memories about sick pets. Some of us have stayed in the hobby despite the setbacks, while others either became too frustrated, too angry, or too

upset with the loss of life to continue. In those days, there weren't any real "fish doctors," so no one knew what to do when our pets got sick. Medication was a completely hit-or-miss affair; you guessed which medication to use, the manufacturer guessed how much to tell you to put in the tank, and then you guessed whether the medication worked or not. (After all, in the story I've just told, the fish did get better some time after I medicated the tank; did the medication cure them, or did they get better for some other reason?)

But caring for fishes is much easier today. On the treatment side, we know a lot more about fish diseases than we did a decade ago. And although aquarium medications still have a long way to go, we have a better idea about which treatments work and which do not. More significantly, aquarists are now learning how important it is to *prevent* disease.

The turnaround in fishkeeping mirrors our perceptions of human health and disease. Our grandparents said "An ounce of prevention is worth a pound of cure," when they wanted us to wear galoshes on a rainy day. But despite that cliché, our medical system—and our

actions—focused more on treating diseases than preventing them. Most of us proceeded on our merry way with the assumption that if anything went wrong, a pill, an injection, or an operation could restore our health. This desire for a simple cure-all is a longtime American obsession that has fueled the sale of everything from snake oil to laetrile. Allowed to think about our own health in those terms, we naturally take the same approach to our pets.

But many human health-maintenance organizations are now focusing—as their names imply they might—on *fostering wellness* instead of just *treating illness*. We are admonished to stop smoking, eat properly, exercise regularly, and reduce or learn to cope with stress. Why is this happening? The medical community, in addition (we hope) to having our best interests at heart, keeps a sharp eye on the bottom line: it has finally figured out that it is both easier and far less costly to keep healthy people healthy than it is to make sick people well.

The same reasoning holds true for fishes. Keeping healthy fishes in good shape is fun and rewarding. Diagnosing and treating fish diseases can be difficult, frustrating, and expensive. Failure to cope with disease is the main reason that so many fish tanks are sold at yard sales.

That's why this chapter pulls no punches in discussing the problems involved in diagnosing and treating fishes. By explaining how difficult diagnosis and treatment are, I hope to convince you to work harder to keep your fishes healthy. Please note that I can't present a comprehensive discussion of fish diseases in a single chapter; I'll only deal with the most common ones here. I encourage you to consult at least one of the specialized reference books on disease suggested on page 225.

# AN OUNCE OF PREVENTION

Bacteria and fungi are always present in fish tanks. "But if bacteria are everywhere, all the time," you may ask, "why aren't fishes always sick?" The answer is simple: Fish, like humans, have an array of natural defenses against infection. The first line of defense is the outer body surface, where mucus that covers scales and skin contains substances with antibacterial and antifungal action. This mucus deters skin infections in much the same way that human tears help keep delicate eye tissues out of trouble. If infectious agents penetrate these outer defenses, fishes also have a body-wide immune system that—though neither as complex nor as effective as ours—enables them to defend themselves under many conditions.

That's why many (though not all) aquatic troublemakers can only cause problems if they find an opening in fishes' armor through which to launch their assault. They may find those openings in wounds inflicted by careless handling, fights with other fishes, or parasites. Or they may find an Achilles' heel (Achilles' fin?) in fishes whose immune systems have been disabled or impaired by stress. Avoid the errors that lead to those breaches in body defense, and you'll be most of the way toward maintaining your pets in the best-possible health.

**Improper Tank Conditions**  Stress can cause illness directly, or it may weaken animals sufficiently to give disease-causing organisms the opening they need. When this is the case, particularly if the problem is detected early, improving water quality or eliminating

overcrowding may allow fishes to recover without medication. Failure to eliminate the sources of stress, on the other hand, ensures that the disease will get worse, regardless of medication. Even if sick fishes are removed to a hospital tank and cured, they will relapse if returned to the conditions that upset them in the first place.

**Dietary Deficiencies**  Highly specialized feeders (particularly certain reef fishes and cichlids) kept on improper diets become malnourished, and develop infections that would not otherwise occur. Diets lacking in vitamin C, as discussed in Chapter 9, are linked to a syndrome called "head and lateral-line disease" in tangs, certain angelfish and other plant-eaters. A combination of vitamin deficiency and poor water conditions are also implicated in "hole-in-the-head" disease in discus. To avoid these problems (and in mild cases, to overcome them) feed herbivores adequate quantities of such fresh greens as romaine lettuce, and avoid ultraspecialized feeders of other types.

**Live Foods**  As important as they are in balanced diets, they can also be sources of contagion. Wild-collected plankton and marine algae can carry parasites that wreak havoc in your marine tank. Daphnia and *Tubifex* worms can harbor diseases that can be just as problematic in your freshwater setup. There are two ways to get around this problem. You can culture live foods yourself, or you can purchase them from sources that culture, rather than collect them. Alternatively, you can feed saltwater organisms (such as plankton or brine shrimp) to freshwater fishes, and provide freshwater foods (such as daphnia and *Tubifex*) to saltwater pets. Many parasites cannot tolerate changes in salinity, and for that reason cannot infect animals in the "wrong" environment. (Because the food can't survive in the wrong salinity either, you must be careful not to foul the tank by overfeeding.)

## THE IMPORTANCE OF QUARANTINE

Although I've mentioned quarantine earlier, I want to stress it again in this context of health and disease. Novice aquarists have much more trouble with disease than they need to because quarantine seems either too bothersome or too expensive. Admittedly, it requires extra time and equipment. But when fish after fish is added to a community tank without quarantine, sooner or later, a disease is added, too. Recall that virtually all wild fishes carry parasites and diseases, although the former are often few in number and the latter are often present only as latent infections that cause little or no trouble. Even fishes from aquaculture farms occasionally carry parasites or pick up diseases in improperly maintained dealers' tanks. For that reason, any fish added to an established tank is a potential source of trouble.

That's why all fishes, fresh and salt, should be quarantined in a separate tank for observation for at least two weeks prior to adding them to an established aquarium. Wild-caught marine fishes, regardless of apparent health, should not only be quarantined, but treated as though infected to purge them of external parasites (page 215). This treatment is not com-

pletely harmless, and some fishes may, in fact, perish while in quarantine. But if you've got five or ten beautiful (and expensive) pets in a community tank, it's worth the risk to the newcomer to preserve the established community.

## Sick Bay: The Hospital/Quarantine Tank

Every hobbyist should have a spare tank for quarantining new acquisitions. An extra tank can also serve as a hospital in which to isolate and treat fishes that become ill in community tanks. The quarantine/hospital setup doesn't have to be attractive because it won't be a permanent addition to the household, and can, in fact, be set out of the way in a spare room or corner.

This tank should be sized for the largest fishes it might house, and equipped with a cover and heater. It should have ample aeration and mechanical filtration, but no chemical filtration (which would remove medication). Keep it bare of decorations, both to simplify determination of tank volume and to make it easier to observe your patients. If a fish under treatment is particularly nervous, include an inert shelter such as a plastic flowerpot or a piece of PVC pipe. Do not use any pieces of coral or limestone gravel; these will bind to certain medications and remove them from action.

Because this tank is set up only when needed, and because it will often contain medications that interfere with beneficial bacteria, biological filtration can be a problem. Equip it, if possible, with a mechanical filter that has

been operating in an established, well-stocked, disease-free aquarium. Such a filter will come equipped with a population of beneficial bacteria that will help keep levels of nitrogenous wastes under control during the treatment period. Despite this precaution, nitrogenous wastes will probably still accumulate, stressing your already sick fish. Plan, therefore, to change water regularly, redosing each time with medication to maintain drug concentrations at therapeutic levels.

**Quarantining Freshwater Fishes** Maintain the quarantine tank at about 78° F unless that temperature stresses the particular species involved. Feed sparingly but regularly, and monitor nitrogenous wastes. Change 25 percent of the tank water weekly unless wastes begin to build up, in which case change 50 percent of the water daily.

Keep the fish in quarantine for a month, watching carefully for signs of disease. If infections occur, treat as necessary and continue quarantine until you are certain your new acquisition has a clean bill of health. Make certain its water is similar in composition to that of its final destination, and make the transfer to the community tank gently.

**Quarantining Marine Fishes** All wild-caught marine fishes should be treated as though infected. The quarantine tank should be set up as described for freshwater systems above, with special emphasis on incorporating a filter with a mature culture of beneficial bacteria. Establish a copper concentration of 0.03

mg/l (see page 225). Do not overload with fishes, as the tank's stressed biological filter will not be able to handle much waste.

Before placing a newly acquired fish into the quarantine tank, give it a freshwater dip. Prepare chlorine-free freshwater, adjust its pH to 8.3, and equalize its temperature to the water in which the fish is swimming. Gently remove the fish from its shipping bag and cradle it in a soft net in the freshwater container for a minimum of two minutes. If the fish shows no signs of shock or distress, continue the dip for as long as ten minutes. If the fish does show distress—by gasping for breath, thrashing about, or appearing to go limp—remove it earlier and place it in the quarantine tank. Repeat the freshwater dip twice at three-day intervals.

Monitor the fish for signs of disease for two to three weeks, feeding sparingly but regularly. Be certian that nitrogenous wastes are kept under control; if ammonia or nitrite levels rise, perform 50 percent water changes daily. If, at the end of the quarantine, no signs of disease are visible, make certain water conditions in the quarantine tank match those in the destination tank and gently make the transfer.

## BEFORE YOU CALL THE DOCTOR

If, despite reasonable precautions, your fishes start acting sick, don't rush to medicate them. Randomly adding medication to your tank is likely to do more harm than good, for reasons to be discussed shortly. Unless you can unequivocally identify a specific pathogen on your fishes, water quality, rather than medicine, should be your first concern.

**Check for Subtle Pollution**   Unexpected contaminants (page 28) often cause stress and disease. Culprits range from dishwashing detergents that accidentally contaminate aquarium equipment to household ammonia, cleaning solvents, paint fumes, insecticides, and cigarette smoke. Make certain that none of these are entering your aquarium.

**Check Water Quality and Change Water**   All important parameters of water quality—from pH to salt concentrations to organic compounds in the water—change over time. Your biological filter, while eliminating highly toxic ammonia and nitrites, produces less toxic (but not totally innocuous) nitrates. Your fishes also give off substances that affect their own health and the health of their tankmates if they accumulate in high concentrations.

If you've been keeping a log, you can tell at a glance if your pH has been dropping or if your biological filter hasn't been working. If you haven't been logging, pull out your test kit and check every parameter.

If poor water quality is the problem, make several major water changes. Siphon water from the bottom of the tank and replace it with new water of proper composition. Even if your fish really are infected with a disease-causing organism, water changing helps for two reasons. Obviously, it reduces stress from poor water. Less obviously, it helps remove diseased organisms from the tank. Because many parasites have reproductive stages that hang out at the bottom, siphoning off bottom water will lower the parasite population.

Take care not to shock fishes with drastic changes in water characteristics. If the tank's pH and hardness are close to those of the water you'll be adding, change between 50 and 75 percent of your water daily for several days. Keep checking water quality until conditions are acceptable, and then be certain to stay on a regular water-changing schedule from that point on.

But if your tank pH has dropped far below that of the water you plan to add, begin with 20 percent daily water changes to adjust the pH gradually. Once tank pH is within 0.2 pH units of the new water, make the major changes prescribed.

You should then, of course, figure out what went wrong, and make certain that the problem doesn't happen again. Were you lax in maintenance procedures? Did a fish die unnoticed in a clump of plants and foul the water? Did your undergravel filter stop pumping for some reason?

You may discover that massive water changes solve the problem without medication. If they don't, take steps leading to the use of fish drugs. If only one or a few fishes are affected, set up a hospital tank as described on page 213, and while that tank is settling in, proceed with the diagnosis.

## DISEASE-CAUSING ORGANISMS IN AQUARIA

To deal with sick fishes in the most effective (and least expensive) way, you need to be familiar with the organisms that cause major fish diseases. Luckily, only a few rare fish diseases are caused by viruses. I say luckily, for, like certain types of cancer in humans that these diseases superficially resemble, they do not respond to either antibiotics or other standard medication.

## Bacterial and Fungal Infections

Bacteria and fungi, two groups of organisms that are found almost everywhere, appeared on earth hundreds of millions of years ago, and have been evolving on many different ecological tracks ever since. The vast majority of them are harmless, and many are essential in nature. But some of them, the ones we call pathogens, have adapted to making their living at the expense of other organisms. These organisms are placed by biologists into two distinct kingdoms in the world of living things. Bacteria belong to the kingdom Monera, and fungi belong to the kingdom Fungi. This classification testifies to their biological distinctiveness; belonging to separate kingdoms, these organisms are fortuitously very different sorts of creatures from members of the animal kingdom such as ourselves and fishes.

Why should differences between bacteria, fungi, and animals be lucky for us? Largely because those members of other kingdoms handle some of life's essential processes differently than we do, we can use drugs that monkey with their life functions but don't mess up our own. That, in turn, is why we can swallow antibiotics and swab antifungal agents on our skin to control infection without killing our own tissues.

Bacteria have been evolving for millions of years longer than the rest of us living creatures. For that reason, many of them differ from one another far more than, say, a fish differs from a human, or even from a butterfly. This bacterial diversity is mostly biochemical rather than physical, so it is largely invisible, even under electron microscopes. Yet it has important ramifications when it comes to treatment. Because different bacteria "work" differently, they are susceptible to different medications. An antibiotic that slaughters one species may not even discomfit another, which is why treatment of bacterial disease (in either fishes or other animals) should never be undertaken without accurate diagnosis; you want to target a specific beast with a specific drug.

## Parasites

The word "parasite" is a general term usually used to refer to disease-causing organisms other than bacteria and fungi. Several of the most common and most destructive parasites on aquarium fishes are single-celled organisms belonging to the kingdom *Protista*. Others, much less common in home tanks, are more complex animals that can be an inch or more in length. As a group, parasites can attack healthy fishes fairly easily, an ability that causes some of the most frustrating health problems in aquaria. To make matters worse, parasites perforate hosts' outer defenses and cause general weakness, making it easier for bacteria and pathogens to enter and cause secondary infections.

Several parasites have evolved ways of life that—although they enable both parasite and host to survive in nature—are deadly under aquarium conditions. Many have life cycles involving at least two stages: One that lives on the fish and causes problems, and another that leaves the fish in order to reproduce. When the reproductive stage leaves the fish, it falls to the bottom and multiplies prodigiously, often releasing hundreds—or even thousands—of offspring within a few days.

In nature, where lots of space and plenty of water separate parasites and hosts, relatively few of these new little nasties find meals. If one does happen to latch onto a fish, that single parasite hangs on for a while, leaves to reproduce, and may or may not be replaced in time by a few others of its kind. This low-level, sequential infestation has a negligible effect on the fish's overall health. In the confines of your twenty-gallon tank, on the other hand, *most* of those swarming young parasites find one of your fishes to latch onto. Thus, once the parasites are present in the tank, the infestation quickly gets out of control.

## Internal versus External Infections

Infections and infestations in fishes can be grouped into two broad categories:

**External Ailments** These affect fins, skin, eyes, lips, or other exposed body areas. These are the diseases most easily diagnosed, and—because the disease-causing organisms are on or close to the surface of the fish—are the most susceptible to drugs added to aquarium water.

**Internal Infections and Infestations** These affect the gut and other internal organs. These infections are often very difficult for hobbyists to diagnose and treat. First, because they are located inside the fish, they are not exposed to waterborne medications unless those medications are absorbed into the fish's body. Second, because they occur internally, these infections may not cause obvious symptoms until the fish is so far gone that truly heroic treatments are needed to save its life.

# DIAGNOSING AND TREATING FISH DISEASES

*They do certainly give very strange and new-fangled names to diseases.*
> *Plato,* The Republic

If your fish are acting sickly and white spots, unusual amounts of body slime, or fuzzy white growths are apparent on various parts of their anatomy, use the descriptions of common diseases that follow to diagnose your pets' ailment. If you can find none of the symptoms described on the disease pages, ask for professional advice. Knowledgeable input will save you not only time and money, but probably several treasured pets as well.

To ask for advice efficiently, you must summarize a lot of critical information. To do that, fill out the Disease Report Form on page 208. With all those details summarized in one place, you can turn to an experienced aquarist, a knowledgeable pet-store owner, or the expert staff of FISHNET for help. Although filling out the form may seem like a bother, no one will be able to give you much useful help without that information. The folks on FISHNET wisely have a policy of not making recommendations without that information, and other responsible individuals will do the same.

## ICH

**What to Look For**  Small, but clearly visible and individual white spots on the fins, skin, and gills of either freshwater or saltwater fishes. In the early stages of infestation, fishes often scratch themselves against rocks or other aquarium decorations. In heavily infested fishes, spots may be so close together in places that they look like solid white patches on the body surface. Long-standing infestations are often accompanied by secondary bacterial or fungal infections.

**Disease-Causing Organism**  In freshwater, the culprit is *Ichthyophthirius multifiliis;* in saltwater a virtually equivalent disease is caused by the aptly named *Cryptocaryon irritans*. Both parasites are protozoans that burrow into the skin of the fish and form the white cyst that is visible to the eye.

A massive ich infection

**What Went Wrong?**  The introduction of parasites on newly acquired fishes is always a possibility, unless new acquisitions are quarantined. Both of these parasites often infect wild fishes in nature, but in relatively low numbers. Their life cycles, however, ensure that even a few of these parasites introduced into an aquarium can wreak havoc in a short while. Ich is one of the primary reasons to quarantine both freshwater and marine fishes before introducing them into an established tank. Overcrowding and resultant stress, along with poor water quality, exacerbate the course of the disease and promote epidemics.

An ich infection

## What to Do

QUARANTINE:  Quarantine all new acquisitions for at least two weeks to check for the presence of these and other parasites. Hold plants and invertebrate live foods in a container free of fishes for at least a week at a temperature of 68° F to eliminate the free-swimming stages that must find a host in order to survive.

DRUG TREATMENT   If an outbreak of ich is caught quickly enough the addition of a proprietary remedy such as Rid Ich (from Kordon) or Desafin (from Tetra) should control it. Check the available remedies for the recommended active ingredients and instructions. Calculate your tank volume as described on page 36, and double-check to make certain that the manufacturer's recommendations provide therapeutic dosages. If tank temperature is near 70° F, maintain the therapeutic dose for five full days *after* all spots have disappeared from all fishes. At higher temperatures, parasites pass through their life cycles more rapidly, and treatment time can be shortened.

OTHER ACTIONS:  Normal drug treatment affects only the free-swimming stage of the parasite; the encysted individuals on your fishes' bodies are immune. Saltwater fishes suffering from severe infestations, however, may benefit from two- to three-minute dips in freshwater.

## VELVET DISEASE AND "OODINIUM"

**What to Look For**  Velvet and *Oodinium* are characterized by a thin white to yellowish-gray film that covers the skin, fins, and gills. At early stages of infection, encysted parasites form a very fine coating that looks like powder on the fish. In some cases, however, a heavy infestation on gill filaments may cause serious damage without spreading to more visible areas. Infected individuals may scrape against objects in the tank, and often exhibit problems breathing.

**Disease-Causing Organism**   In freshwater fishes, *Oodinium* is the culprit, while in marine fishes *Amyloodinium* is responsible. (This in spite of the fact that the disease in marine fishes is still commonly called "Oodinium.")

**What Went Wrong?**  Like ich, these parasites are often introduced on newly acquired specimens, a fact that emphasizes again the importance of quarantine. Overcrowding and poor water quality encourage transmission and debilitating infection, but the disease can also spread to perfectly healthy fishes.

## What to Do

DRUG TREATMENT In freshwater tanks, drugs marketed for ich usually work on these organisms as well. Check the available remedies for the recommended active ingredients and instructions. Calculate your tank volume as described on page 36, and double-check to make certain that the manufacturer's recommendations provide therapeutic dosages. Unfortunately, both these parasites can live without hosts much longer than the organisms that cause ich. In marine systems, a monthlong treatment of copper is usually necessary. If the main tank contains large quantities of coral and gravel (which binds and removes copper from the water), it is best to remove fish to hospital tanks and raise the temperature of the home tank to slightly above 86° F. This speeds up the life cycle of the parasite and causes unattached individuals to die sooner.

OTHER ACTIONS As is the case with saltwater ich, a two- to three-minute dip in freshwater (combined with long-term drug therapy) often offers fishes some relief from severe infestations.

## FIN AND TAIL ROT

What to Look For This syndrome, true to its name, is characterized by fins and tails that become ragged at the edges and gradually disappear.

Disease-Causing Organism Fin and tail rot can be caused by any of several types of common aquatic bacteria.

What Went Wrong? This disease, one of the most common of all complaints among beginners' aquaria, is far more common than it should be. The organisms that cause it are almost always present in aquarium water; they can infect fishes only if the animals are stressed and/or injured by bad handling, poor water quality, or squabbling among tankmates. Once the infection is under control and conditions are corrected, damaged fins usually grow back in a matter of weeks.

## What to Do

DRUG TREATMENT Use a proprietary aquarium antibiotic that contains either oxytetracycline or nifurpirinol. Check the available remedies for the recommended active ingredients and instructions. Calculate your tank volume as described on page 36, and double-check to make certain that the manufacturer's recommendations provide therapeutic dosages. Because of antibiotics' side effects—as well as their high cost when used in therapeutic doses—avoid dosing your community tank if possible. If only a single fish is affected, remove it to a hospital tank for treatment. Only if you're certain that several fishes in your community tank are infected should you treat it.

OTHER ACTIONS Correct water-quality problems and eliminate unruly tankmates, or the problem will recur. If you are keeping livebearers in soft water that tends to get acid, watch pH and add salt to the water as described in Chapter 6.

A female Swordtail whose dorsal fin has eroded away from a bacteria infection

Combined bacterial and parasite problems

## MOUTH AND BODY FUNGUS

**What to Look For** True fungal infections are characterized by white cottonlike growths on lips or other parts of the body.

**Disease-Causing Organism** Several common aquatic fungi.

**What Went Wrong?** Like bacteria that cause fin rot, fungi that cause this problem are nearly always present in tanks, but rarely bother healthy fishes. Usually, they require "openings" in fishes' external defenses in the form of wounds caused by poor handling, fighting, or parasite infestations. Poor water quality and overcrowding make it easier for these infections to spread.

## What to Do

**DRUG TREATMENT** Because fungus usually infects only one fish at a time, remove affected individuals to a hospital tank for treatment. Treat with a proprietary remedy incorporating malachite green as per directions on page 223.

**OTHER ACTIONS** Correct conditions that led to infection.

Ulceration of the head and gills

## "HOLE-IN-THE-HEAD" AND HEAD AND LATERAL-LINE DISEASE

**What to Look For** This syndrome starts innocuously, with a subtle enlargement of the lateral-line pores around the head of the fish. As the situation worsens, skin around the pores loses pigmentation and acquires a raw and ragged look. In freshwater aquaria, large cichlids and gouramis are the most likely targets, while in marine tanks tangs, surgeonfish, and angelfish are all susceptible. Animals often live for long periods while infected but look horrible, and severe infestations can be fatal.

**Disease-Causing Organism** It is difficult to prove that a single infectious agent is always associated with this syndrome; a protozoan called *Hexamita* is often—but not always—involved.

**What Went Wrong?** This disease was a mystery for many years. Today, many aquarists believe that it is brought on by a long-term nutritional deficiency and then aggravated by invading protozoans. In certain cases—among tangs, surgeonfish, and angelfish, for example—the syndrome is often associated with a lack of fresh plant material in the diet.

A White Ryukin with mouth fungus and tail rot

Mouth fungus

219

## What to Do

DRUG TREATMENT   If you are certain that the disease has progressed far enough that *Hexamita* is involved, metronidazole (Flagyl) is one of the few medications that have any demonstrated action. Obtain the drug by prescription  dose as described on page 224, and correct conditions that led to the disease.

OTHER ACTIONS   Mild cases can often be cured without medication if sufficient vitamin C is added to the diet. For the herbivorous fishes in whom this syndrome is most common, that is easily accomplished by regularly offering fresh leaves of romaine lettuce.

## DROPSY

**What to Look For**   Swollen body, reddish areas at fin bases, and fins that protrude like the scales of a pinecone.

**Disease-Causing Organism**   It is still not clear precisely what causes this disease; bacteria and viruses have been implicated (but not conclusively), although nutritional problems are also suspect.

**What Went Wrong?**   This may well be the most mysterious of fish diseases. In some cases, lack of proper foods or poor water quality seem to be at fault, but one or two individuals may become infected in a clean aquarium filled with healthy fishes.

## What to Do

DRUG TREATMENT   None definitively successful; isolate affected animals and try nufuriprinol as directed.

## Larger Parasites

There are a number of larger parasites that attach themselves to fishes on occasion. These include several types of wormlike animals and several aquatic equivalents of the fleas and lice that pester dogs and other terrestrial animals. These are sufficiently rare that in all my years of fishkeeping, I have encountered them only two or three times.

Because these parasites live either on the outside of a fish's body or on its gills, they are exposed directly to medication in the water. Most can be controlled by Trichlorofon (page 224). Treatment is relatively simple; make certain you add the right medication at the right concentration, you've got a good chance of eliminating the problem.

# MEDICATIONS:
## Uses and Abuses

*There are some remedies worse than the disease.*

Pubilius Syrus, circa 42 B.C.

Independent of the need to select the proper drug to fight a specific pathogen, there are several serious problems with medications commonly used in aquaria.

## Efficacy

Although there are several excellent medications on the market, many don't work as advertised. There's no FDA for fishes to prevent manufacturers from making unsubstantiated claims, and *Consumer Reports* has yet to do an exposé on proprietary fish remedies. As a result, you can't walk into a pet shop and distinguish effective medications from aquatic snake oils. Although aquarium drug companies get defensive about their marketing strategies, too many products stress false or exaggerated claims rather than explicit and truthful information on drug action. The hype involved in this part of the aquarium business is disgraceful.

The curative abilities of many aquarium medications have not been tested at all, while others have not been subjected to the rigors of well-designed experiments. Such experiments, which do exist in the professional aquaculture literature, can provide vital information on product effectiveness. Unfortunately, not all people who run aquarium drug trials understand experimental design, and badly designed experiments provide little more than circumstantial evidence for product effectiveness. Take the personal experience I described at the beginning of the chapter. I had a sick fish. I added medication. The next day, the sick fish died, and the other fishes looked worse. But the day after, everyone looked better. Had the medication cured them? At the time, I thought so, and I used to swear by the medication that seemed so effective.

But look at the "data." The day after I added the medication, everyone looked worse. They didn't start looking better until I "cleaned" the tank, in the process replacing a lot of the water. And they looked better yet when I changed still more water. In reality, the medication might have had nothing to do with that particular cure, and may even have made matters worse by killing the biological filter.

To *prove* that the medication had cured the fish, I would have needed to conduct a controlled experiment, involving two identical tanks, stocked the same way, with the same disease problem. Into one tank (the experimental setup), I would have added the medication. Into the other (the control) an equal amount of distilled water. I would then have had to treat both tanks in the same way (including feeding and water changing) and record the results.

*If* the fish in the medicated tank got better, *and* the ones in the unmedicated tank showed no improvement or got worse, *then* I would have had evidence that the medication had saved the day. But looking back on the experience, it's likely that the fishes in the unmedicated tank would have done better; the disease was probably brought on by overcrowding and poor water quality, and frequent water changes allowed the fishes to fight the infection on their own.

If your fish have contracted something other than the easily diagnosable ailments listed above, you will minimize frustration, expense, and loss of fishes by using one of the books listed at the end of this chapter. Each has at least one author who is a professional in the field of fish health, and each has a wealth of practical and scientific advice on curing sick fishes. Once again, I strongly recommend that anyone with access to a computer join the FISH-NET forum on the CompuServe network; the staff is extremely knowledgeable and offers top-notch advice—usually within hours—to hobbyists in distress.

In some cases, you'll need a prescription from a friendly doctor or veterinarian to purchase the drug of choice from your local pharmacist. Although that may seem like a bother, it means you'll get the right medication for the job, that the medication will be fresh, and that you'll have a clear indication of the strength of the preparation.

## Problems with Effective Versus Recommended Doses

Another problem with certain fish medications is that doses recommended in product literature do not always provide therapeutic concentrations in the aquarium. For some reason, recommended doses for several aquarium antibiotics are as much ten to one hundred times lower than the minimum effective doses published in the scientific aquaculture literature. The reason for this problem is not altogether clear, although it may be another product of inadequate experimental design. It may also be the case that manufacturers recommend low doses because they know that truly therapeutic doses can be marginally toxic to fishes. They may thus make low recommendations to be on the "safe side" in terms of consumer complaints. If a medication kills fishes, after all, consumers complain. But if medication doesn't really cure the disease, any number of other factors may be to blame.

For this reason, be certain that you are applying the correct medication at the correct dose; too little won't eliminate the offending organisms, and too much may kill your fishes. The best information on drug dosage comes from the scientific literature, which is presented in the metric system of measurement. This system is straightforward and consistent, and you should have no trouble learning to use it.

First, calculate the true volume of your tank in liters. This is necessary because the sizes of tanks in gallons are not true measures of their capacity. Begin by measuring the *inside* of your tank with a metric ruler. If you haven't got one, multiply the dimensions in inches by the conversion factor 2.54 cm/inch. Calculate the capacity of the tank by multiplying length times width times the actual height of water in the tank. If you are using a bare hospital or quarantine tank as I recommend, that's the number you'll need. If you are treating fish in an aquarium holding lots of gravel, rocks, and driftwood, you must estimate the volume of water displaced by those decorations and subtract that from the total. A good rule of thumb is to decrease the volume of a well-landscaped tank by 15 to 20 percent of its calculated value.

Next, check the recommended dosage for the drug of choice. Several are given here; others can be found in the specialized source books listed at the end of the chapter.

The trickiest part is to determine the concentration of the active ingredient your medication contains. If you've got antibiotics by prescription in a vial from a druggist, the active ingredients will be clearly described. Over-the-counter aquarium medications in pet stores, on the other hand, may or may not be so clearly labeled. Some packages might provide a clear statement that each pill contains 200 mg of the antibiotic nifurpirinol. On the other hand, the label may simply state that an active ingredient, such as trichlorofon, represents 10 percent of each 200 mg tablet. In that case, a simple calculation tells you that each tablet contains 20 mg of the drug.

Finally, multiply the volume of water in your tank by the recommended dosage (in mg/l) to find the total amount of medication you must add to the tank. To achieve a dosage of 50 mg/l in a 40-liter tank, for example, requires a total of 50 mg/l $\times$ 40 l or 2,000 mg of the drug. If each tablet contains 200 mg, you must add ten tablets.

In all cases, observe both my general recommendations and the specific advice of the drug manufacturer regarding the total length of the treatment period. This is important whether you are dealing with parasites or bacteria. Drugs often target one specific stage of a parasite's life cycle while leaving other stages unharmed. You must therefore be certain that all the parasites in the tank pass through the vulnerable stage while medication is present.

Finally, several of the most commonly available aquarium antibiotics are not absorbed by fishes directly from the water to any degree. For that reason, these drugs can be effective only against bacteria growing *outside,* on the surface of the skin, fins, or gill filaments. To treat internal bacterial infections, you must use either one of the few drugs that is absorbed internally, or add the proper medications to your fishes' food to make certain that they swallow it.

## Side Effects

Any informed consumer of medication inquires about side effects, which can range from innocuous to fatal. The situation is the same in fishes, but those animals haven't the communicative powers to tell you when something is not agreeing with them. Unfortunately, many medications effective against aquatic parasites are often also toxic to fishes. Luckily, these drugs usually kill parasites at much lower doses than they kill fishes, but even nonlethal doses may place fish under stress. This is another reason to use medications cautiously and only when definitely indicated; indiscriminate treatment may stress fish further while not affecting the disease.

## Medications and Nitrogen Cycle

In part because diagnosing bacterial disease is so difficult, many antibacterial medications are intentionally broad-spectrum, meaning that they affect a variety of bacteria. For fishes in isolation, such medications are excellent; given the vagaries of diagnosing bacterial infections, the broader a drug's action the better the chance that it will kill whatever is ailing your fishes. For community tanks with biological filters, on the other hand, broad-spectrum antibacterial drugs can be problematical, for they may inhibit or kill beneficial bacteria. The resulting rise in ammonia and nitrite levels may cause more serious problems in the tank than the pathogen! For this reason, use antibiotics in separate treatment tanks whenever possible.

## Medications and Invertebrates

In freshwater tanks, fishes are almost always a hobbyist's main concern, with the exception of an errant snail or two. In marine tanks, on the other hand, invertebrates are often an important part of the show. Copper, often used to help rid fishes of parasites, is useful precisely because it kills a wide range of invertebrates—including some you might want to keep alive, such as sea anemones or crabs! Overdoses of copper are also potentially toxic to fishes. For these reasons, always use copper carefully and never add it to a tank containing invertebrates.

## Bacterial Resistance to Drugs

Bacteria have the disconcerting ability to evolve resistance to antibiotics when exposed to them at low doses or for brief periods. For that reason, failure to maintain a full therapeutic dose for the full recommended treatment period will encourage the development of a resistant strain in your tank. Despite your best efforts in that regard, you may find that a correctly identified bacterial infection may not respond to treatment, not because you have done anything wrong, but because a number of common aquatic pathogens have already become resistant to the antibiotics most commonly used in the aquarium trade. FISHNET and the better trade magazines will keep you apprised of such problems as they are discovered.

## A SAMPLER OF USEFUL MEDICATIONS

Generic Name:
MALACHITE GREEN AND FORMALIN

### USE
External parasitic infestations (such as ich) and external fungal infections.

### DOSAGE
These two medications used together work far better than either works on its own. Therapeutic dosage when delivered as a pair should be roughly 0.05 mg/l of malachite green and 15 mg/l of formalin.

### PROPRIETARY PRODUCTS
Rid-Ich (from Kordon) and Desafin (from Tetra) both deliver this medicinal pair in the appropriate combination and at the recommended dosage. These medications are also available individually and in other formulations, but proper dosage is difficult to determine from product package information.

### CAUTIONS
Malachite green is toxic to certain fishes (such as black ghost knifefish). Formalin is toxic to most freshwater and marine invertebrates.

Generic Name:
## TRICHLOROFON (MASOTEN)

USE
Large parasites.

DOSAGE
0.25 mg/l; specific treatment regimen varies with the specific parasite.

PROPRIETARY PRODUCTS
Life-Bearer (from Aquarium Products); follow manufacturer's instructions for proper dosage.

CAUTIONS
Trichlorofon is toxic and easily absorbed through human skin, so use it with care and keep out of reach of children. Toxic to freshwater and marine invertebrates.

Generic Name:
## METRONIDAZOLE (FLAGYL)

USE
Infestations of flagellated protozoa such as the *Hexamita* often associated with head and lateral-line disease. If delivered internally, effective against protozoan infestations in the gut.

DOSAGE
For external treatment, maintain concentration of 7 mg/l.
For internal treatment, mix with food in ratio of 1 to 100 (10 mg drug/gram of food).

PROPRIETARY PRODUCTS
This drug, used to treat gut infections in mammals (including humans), is available only by prescription through a veterinarian.

CAUTIONS
As with all prescription drugs, use only as directed and keep out of reach of children. Although used by prescription for certain human ailments, this drug can have serious side effects if swallowed.

Generic Name:
## OXYTETRACYCLINE

USE
External, bacterially caused fin and tail rot.
Certain internal infections.

DOSAGE
For external infections, 20 mg/l for long-term treatment. 50–100 mg/l for 1-hour baths.
For internal infections, mix with food and administer daily at rates of 50–75 mg/kg of fish body weight.

PROPRIETARY PRODUCTS
Several widely available products contain this drug, but following package instructions will not deliver therapeutic dosage; adjust application accordingly.

CAUTIONS
Because this is one of the most widely used aquarium antibiotics, many strains of aquarium bacteria have developed resistance to it. Not as active in hard, alkaline fresh water or saltwater.

## Generic Name:
## NIFURPIRINOL

### USE

Because this is one of the few antibiotics absorbed by fishes from tank water, it is effective against a variety of both internal and external bacterial infections.

### DOSAGE

0.1 mg/l.

### PROPRIETARY PRODUCTS

Furanace (from Aquarium Products) used as directed, delivers this drug at the recommended dose.

### CAUTIONS

Because this product is destroyed by exposure to light, the treatment tank should be kept as dark as possible. (Use low-level illumination for a while around feeding periods so your fish can eat properly.)

## Generic Name:
## COPPER (USUALLY AS COPPER SULPHATE)

### USE

Commonly used against external protozoan infestations such as *Oodinium,* particularly in marine aquaria.

### DOSAGE

0.15–0.3 mg/l.

### PROPRIETARY PRODUCTS

A popular aquarium medication, copper is available in many formulations. Use only those that list copper concentration on the package so that you can measure out the appropriate dose.

### CAUTIONS

Copper is quite toxic to freshwater and marine invertebrates, some plants, and some algae. It may also interfere with the action of bacteria in your tank's biological filter. At levels about 0.4 mg/l, copper is also toxic to many fishes. Before using copper, be certain to buy a good-quality copper test kit to monitor dose levels. Note that because copper is removed from solution by coral, dolomite gravel, and organic matter, it is far easier to create and maintain the proper therapeutic dose in a clean hospital tank.

## Sources for Additional Information

Chris Andrews, Adrian Exell, and Neville Carrington, *Manual of Fish Health* (Morris Plains, NJ: Tetra Press, 1988).

Edward Kingsford, M.D., *Treatment of Exotic Marine Fish Diseases* (St. Petersburg, FL: Palmetto Publishing Company, 1975).

Steve Meyer, "Fish Disease and Treatment, Parts I and II," *Aquarium Fish Magazine,* June and August 1989.

George Post, *Textbook of Fish Health* (Neptune City, NJ: Tropical Fish Hobbyist Publications, 1987).

*This list is adapted from an excellent pair of articles by Steve Meyer in* Aquarium Fish Magazine.

# APPENDICES

## MAIL-ORDER SOURCES

The number of aquarium-related companies, large and small, that ply their trade through the mails has mushroomed over the last decade. In the following abbreviated list, I have listed only major suppliers that I feel are both reliable and well-stocked with a wide range of products. Prices at many vary monthly, and seasonal specials are common. Catalogs are generally either provided free of charge with orders or may cost a few dollars. Many smaller, more specialized firms offer products ranging from multibulb light fixtures to high-tech filtration systems. Most advertise regularly in aquarium journals. Inclusion in or exclusion from this list does not imply endorsement or lack thereof.

AQUATIC SUPPLY HOUSE
42 Hayes St., Dept F
Elmsford, NY 10523
800-777-PETS, Ext. F

(In NY 914-592-3620)
Fax: 914-592-8658

DALECO
3340 Land Dr.
Fort Wayne, IN 46809
Phone or fax: 219-747-7376

DISCOUNT AQUARIUM
3504 N. High St.
Columbus, OH 43214
Orders only                800-433-4619
Orders in Ohio only        800-533-5115
Customer service           614-447-0032

MAIL ORDER PET SHOP
4219 So. Market Ct. #H
Sacramento, CA 95834
916-923-0103
                *and*
60 So. Second St. #M
Deer Park, NY 11729
516-595-1717

Customer service line   800-326-6677
Order line              800-366-7387

PET WAREHOUSE
P.O. Box 20250
Dayton, OH 45420
800-443-1160
24-hour fax: 513-252-7388

THAT FISH PLACE
237 Centerville Rd.
Lancaster, PA 17603
800-233-3829
(In PA, 800-222-FISH)
Fax: 717-295-7210

## SELECTED JOURNALS AND BOOKS

### Aquarium Journals

Because these magazines differ widely in style, content, and editorial philosophy, I would suggest that you evaluate all of them. Either subscribe to all three for one year, or pick up a few single issues of each to see which you like best. After you've been keeping fishes for a while, you will find them to be redundant, although fanatics often subscribe to all three.

*Tropical Fish Hobbyist* and *Freshwater and Marine Aquarium* carry much higher volumes of advertising, and are therefore good windows onto the world of mail-order aquarium merchandising. If pressed to recommend only one publication to beginners, however, I would choose the slimmest and least flashy of the bunch—*Aquarium Fish Magazine*—for reasons described below. Note that in addition to these general-interest publications, many aquarium specialty societies have their own newsletters.

#### AQUARIUM FISH MAGAZINE (AFM)

Published monthly by Fancy Publications. Subscription orders to *AFM*, Subscription Department, P.O. Box 484, Mt. Morris, IL 61054-0484.

This is the "new kid on the block," and as such, is trying harder. Neither as flashy nor as large as its older competitors, *AFM* is cleanly laid out, well-organized, and contains (for my money) the most clearly and professionally written articles in the business. Several FISHNET members write for *AFM*, informing their pieces both through constant interchange with aquarists around the country and through their considerable scientific and writing skills. Emphasizing concise, clearly written presentations, *AFM*'s articles offer the best explanations of aquarium management techniques that I've seen anywhere.

#### FRESHWATER AND MARINE AQUARIUM (FAMA)

Published monthly by R/C Modeler Corporation. Subscription orders to P.O. Box 487, Sierra Madre, CA 91024.

This lively, well-illustrated, and friendly publication carries many interesting articles and useful, monthly columns written by a wide range of aquarium professionals. The subjects covered span a wide enough range of topics that even this jaded old fishkeeper can usually find something of interest in each issue. *FAMA* and *T.F.H.* seem to vie with each other to get the best pictures of the most recent additions to the hobby.

#### TROPICAL FISH HOBBYIST (T.F.H.)

Published monthly by T.F.H. Publications, Inc. Subscription orders to One T.F.H. Plaza, Neptune City, NJ 07753.

This oldest and largest of the aquarium publications is profusely illustrated and contains many articles written by professional ichthyologists. Subjects covered range from useful information on breeding unusual species to egocentric travelogues of questionable informational content. Often contains useful information, but quality and writing level varies enormously from article to article.

## A Sampling of Aquarium Fish and Plant Encyclopedias

Axelrod, H. R., and Burgess, W. E. 2d ed., 1986.
*Dr. Axelrod's Atlas of Freshwater Aquarium Fishes.*
T.F.H. Publications.

Extensive, as inclusive as one could ever hope such a book to be, and profusely illustrated. Organized zoogeographically, which means that fishes are grouped first by native habitat and then by family. That organization, which splits wide-ranging fish families into several scattered areas, may help advanced hobbyists who know, for example, that certain cichlids hail from South America, while others live in Africa. Beginners, on the other hand, may become confused. A few basic cultural requirements are included for each species, but this is basically a photo identification atlas.

Van Ramshorst, J. D., ed. 1978.
*Aquarium Encyclopedia.*
HP Books.

This beautifully illustrated and authoritative volume inadvertently highlights, through pictures and description, the differences between accomplished European aquarists and most of us here in the United States. Extensive material on aquatic plants is accompanied by photos of lushly planted tanks. Striking photos of a wide variety of fishes, organized by family, are followed by good cultural information. An excellent reference atlas.

Ratraj, K., and Horeman, T. J. 1977.
*Aquarium Plants: their identification and ecology.*
T.F.H. Publications.

The best book I have seen to date on aquarium plants and their management. Not a coffee table volume by any means, but well illustrated, clearly written, and chock full of useful information.

## SPECIALTY FISH ORGANIZATIONS AND SOCIETIES

If you decide to specialize in a particular species, there are many organizations devoted to the study of specific fishes. Listed below is just a sampling of these many societies. When writing for information, send a self-addressed stamped envelope.

AMERICAN CICHLID ASSOCIATION
ACA Membership Committee
Glenn Eaves
P.O. Box 32130
Raleigh, NC 27622

AMERICAN FISHERIES SOCIETY
5410 Grosvenor Ln.
Bethesda, MD 20814

AMERICAN KILLIFISH ASSOCIATION
Ronald Coleman
903 Merrifield Pl.
Mishawaka, IN 46544

AMERICAN LIVEBEARER ASSOCIATION
Timothy J. Brady
50 N. Second St.
St. Clair, PA 17970

APISTOGRAMMA STUDY GROUP
Donald Frisque
1845 Jaynes Rd.
Mosinee, WI 54455

AUSTRALIA-NEW GUINEA FISHES ASSOCIATION
Bill Richardson, Secretary
P.O. Box 637
Warragul, 3820
Victoria, Australia

BRITISH CICHLID ASSOCIATION
Howard Barnfather
100 Keighley Rd.
Skipton, N. Yorkshire
BD23 2RA England

BRITISH DISCUS ASSOCIATION
c/o F. W. Ashworth
41 Pengwern
Llangollen, Clwyd.
LL20 8AT England

BRITISH KILLIFISH ASSOCIATION
A. Burge
14 Hubbard Close
Wymondham, Norfolk
NR18 ODU England

BRITISH MARINE AQUARISTS' ASSOCIATION
E. Storey
139 Bradford Ave.
Greatfield Est. Hull. N. Humberside
HU9 4LZ England

CANADIAN ASSOCIATION OF AQUARIUM CLUBS
Sarah Langthorne
95 East 31st St.
Hamilton, Ontario
Canada L8V 3N9

CATFISH ASSOCIATION OF NORTH AMERICA
Todd Marsh
P.O. Box 45
Rt. 104A
Sterling, NY 13156

CICHLASOMA STUDY GROUP
Audrie Ward
6432 S. Holland Ct.
Littleton, CO 80123

COLLECTORS OF AQUATIC LITERATURE
Paul Harvey
4459 Shellflower Ct.
Concord, CA 94518

DISCUS STUDY GROUP
Ellen Halligan, Treasurer
73-47 184th St.
Fresh Meadows, NY 11366

FEDERATION OF AMERICAN AQUARISTS SOCIETY
Sally Van Camp
923 Wadsworth
Syracuse, NY 13208

GOLDFISH SOCIETY OF AMERICA
Betty Papanek, Membership Chairman
P.O. Box 1367
South Gate, CA 90280

INTERNATIONAL AQUARIUM SOCIETY
P.O. Box 373
Maine, NY 13802–0373

INTERNATIONAL BETTA CONGRESS
Stefan L. VanCamp
923 Wadsworth St.
Syracuse, NY 13208

INTERNATIONAL CHARACIN ASSOCIATION
D. G. Sidebottom
18 Harry St.
Werneth, Oldham, Lancaster
OL9 7TA England

INTERNATIONAL FANCY GUPPY ASSOCIATION
William St. Clair, IFGA Membership Chairman
2312 Pestalozzi
St. Louis, MO 63118

INTERNATIONAL SEAHORSE & MARINE
INVERTEBRATE SOCIETY
P.O. Box 373
Maine, NY 13802–0373

NORTH AMERICAN DISCUS SOCIETY
Bob Wilson
6939 Justine Dr.
Mississauga, Ontario
Canada L4T 1M4

NORTH AMERICAN FISH BREEDERS GUILD
Jeff McKee
4731 Lake Ave.
Rochester, NY 14612

NORTH AMERICAN NATIVE FISHES ASSOCIATION
Bruce Gebhardt
123 W. Mt. Airy Ave.
Philadelphia, PA 19119

SEAHORSE HOBBYIST SOCIETY
2821 Hollins Ferry Rd.
Baltimore, MD 21230

THE RAINBOWFISH STUDY GROUP OF NORTH
AMERICA
Sherry Bresett
2651 Larkin Ave.
Lakeport-Canastota, NY 13032

# FISHNET FORUM ON COMPUSERVE

Anyone with an interest in aquaria, a home computer, modem, and communications software should immediately dial 800-848-8199 for a trial subscription to the CompuServe network. The FISHNET forum (type "Go Fishnet" at any CompuServe main menu prompt) is the best place to keep up on the very latest in the hobby, to interact with other aquarists around the country (around the world, even), and to seek advice on complex issues concerning aquarium technology and disease treatment.

Many members are well informed professionals who donate astonishing amounts of time to the service. Others cover the range from rank beginners to accomplished aquarists. Virtually no messages stand for more than an hour or two without at least one comment, and many turn into long debates about the merits of various treatments and approaches to the hobby. Extensive "libraries" on-line offer members the sorts of specific information that beginners often have trouble finding on their own. FISHNET's intensely interactive style makes it far better than magazines as a source of controversial information. No one gets away with anything; the slightest bit of ill-considered advice is quickly demolished, often with great wit.

# INDEX